Unexpected

Unexpected

THE AUTOBIOGRAPHY

Greg Rutherford

with Sean Ingle

SIMON & SCHUSTER

London · New York · Sydney · Toronto · New Delhi

A CBS COMPANY

First published in Great Britain by Simon & Schuster UK Ltd, 2016
A CBS COMPANY

1 3 5 7 9 10 8 6 4 2

Simon & Schuster UK Ltd
1st Floor
222 Gray's Inn Road
London WC1X 8HB

www.simonandschuster.co.uk
www.simonandschuster.com.au
www.simonandschuster.co.in

Simon & Schuster Australia, Sydney
Simon & Schuster India, New Delhi

A CIP catalogue record for this book is available from the British Library.

ISBN: 978-1-4711-6252-7
eBook ISBN: 978-1-4711-6253-4

Typeset in Bembo by Rules
Printed in the UK by CPI Group (UK) Ltd, Croydon, CR0 4YY

Simon & Schuster UK Ltd are committed to sourcing paper that is made from wood grown in sustainable forests and support the Forest Stewardship Council, the leading international forest certification organisation. Our books displaying the FSC logo are printed on FSC certified paper.

For my granddad Jim and my son Milo –
I hope I've made you both proud, and
will continue to strive to do so.

To Susie, you have shown me the true meaning of love.
Now and always.
P.S. Thank God for Twitter.
Oh, and my ability to bowl. I definitely won both games!

And finally, to my parents, Tracy and Andrew –
quite simply, thank you.

CONTENTS

INTRODUCTION

It's just another competition. That's what they tell you. That's what you're supposed to think.

Try telling yourself that when you are stood on the runway of London 2012 men's long jump final, when 80,000 people are whipping themselves into a frenzy at the very sight of a British vest, when what you do in the next few seconds could completely change your life.

The stakes are that high. This is a moment for which I've built every muscle fibre, for which I've conditioned every thought and action for seven years. Barely anybody outside athletics circles knows who I am; they certainly don't know the journey that brought me to this moment: the 17 hamstring tears, the numerous other setbacks, both in my athletic and personal life. To ramp up the pressure further, just 36 hours earlier I called my best friend to ask for advice, panicking as I'd gone into an overdraft I didn't have.

Of course it's not just another competition.

The enormity of the challenge hits home on my first jump. Usually I can block out the noise of the crowd as I throw myself down the long jump runway. But this time their roar is not just deafening, it's terrifying. The cheers reverberate in my chest and get in my head, and before I know it I've jumped 6.28m – around two metres short of what will be required to become Olympic champion.

I get it right in the second round, jumping 8.21m, but that surely will not be enough given many of my rivals have jumped at least 15 centimetres further in their careers. Yet, there's a possibility that if I can pull a massive leap out of the bag, the pressure on my opponents' shoulders will be just as intense as the atmosphere in the stadium.

The third round comes and goes. I'm still leading. But I need to produce more.

As I stand on the runway for round four, I look across the track to see Jessica Ennis crossing the line in the 800m, the last event of the heptathlon. The noise which greets her victory is the loudest I have heard in my life. It's as if a plane has broken the sound barrier above Stratford.

Suddenly I have a blunt moment of clarity. You know what? I want a gold medal of my own.

I clap my hands above my head, feeding off the wild spike in the crowd's adrenaline. I shrug my shoulders, shaking the tension from my body like sand off a beach towel. Finally, I crouch into my starting position, a position I've practised and held thousands of times before. I pause and begin to rock back and forth. I take a deep breath and tell myself that I will dedicate this next jump to my grandfather Jim, a wonderful and caring man who died of cancer in 2008 and was my biggest inspiration.

Everything that happens next is too fast to take in; when a jump goes right it's just instinctive, it knits together perfectly.

It takes me 20 steps to travel the 45 metres to the take-off board, by the time I jump I am travelling at over 20 miles an hour. As my pace quickens, I get the sensation that this is a good one, this is all coming together. Then I hit that sweet spot on the board.

In a blur I land in the sandpit, roll, and rise to my feet as quickly as I can. It feels big – but how big? Sometimes feelings are misleading. The scoreboard flashes up with 8.31m. The fourth best jump in my life just when it matters most. The crowd go crazy again. Inside, I'm doing the same, but I'm careful to rein in my emotions. There's still two rounds to go. I must have at least bagged myself an Olympic medal, but I don't think it will be enough for gold.

Throughout the competition I have been chatting to Mitchell Watt, the Australian jumper, one of my best mates on the circuit. Right now, though, he is also my most dangerous threat. In 2011 he topped the world rankings with a monster 8.54m leap. If he can connect, he'll surpass me. He knows it, and I know it.

But the fifth round comes and goes, and I'm still ahead. The crowd's expectations are rising, as are my stress levels. That's the thing with the long jump. You might be winning, but you can't be sure of victory until the final jump from the final jumper, and any one of them could produce something.

Meanwhile on the track, just a few steps away, the men's 10,000m begins. In 28 minutes, Mo Farah will be storming down the home straight to win another gold medal for Britain. But all my focus has to be on the seven opponents next to me.

The last round. Seven men left with a chance of gold. Six. Five. And then four. Now it's only three. The medal standings haven't altered, which means I definitely have a bronze medal. But Mitch, the biggest barrier to my success, is on the runway.

He sprints hard, hits the board and jumps high into the air and looks like he has flown out to at least eight metres without much effort. Even I want to admire it, while desperately hoping he sinks like a stone. And then, as if by divine intervention, that's what happens. He drops into the pit and I know it's not enough even before the scoreboard flashes up 8.16m.

My heart jumps. I am now guaranteed silver. The American Will Claye is next. His personal best is 8.26m, so he needs the jump of his life to take my gold medal.

But it doesn't happen for him. Will runs straight through the pit, and in that split second his failure becomes my greatest moment of success. All of a sudden I am drowned by waves of joy. Everything I have ever wanted has suddenly just happened to me.

I don't know whether to laugh, cry, run around, or jump in the crowd. Perhaps I could do them all at once? The overriding feeling is one of relief. I've always been the nearly guy, the maybe guy, the probably not guy. And now I am Olympic champion, on home soil, as part of a historic night in British sport.

After I finish my lap of honour, I stand under the Olympic flame so I can watch Mo cross the line to win the first of his two gold medals at London 2012. I feel the heat of the flame on my neck as I see the final act of one of the greatest moments of British sport from the best seat in the house. Incredibly, Great Britain have just won three gold medals in 46 minutes. No wonder the next day the papers are calling it Super Saturday.

Given what I've been through to get to that point, I don't intend to stop there. As I defiantly tell reporters straight after the competition: This is just the start.

CHAPTER 1

No Christmas, No Birthdays

I hate sports autobiographies. Most bore me to death. So before I started writing this, I had a clear condition in my mind: I had to be brutally honest. I didn't want this to be a conventional, sugar-coated, bland tale of a developing sportsman. All the mistakes, all the stupid things I did growing up – and there are a great many – made me what I am today. As did my unconventional upbringing. As did the odd smacking.

I would have been about five when I realised my family were different. All my school friends were looking forward to something called Christmas and getting presents from someone called Father Christmas. But when I asked my parents about it, their reply was short. I was told it was just not something that we do, and it was made extremely clear that I should not bring the subject up again.

Their reaction was just as bad when it came to birthdays. These were also banned, or at least celebrating them was. I wasn't even allowed to go to other people's parties because it was against my parents' Jehovah's Witness faith.

Easter was also off the list – it was not mentioned in the Bible, so it was not to be celebrated. So you see the underlying theme of the household in which I grew up.

We weren't well off, either. At least by most people's standards. Whenever times got tight, as they often did for a family reliant on my dad Andrew's income as a self-employed builder, lunches would often consist of tins of beans or dried pasta with grated cheese on top. My mum Tracy would do an incredible job of rustling up a stew with whatever cuts of meat we could afford. Though I must say, we ate her casserole so many times that it brings an involuntary gag reflex when I think of it now. On Sundays, however, she would make amazing roast dinners.

With this in mind, one of the most surprising and amusing aspects of being in the public eye is that people think I'm posh. I guarantee you that whenever I venture any opinion on social media, the abuse I get is usually directed either at the colour of my hair – there's not much I can do about that – or at my apparently privileged upbringing. I get stuff like 'Greg Rutherford has thrown his posh toys out the posh pram again' all the time. If they could go back in time to when I was born into the world on 17 November 1986, weighing a whopping 9st 6lb – yes, my poor mum! – they would discover that the reality was somewhat different.

Originally, my mum had wanted to call me Dennis and, funnily enough, she now has a cat of that name who is a big fat bruiser, but in the end my parents agreed to call me Gregory

James Rutherford instead. My mum would never say this, but I think she wanted a name that sounded a bit fancier than we actually were, given that we were the definition of a working-class family from Bletchley, Milton Keynes. She called my elder brother Robert Andrew Rutherford, which I guess also has a relatively well-to-do ring to it.

I'm proud of my upbringing, but financial struggles come with a cost, and the strain on my parents often put pressure on other areas of their lives. I don't think it helped that I was such an energetic child, relentlessly refusing to sit still and always exploring. My brother Robert, however, was an easy baby by all accounts – put him on a rug in the front room with some toys, and he wouldn't move all day. But a couple of years after him, my mum had me: a child who literally would not stop, every hour of the day, and the night.

She tells of how I was constantly climbing and falling from particularly precarious locations. Though I actually learned to walk quite late, at around 15 months, my mum always says I used to be a total nightmare. And now, seeing my son Milo, who is apparently just as energetic as I was at his age, it really can't have been easy for her, especially with my dad working outrageously long hours.

According to my parents, my early childhood was one dramatic episode after another. If I wasn't falling off something or pulling something over, I was cracking my head open. When I was about four, I tried to cut my own hair with scissors, and my mum went mental. She marched me to a brutal Italian barber's in Bletchley. The barber took one look at me and said, 'Well, I can't do anything with that,' and roughly shaved my head. The problem was – apart from the fact that I now looked like a little ginger hooligan – I also had lots of scars all over my head from my mishaps past and present, so in trying to avoid her child looking like he was homeless, the shaving of my head only made me look like a thug instead.

As happens in any normal school, when I was young I would be thrilled to receive birthday party invitations from friends, and I used to go home and beg my mum to allow me to go. Every time the answer was the same: no. I used to plead with her, promising, 'I won't sing "Happy Birthday" and I won't eat the cake, I just want to play with my friends,' but it never worked. The first time I went to a birthday party I was in my late teens.

I hated this restriction, and what my parents never perhaps appreciated was that in my mind their adherence to this rule was almost deliberately breeding a level of segregation from my current and future friends. Naturally, on the Monday at school everyone would be talking about the party they had gone to at the weekend. Except me. I really cannot overstate just how much I hated it. It was horrible.

Their stance does, to a lesser extent, remain today. Even when it was my son Milo's first birthday in 2015, my mum was there and actually made him a beautiful rainbow cake, but I suspect she felt uncomfortable getting involved; she didn't buy any presents or anything like that. My dad wasn't even there at all, nor were my grandmas. It was just Susie's side of the family and friends. On the one hand, it was a bit sad. On the other, my parents were baptised Jehovah's Witnesses, they met through their faith, so I have to respect this, much though I wish it was not the case.

Christmas would just be a normal day too, which is quite a difficult task considering so much in our culture in the UK is defined by the build-up to the festivities in December. We would sit in our house, doing nothing. My parents would completely ignore it. As a result, I never grew up with the childhood fantasy of a jolly man with a bushy white beard and a red-and-white costume bringing you presents – Father Christmas was simply never mentioned. Just as well, given I never received presents anyway!

I remember being at school and seeing my classmates getting excited about Santa coming, and I'd actually be thinking these kids are all stupid – Father Christmas doesn't even exist. I suppose the one benefit of being from a Jehovah's Witness family was that I never had to experience the letdown of finding out he wasn't real . . .

Christmas meant only two things: leaving school a few days early because everyone was involved in the nativity play and other Christmas-related activities in which I was not allowed to participate, and better TV. Even then we were banned from watching anything to do with Christmas, so that upside was quickly diminished.

I remember one Christmas Day morning, I actually took a glass and put it against the wall in our front room to listen to next door's kids opening their presents. I stood on a chair with the cup pressed to my ear and my head close against the wall, feeling incredibly jealous of their excitement as they unwrapped their presents while, at the same time, really trying to be as happy as I could be for the two little girls who lived next door.

The mention of this story to my partner Susie has her welling up. But at the time, I didn't know any better. It wasn't so much a sad occasion for me at the time; it was simply my reality. The 25th of December (which was my staunch Jehovah's Witness grandma's birthday as well) for us was a normal day, with a normal dinner, some TV, and then bed. Even now, I feel really awkward opening presents in front of people. It's a kind of hangover that's developed because it was just something so alien to me when I was growing up. Conversely, nowadays, I am probably completely over the top when it comes to buying gifts for others. I'm just not experienced enough to get the art of gift-giving right.

It was only when I was about nine or ten that I started questioning my parents' decision to put a blanket ban on celebrating the days that everyone else did as a matter of course. I couldn't understand what was so wrong about everyone getting to see their family, having treats to eat and trying to have an enjoyable time. A great many people aren't religious, but most recognise that any occasion that brings a family together and makes them happy is a lovely thing, regardless of any spiritual or other connotation it may have. Alas, my parents disagreed.

And there was certainly no room for magic or fantasy in our house, of the kind that really light up a young child's eyes. If I asked about a tooth fairy my parents would be like, 'Don't be stupid – there's no such thing.' And Halloween was a massive no-no. My mum, especially, was very anti entertaining the notion of ghosts or the supernatural, even when presented in a tongue-in-cheek way.

Coming from a Jehovah's Witness family meant that we would attend meetings in our places of worship, Kingdom Halls, on Tuesdays, Thursdays and Sundays, as well as going around people's houses knocking on doors – yes, the activity everyone associates with Jehovah's Witnesses was part of my life growing up. I don't really remember people's reactions to it, because I guess I was quite young. To me, it was the fact that I was spending time with my dad, and seeing him interact with other people, that mattered. I didn't realise that we were actually annoying a lot of people by knocking on their door of a Sunday afternoon.

A few times a year, we would also travel to the Ricoh Arena, a stadium in Coventry, for large gatherings of Jehovah's Witnesses. Like most kids, I didn't enjoy being forced to go somewhere and sit all day to listen to somebody harp on about something I had no idea about, just because my parents had made me go there. It was, as I guess most religious ceremonies are for kids, incredibly boring. I have a vivid memory of going to one gathering in the late 1990s, and there was this boy about the same age as me making a speech. I remember my grandma turning to me and saying, 'Don't you wish one day you could be like this child?' But all I thought was, 'Oh my God, no – this lad is a complete tool!' Naturally, my actual reply was more like, 'Yes, Grandma, of course, that would be lovely.'

CHAPTER 2

Tough Times

My sister Natalie came along six years after me. She was born with a dislocated hip, which should have been relatively easy to fix, but it wasn't picked up immediately and so she ended up having several operations, one of which went disastrously wrong. Thankfully, she recovered, but my parents' perspective switched in many ways, and my poor dad in particular suffered immensely. As a parent now myself, I can't begin to imagine what they went through, but I can perhaps start to empathise with the stress they were under and how that subsequently and inevitably filtered down to how family life was sometimes not so harmonious.

Of course, when we were growing up, Mum and Dad did everything in their power to give us the best opportunities they could. Our lives were not always easy, but my dad in particular had it far harder, for he grew up on the poverty line without a father. My grandma worked three jobs, yet she always struggled to keep her family's head above water. My dad tells the story of just how resourceful his mother was when he was little: if they had cereal in the morning, she would put milk in my dad's bowl and then, when he had finished his breakfast, he would pass the bowl to her. She would then put cornflakes in the same bowl, using the last dregs of the milk to save money.

I can't comprehend that. We always had milk in the fridge. We always had cereal. And even if we had cheap meals – 7p tins of Netto beans on toast made from long-life bread sticks in my mind as a staple – we never went hungry as my mum could always make something tasty from the cupboard, and she's a fantastic baker. My dad has worked himself to the bone almost every day of his life for over 40 years, which is not conducive to forging strong family bonds, but at the same time was perhaps a natural response to his upbringing. Like every parent, he wanted a better future and life for his kids than his own, and I admire his work ethic.

However, for someone who was very working class, my dad did have an unusual second job – as a ski instructor. I know it sounds really odd, but it was one of those things that happened completely by chance. Because Dad didn't come from an affluent household, as a kid he never got to go on holiday. But one year, another Jehovah's Witness family from Harpenden, in Hertfordshire, kindly told my gran they wanted to take him on their annual skiing trip. He went, caught the bug, and he was such a natural that when he got older he qualified as an instructor so that he could sometimes teach at the Hemel Hempstead dry ski slope after he had finished his building work for the day. He would help out there when we were little and would take us along to learn. So while it sounds quite bizarre, from a very young age my brother and I learned to ski – and still love it to this day.

My mum's upbringing was slightly different. She grew up with both parents: my granddad, who was one of the gentlest and kindest men you could ever imagine, and my grandma Carole. Life was more harmonious, but thanks to my grandma's often fiery nature and outspoken behaviour, it could occasionally be volatile. She's a wonderful woman – but she certainly knows her own mind!

I must stress, there were plenty of fun times in my childhood, too. I have a distinct memory from when I was very young of my brother and me waking up super-early to surprise my dad by sneaking downstairs. This must have been about 5am, because we didn't see him much in the early years as he was working so much. It was a rubbish surprise looking back now, just being downstairs in the house at a time of day when normally we wouldn't. It's funny what a powerful mental impact something so simple can have on a child; he was probably only mildly taken aback and then got on with his day.

Some of my fondest memories, as for many young boys I'm sure, are of being out the back of my house, playing football in the road with my dad. It didn't happen that much, but I cannot tell you how I loved those moments. More often than not, though, on a Sunday afternoon I would beg him: 'Oh, Dad, can we go play football?' Obviously, the poor bloke was totally knackered from work and he'd say, 'I'm too tired, I need to have a rest,' and just as the times we did play gave me so much joy, I'd really feel the disappointment.

While music wasn't a big thing in our house, Mum had a record player in the front room and now and again she would put on the vinyl and dance around to the Bee Gees and Abba while she was cleaning, which was fun to witness.

But, when things did get tough for my brother and me, they got really tough. To put it mildly, our house became a volatile place to live, with a lot of shouting, and smacking. One day my dad would be fine, the next he wouldn't speak to anyone. My parents would have blazing rows. And, far more often than I would have liked, I felt I took the brunt of the fallout.

To make matters worse, like a lot of people neither of my parents was good at showing their emotions properly. Often we'd hear them shouting at each other, which is difficult for any child. Of course, everybody argues and has the odd fight, but for years it felt very explosive. It was particularly tough in the early nineties, when the bottom fell out of the building trade and my dad had no work. He was desperately having to pick up jobs wherever he could just to keep us afloat, and it must have been so tough for them both, especially with children to consider.

However, it wasn't only personality clashes that were causing full-scale eruptions in the Rutherford household.

It all started when my sister was learning to walk and my parents noticed that she had a limp. When the hospital got round to scanning her hips, they saw that her ball-and-socket joint hadn't developed, which meant the head of her femur was not sitting properly where it should. 'Clicky hips' is one of those conditions that are much harder to treat non-invasively and successfully if not spotted early on, soon after a baby is born. Natalie was two and a half by the time the doctors tried to fix it, which meant she needed major surgery on numerous occasions. So with two young children, and a third in and out of hospital, as you can imagine, the stress naturally seeped into every aspect of my dad's life, making the situation at home highly pressurised.

Nowadays my dad is a different person. If you were to meet him you would say he's funny and great company, and most of the time he is. Along with my mum, he is one of my biggest supporters. When I won gold at London 2012 they wore 'Go Greg!' T-shirts to the stadium. I also get on well with my sister. But for a long time Natalie and I had a very fractured relationship. We weren't close at all.

For the first three years of my sister's life I doted on her like there was no tomorrow. We didn't have much, but any money I ever got I used to buy her presents. I wanted to look after her, just like any brother would when seeing that his little sister is unable to do everything he can do. It was horrible to watch Natalie endure those horrible operations, until her hip was finally fixed when she was ten.

However, at a certain point for a short period, something changed. Suddenly, she seemed to take great pleasure in seeing me get hit. I'm not sure why she did it: she was clearly suffering a lot of pain in her life and maybe this was one way of gaining control. My parents always doted on her, understandably, and she got into far less trouble than Robert and I did – we set the bar high.

For whatever reason, as she grew older Natalie picked up on the fact that my dad was hypersensitive and she used it to make my life a misery. For example, we'd be watching the TV and she'd hear my dad come in from work. Suddenly she would make a noise, as if she was hurt. Then next thing I knew my dad would come running in and smack me or shout at me. It was a really bizarre time.

In that period my dad hated being in the house because it meant he had to face up to life again. But every time I heard my little sister going 'Wah!', I'd look at her and I knew what was coming. There would be pure desperation at first, then pure pain as I took a hiding.

Usually, I would shout back because that is my personality. I would get a smack and then be sent on my way, crying, back up to my room, again and again and again.

It went on for years. My parents never hit us to the extreme, but it still hurt. And there was the mental torture of it too, because I felt my sister appeared to delight in me being punished. Occasionally I would even see her smiling at me as my parents' blows landed. I can't describe the anger I felt as a result while growing up and didn't understand that she was still very young. Thankfully, as we got older Natalie made a full recovery and, slowly, we built a few bridges and became much closer. She's now a wonderful aunt to my son, who absolutely adores her.

It wasn't only Natalie who was to blame for the smacks my brother and I suffered. A smacking was something very easily dished out in our house for any scrape either of us got into. I remember speaking to my friends, and it seemed they only got punished if they did something really bad. I recall one lad telling me that he threw a brick at a bus once, smashed the window with it, and his dad hit him. I thought, 'Well, fair enough, of course you are going to get hit for that.' However, my parents' reaction to something even moderately bad was to smack us. We'd run away from my mum and she'd have to chase us around the house waving a wooden spoon at us.

When I think back on it now, I laugh. Honestly, I do – although at the time it was less funny. Often my brother and I would run off, and then my mum would try to grab us. I guess we became relatively desensitised to it, or had too much bravado. When she hit me I would say, 'That didn't hurt,' because I didn't want her to see it was having an effect. So she would hit me again, harder still. Of course, I ensured that my answer didn't change. 'That didn't hurt.' But now I said it through gritted teeth because it did, really. I was just trying to save face.

As much as my mum did smack me, often she was very much an ally. She would make my dad come and apologise. When we were kids, if my brother or I ever apologised to my dad for doing something wrong, he would say, 'You don't mean it because you keep doing it.' I wanted to say to him, 'Well, you hit us and then you come and say sorry but then you will do it again the following day, so you obviously don't mean it either.' Of course, I didn't dare point out the irony because he probably would have smacked me again.

Given what happened in my childhood, it's perhaps not a surprise that I find most religion very frustrating: there seems too little emphasis on the 'love thy neighbour' part. So when people ask me if I'm religious I say no. That is not to say that I don't believe in a God. It's just that I believe everyone should lead the life that makes them and others happy. Whether you are someone of faith or not, as long as you are also being a good and respectful person who thinks of others, who – apart from the fanatics out there – can say that is wrong?

Yet I am not sure whether what happened during my upbringing has had a lasting negative effect, which may sound odd given what I have just described. Then again, my athletics success superseded anything that had gone before it. When you have been lucky enough to travel the world, learn so much about life, meet a wonderful partner and have a brilliant son, you realise there's no point in looking back in anger, and I love and appreciate my wonderful, highly supportive parents for everything they have done.

That is why I have always tried to live in the present as much as possible. And I guess one positive consequence of the regular smacks I received as a child is that I have always been willing to speak out against injustice and am prepared to be critical of anything I perceive to be wrong. That is why you will see me react to certain stories in the media, such as the Russian doping scandal or when Tyson Fury launched his rant against gay people.

Fury might have been heavyweight champion of the world but I couldn't just stand by while he compared homosexuality to paedophilia and also made clear his abhorrent sexist views. My comments led to a backlash on social media, with a lot of people reacting in a less than positive way, but there was absolutely no way I couldn't respond.

And looking further on the bright side, my childhood has given me a far better understanding of how people can react under extreme stress and pressure. Since becoming a parent I've been determined never to be like that with Milo, or any future offspring my partner Susie and I might have. Because my experience of going through this level of stress as a child was never easy. But it has also made me realise how much courage they had in a time of adversity, before coming through in the end.

CHAPTER 3

Always Hearing the Word 'No'

Shortly before my fifth birthday I started at Holne Chase primary school in Milton Keynes, and quickly became the little ginger kid who got picked on. You won't be surprised to hear that I didn't have a good time there. Like most kids of that age, I didn't have a strong identity and I wasn't confident enough to be the leader, and so I would always be following other children who were considered the cool kids. Sadly, I would often be the butt of all their jokes too. My overall memory of my first school years is of being bullied quite a lot.

What made the three years I spent in Holne Chase bearable was that I developed a massive obsession with history, particularly the early medieval period. The school had a mini-library and I was always looking at books that had pictures of knights, sword fights, jousting and archery. I'm really painting you a picture of the cool kid at school here, aren't I? I particularly remember one book which contained all the various suits of armour from different parts of Europe, as well as re-enactments of battle scenes, which really sparked my imagination.

I became fascinated by the idea of knights and battles, and how different the world was back then – a lot of the history was from around the area in which I lived. And because my dad would always have wood, hammers, nails and other tools lying around, this enterprising child soon learned how to use them to make swords, shields and anything else from that period that I considered cool. Whenever we were sent something in a cardboard box I would try to turn it into some form of armour. You might think I'd have grown out of my obsession with this period, but even to this day I am still fascinated by medieval history. If I get a chance to watch TV, I drive my partner Susie up the wall because I will only want to watch *Time Team* or some other history programme. Needless to say, it does annoy her a bit – mainly because they're often repeats.

Primary school was also when I first discovered I had athletic ability. Racing one another in the playground is somehow a key factor of life in primary school and I soon found that I could win easily, every time. Even then, though, there were times when some of my classmates would try to belittle me, and from this I can draw parallels with my sporting achievements to date – no matter what I do, there seem to be more detractors when it comes to my performance compared to others. I don't know why.

I recall there was this one other kid who was relatively fast, yet I still beat him in a race. But then everyone went around saying, 'Oh no, no – he's faster than you.' There was no reason for it, except that I was always the kid who must get put down even when I did well. That used to frustrate and annoy the hell out of me. I used to think: 'I have proven that I am better but you still won't accept that.'

That mindset has never left me. I have always been the underdog, trying to prove my worth, whether it's to my classmates at Holne Chase or the critics I've had in my athletics career. Some people still think my London 2012 gold medal was a fluke, that my World Championship victory in Beijing in 2015 was lucky, and that there was something fortunate about my European and Commonwealth titles too. I used to lament this attitude, and I must be honest that after London 2012 in particular it did bother me. However, nowadays it only fuels my desire to win. The desire to prove people wrong is a powerful motivator.

And I have always used sport as my main weapon. As a kid I used to tell myself: 'You might be a bit bigger or stronger than me; use your better grasp of the English language to poke fun at me; or make the kids laugh at me, but I can run faster than you.' It wasn't much, admittedly, but it gave me something to cling on to even when times were tough, and it slowly helped build my self-confidence.

My first school was a combined school, so I could have gone through to year seven but I left after year three. In year two, I had a horrible teacher, who, for whatever reason, didn't take a liking to me and that was the beginning of the end. My mum went in and fought for me, but in the end it made sense to take me out and move me to my brother's school.

So when I was seven I went to Two Mile Ash in Milton Keynes, where I was afforded the luxury of a fresh start because nobody knew me. I was determined to reinvent myself and not be picked on so much, and luckily I made friends with some nice people and started to enjoy myself a bit more at school.

What really hit home by going to this new school was the difference in our family circumstances. Because its catchment area included some particularly affluent parts of Milton Keynes, I had a few friends who had rich parents and nice detached houses. Some of them had football goalposts in their gardens, which blew me away. To a sporty child, this was the biggest sign of wealth imaginable!

Many of my friends also had Nike trainers or cool gear, something I could only dream about. There was one time, after our dog Franz (named after the famous Austrian skier Franz Klammer) got put down, when my mum took us out and bought me this green T-shirt with a big Umbro sign on the front. I remember thinking that was quite a big deal because I had a brand-name sports T-shirt. And at that point I would have been about ten, but I kept wearing that T-shirt until it was way too tight.

My parents' footwear of choice for me was a pair of Ascot trainers with a fake-looking tick on them from the cheap shops in Bletchley, which I hated – and at my middle school I used to get torn to pieces for wearing them. Once, though, we went to JD Sports because I needed some new trainers and I'll never forget it: there was a discount bin and my mum managed to find a 'pair' of Nike trainers – one foot was size seven and one was size eight. They were super-cheap because they were clearly just leftover odd trainers, but I didn't care. I was thrilled to own a pair of Nike shoes, like you would not believe. It was such a big deal to me. This memory is one that stays with me now as a professional athlete, to never take for granted the free and abundant clothing I'm lucky enough to receive these days.

Thrilled though I was, whenever I played sport, games or any form of PE, I always had to make sure that the Nike insoles were out of sight of my classmates when the trainers weren't on my feet, because I was petrified that somebody would see that they were different sizes. This was the sort of thing that these kids would absolutely kill you for, and I was perpetually worried about having more people rip me for something, even though these trainers were my pride and joy because they were Nike.

Away from sport, my brother and I used to spend a lot of time in our own room: I loved Lego and figures, and when we were a bit older we'd quite often go to a car-boot sale on Sundays – my dad would give us a pound to buy a couple of toys.

I have one particular memory from those trips: my dad brutally haggling people down because he is the tightest man alive. We went up to this stall where this bloke had an old pair of grey New Balance trainers. These caught my dad's eye, and he asked how much how much they were – 50p. Now, any reasonable person would probably think this was a bargain, but not my dad. 'I'll give you 20p,' came the reply. My dad is quite jolly, and if you met him you'd view him only as nice, but sometimes he can give you this look that is so intense it's quite scary, and he used it here. This bloke, well, you could see his heart dropped and he just muttered, 'Oh. Right. Yeah, OK.' And my dad went off happy because he had saved 30p! He ruined this guy's day for a measly 30p.

It won't surprise you to learn that we weren't really bought much, especially in the early years, because my parents couldn't afford it. They weren't being cruel, just honest – they had no spare cash. The word I heard more than any other during my childhood was 'no'.

'Oh, Mum, can I have that?' 'No.'

'Can we go to McDonald's?' 'No.'

'Can I . . .?' 'No.'

My partner Susie had a similar upbringing, as her family also didn't have much money to spare. Nowadays, we often remark how cheap some toys are, and how you can pick up loads of great wooden ones for next to nothing, or second-hand toys on eBay. It's not a big deal. For our parents, it was different: things were expensive and gifts were luxuries and treats.

That's why I remember one occasion when we went into Milton Keynes so vividly. As normal, my brother and I went through our usual routine of asking for an Action Man, something we knew we were never going to get, but would always ask for anyway. And this time, Mum said yes. Our excitement levels went through the roof. We couldn't believe it. She said yes! It was like the greatest thing ever – we had an Action Man! And because we had so little, that one toy brought me hours and hours of happiness.

For all the worry I had about being teased, bullied or ridiculed at Holne Chase, it was at middle school where my love of sport really started. Two Mile Ash had football and rugby teams, so there was the opportunity to take part in structured sport, something I quickly thrived on. From being the person who was picked on, I became the kid who was picked for most teams. Up front for the football team, on the wing for the rugby team, playing basketball for Shenley Jets and running 75m races for the school in the summer. I wanted to play as many sports as possible, and I probably did.

It was while I was at Two Mile Ash that my family also had its first ever 'present day' – when the family got together and gave you a present. There were only three of them in total during my childhood and they tended to coincide with my dad having a larger bit of work, like a full house extension, to do. Imagine my excitement: no birthday or Christmas presents and now this.

The first one came when I was about eight years old, and I remember my uncle Lee got me and my brother a toy car each: Bert got a Ferrari F40 and I got a 1967 Chevrolet Corvette. My excitement rocketed, but we had to wait for another three years for the next present day, which just so happened to coincide with Princess Diana's funeral, 6 September 1997. We somehow got a bouncy castle in the garden, which was hugely exciting for us, and all my family came over and gave us presents.

I remember the TV had been moved into the dining room so people could watch the funeral. But looking back, I wonder if any of the neighbours saw us jumping up and down on the bouncy castle and thought, 'These guys are a bit odd, they're celebrating that she's died.'

That day I was given a *Now 37* CD while Robert got a CD by Eternal. My brother and I were also lucky enough to get a Sanyo CD player each, and until a couple of years ago my dad was still using one at work, even though it was a complete wreck. I guess the fact that I remember every detail shows you how special and important these moments were.

Our third present day came a few years later, when I was 14

and at Denbigh secondary school, and my mum and dad bought me a PC. As you can imagine, this was a massive deal. By then, my mum had been working as a maternity nurse for some years, which meant there was more money in the house, and they must have felt it would be good for my schoolwork and for the rest of the family as well.

Of course, we had other ideas. I remember my brother getting *Doom* and hiding it from my mum because it was an 18 certificate, and she hated all the shooting games, while I had *Diablo II: Lord of Destruction*, a hack-and-slash role-playing game where you enter hell at one point. My mum wouldn't have liked that much either. I used to be obsessed with that game, but I had to fight off my brother to get on my own computer to even play it, even though by then I was doing so many different sports that I didn't use it nearly as much as he did.

My brother and I butted heads quite a lot as kids. But as we got older, we started to get on really well. We spent a lot of time upstairs in our rooms, hanging out, though it became the bane of my life when my brother developed into a computer games addict – at 7am every day he would sneak into my bedroom, turn the bloody computer on and then wake me up just so he could play.

CHAPTER 4

A Life of Crime?

As I approached my teens I'm pretty sure the smacking I was getting at home lay behind my increasing bad behaviour. I was rebelling because I was being punished all the time. I hated it. One time I was so annoyed and angry that it had happened again that I punched my bedroom wall as hard as I could and split my knuckle. I remember wailing in pain and my mum looked at me and said, 'Well, that was stupid.' She was right, but it summed up my frustration.

From a really young age – as far back as I can remember – I had this feeling of wanting to be reckless, to push the boundaries as far as I could. When I was four or five, my dad began work on building a double garage at the end of our garden. A couple of years later, before he had fitted the window in the storage room on the first floor, I would run and jump right out of the window on to a pile of sand on the floor. Imagine leaping out of your bedroom window: most people would think twice about doing it. Not me.

I loved the feeling of flying through the air. I guess it came in handy when I got older. Probably one of the reasons why I have always pushed my luck is that I've never suffered any bad injuries as a result of my daredevil streak. I have always been reckless – in fact, I still am to this day – but, touch wood, it hasn't cost me. Ironically, it's actually the more mundane task of the long jump that damages my body more than anything more heedless.

Before my brother and I jumped, we always checked to see if the coast was clear. First, we would gaze down at the kitchen. Then the second bedroom. Then, finally, my parents' bedroom. They were the only rooms that the double garage could be seen from, and we knew that usually my mum would be downstairs with my sister. We didn't want our mum to see us, but I'm sure my dad guessed what we were up to.

He was soon doing more than guessing. At that point, Dad was yet to put in the stairs to the top floor. So Robert and I climbed on to this bay window and pulled ourselves up into the top section. It was a bit of an adventure for us – or at least it was until my brother jumped down to the bay window, put his leg through the glass and gashed it badly. I was already ahead of him so I saw him put his hand on his trousers and then lift it up. There was blood everywhere.

I ran in to get my dad. His initial reaction wasn't to say, 'Don't worry, I will take you to the hospital and get it stitched up,' but to go absolutely mental at my brother. It must have been the shock of what he saw. So my brother had blood pouring out of him, but had to endure this dressing-down before he was taken to A&E. That was typical of my dad: his first response was always to go ballistic. The arm around the shoulder came later.

When I was a kid, lots of my friends would hurt themselves, usually while doing something stupid, and they'd get a plaster cast which would always leave me a bit envious. I really wanted one of my own, so that I could get it drawn on and signed by all my mates. Even when I broke part of my hand in a fight in my early teens I was disappointed that I had strapping rather than a cast: because one of my fingers was dislocated, the doctors put it back in and just splinted it, much to my annoyance.

Being vocal isn't a new thing for me. I was always quick to shout when I felt something to be an injustice – even if that injustice was actually just my mum saying it was too late to go and play outside. In turn, that meant I would get hit with the wooden spoon rather more regularly than I would have liked. The way I saw it, maybe at times I was being a little bit of a shit and I deserved a smack or whatever else. But the problem was it was so commonplace in my household, and for nothing, that I wanted to silently hit out.

As I got older, this rebellious streak pushed me in other directions. And because of the religious upbringing, and being so restricted as a result, I butted up against that. Although I was always petrified of my parents finding out about anything naughty I was up to, I also desperately wanted to do lots of the things they wouldn't allow – this is the irony of strict parenting.

Most teenagers go through a rebellious phase at some point. They smoke a few ciggies behind the bike sheds or somewhere, or drink cheap spirits on a park bench long before the law says they should. They might nick the odd sweet or two from a shop as a dare. I did all that. And a lot more.

It started relatively tamely. In the summer holidays when I was 12, a few of us decided we wanted to do an all-nighter – where our parents assumed we were all at a friend's house having a sleepover when in reality we roamed the streets or crashed somewhere we shouldn't until morning. But I first had to get it past my parents.

My first attempt was a complete failure. I went to my mum and said I was going to stay over at so-and-so's house. I had a plan I thought was really clever – if I just threw in an obscure enough friend, someone she didn't know that well, she'd be more likely to believe it than if it was a mate around the corner. But no. My mum, being a relatively wise woman, said, 'OK, that's fine, as long as you get their mum to give me a call.'

Well, I wasn't going to give up there. I persuaded this girl I knew to ring up and pretend to be a mum. Unsurprisingly, we were rumbled. My mum never said outright that she had cottoned on, but it must have been very obvious that she was speaking to a child. Predictably, I wasn't allowed out.

Eventually, though, all-nighters became a very regular thing, especially over the summer holidays. I often found myself at a loose end. Because I didn't go to a school near my house, all my friends lived in a different part of Milton Keynes, so I didn't get to see them very often. That meant, in the holidays, I only had the kids who lived nearby – ones I wasn't that close to – to hang out with. They tended to be a bit rougher and more likely to get into trouble than my schoolmates. And I was all too willing to go along with their plans.

We started by going to the old brickworks in Bletchley, where there were abandoned offices, and breaking into them. We were definitely not the first people to do so. The building had been closed for a while, and every time someone got in, the authorities put new bars on, but they weren't hard to get past.

After breaking in, we always headed upstairs because the ground floor was a real mess: it had been trashed quite a few times and there was a lot of rubbish around. It was also very dark because all the windows had been boarded up and barred. And, as you do as kids, you wind each other up to frighten your mates. We would tell each other that there was some big scary bloke living down in the bottom bit. I wasn't prepared to hang around to find out whether it was true.

Upstairs, there were already some large tractor tyres and pieces of wood that people had pulled up the stairs, so it was easy to create a den. It was there that I tried smoking for the first time. Absolutely nobody in my family smoked but, typical me, I was trying to be rebellious and a bit different.

I remember one of the lads claiming that he had been smoking since he was seven. A few of these kids came from tough backgrounds, where smoking early was normal, so at that point I was way behind some of them in experience. I was desperate, therefore, to look cool even if it meant doing something slightly dodgy. Subconsciously, I also knew I was damaging my own body but I wanted to be bad in order to rebel, so I carried on.

I grabbed the rolled cigarette, took a drag, and immediately hated it. In fact, in all the years that I dipped in and out of smoking, which lasted until I was 16, I always hated it. But I didn't cough, and I felt really pleased with myself. I remember thinking, 'Oh, I didn't cough, most people cough so I'm a bit cooler.' What an idiot!

So I'd broken into a building with a few mates and I had tried smoking. I was 12, and I knew that if my parents were to find out either of those things, let alone both, I would be in fear for my life. Every kid says that, of course, but I genuinely thought that my parents would give me the smacking of all smackings.

They don't even know to this day about a lot of the things I did when I was stupid and young, so it will be interesting to see how they react to reading this. I imagine they still won't be that happy: they have mellowed, but not by much.

Soon this kind of escapade became a habit: we'd break into buildings, have a smoke and – increasingly – end up getting chased by security people or the cops. It happened a lot: security would turn up, then the police, and we would leg it. One time, though, a couple of my mates and I got caught after trespassing and looking for a way in to a school via the roof. We ended up throwing stones from the rooftop, and I was taken home by the police and got a bollocking like you wouldn't believe from my mum. You can imagine her embarrassment when I turned up in a police car. I remember I got walloped – and then grounded.

Really, for the most part we were just bored. We had nothing else to do. Bletchley isn't exactly a hotbed of excitement for any young kid, and especially someone like me who was always on the go and wanting to be active. But soon I was starting to grow tired of just breaking into a building, smoking and every so often getting chased. I wanted to experience a fresh thrill.

That led to the first time I ever stole something. A mate and I went into central Bletchley on our bikes. We went into a shop with a jewellery stand and saw a pair of studded earrings priced nine quid, which would have been relatively expensive back then. They obviously weren't real gold, and I had no intention of actually wearing them. But one minute they were on the shelves, and the next they were in my pocket. It was easy. We had got away with it.

So, naturally, we did it again. And again. I was more of a sheep than a leader. OK, they're nicking a chocolate bar. Right, I will do the same. But quickly I acquired a taste for thieving. Usually, we operated in individual shops on the high street in Bletchley. For some reason, I still remember nicking a bunch of fake gold straps for watches in this one place. We never did anything with booty like this – I would either ditch it in a bush or take it home and put it in a box somewhere. I would find it a year later and think, why on earth have I got this?

Most of the time it was sweets and chocolate: Wham bars, cola bottles, things like that, usually from the local Co-op. It was so easy to do. It didn't have CCTV cameras and cashiers at the till couldn't see you. It was a shoplifter's dream: you just put the sweets up your sleeve and walked out.

Looking back, most of it was just the thrill of doing something wrong. I also thought that if I did bad things, it might make people look at me differently, and I'd get more street cred with the cooler kids. Some of it was more simple: because I had very little money, I couldn't buy many sweets. But I wanted sweets. So I would try to convince myself that I wasn't doing anything wrong. 'It's only a chocolate bar, so it doesn't matter. It doesn't affect anybody.'

And while it might sound odd, I never saw myself as a bad person – I wonder if anyone ever does? I knew that what I was doing was wrong, but it was as if I couldn't stop myself. I knew

I shouldn't be doing it, and it would really upset my parents if they found out. Yet, while I had a conscience, I always somehow managed to override it by telling myself I wasn't nicking anything worth loads of money, or hurting anybody. I might have had an angel on one shoulder, but the devil on the other was whispering in my ear a little louder.

When I scarpered from security or the police after we'd been caught trespassing somewhere, it never felt that serious – just exciting – because of the thrill of the chase. But every time I stole, I did feel remorseful for a while, yet that didn't stop me. I went back and did it multiple times.

The thing is, although I was doing stuff I knew was wrong, I still like to think I was brought up well – I was just rebelling, like so many kids will, reacting against certain elements of my upbringing. I wasn't doing it in a cold-hearted way. I felt guilty doing some things but I also coveted this naughty side: the sensation of the pulse running a bit faster, the body feeling a bit more alive. I found it exhilarating, and I guess that was the point: I craved the rush.

The last time I ever stole was also the closest I came to getting caught. I was just funnelling the sweets up my sleeve at the local Co-op. But I hadn't checked the coast was clear, or noticed that a bloke had come in behind me, so when I finally looked around all I heard was a loud 'Oiiiiiiiiiiii!' I bolted out of the shop as quickly as I could, the sweets falling out of my sleeve as this bloke screamed after me.

As a kid I found this hilarious at first, but I quickly realised that I had been a bit too reckless and silly. I had exposed myself to too much risk and the consequences for me getting caught were probably much greater than for other people, because I knew I'd get absolutely pasted by my parents for bringing shame on the family.

By this stage I was drinking too. Not huge amounts, but certainly regularly at weekends. The first time I tried beer properly, aged about 12 or 13, I didn't like it. It was at the summer training camp for the Bletchley Colts football team, and another player and I went into the clubhouse and saw two Red Stripe beers left by the cricket team, so we nicked them – which seemed a common theme around that time in my life. Before then I'd taken sips of my dad's beer, on the rare occasion he had a drink, but this was the first time I drank a whole one. And I absolutely hated it. It was horrible. But again, that desperate need for me to try to be a bit cool and a bit different kicked in, so I obviously pretended that it was a lovely drink and very refreshing. I was all bravado.

I started drinking more, getting a taste for it I guess, when I was about 14. Snakebite and black. Malibu. Vodka. Red Aftershock. Every so often my brother, who was a couple of years older and much bigger than me, would get us a whole bottle of Teacher's whisky, which we and our friends would also work our way through.

The first time I went to a pub-club was for my 15th birthday. Big Baz, one of my brother's rugby mates, was on the door, so that allowed me to get into the Rat and Parrot in Milton Keynes without worrying about ID. Another friend of my brother was doing something called a 'gas chamber' and so I followed suit: lighting a shot of Sambuca, putting your hand over the top, breathing in the fumes and knocking it back. So that was what

I was up to on my 15th birthday. Some people get a bike; I went out and got totally smashed.

One thing I didn't do very much, though, was fight – although there were a few scrapes here and there.

When I was 14, I had this scrap outside my house with a guy called Russell. My brother and a few other friends were throwing each other into bushes, and so I picked up Russell and tried to do the same. Unfortunately, he missed the bush and landed on the floor. So then he got up and hit me. I wasn't prepared to take that, so then we basically got into a bit of a fight that turned quite nasty. I have to give him credit, though, because he was knocked down at least three times, yet he kept getting up. But I paid the price as I ended up breaking my hand and dislocating a little finger.

That, inadvertently, ended my interest in playing rugby. I was always terrible at saying no to people, and three or four weeks later my PE teacher said that I needed to play for the school in an important match. I'll never forget it: I had this broken hand, which was strapped up and still hurt quite a lot, and I was playing bloody rugby and it was the most ridiculous thing ever. There was this big guy who was smiling at me the whole game; and when I got the ball he grabbed my hand on purpose and squeezed it as hard as he could and I just burst into tears.

Afterwards, I told my teacher, 'You can sod off. I'm not playing for you any more after you put me through that.' So, the unintended consequence of punching Russell and breaking my hand was that rugby became a much less important sport for me. I still did play every now and then, but I never dreamed of becoming a rugby player. It was more for the bigger guys who could take it and didn't mind giving out bits. My brother was much better. He was the star rugby player of our secondary school; he represented the east of England, and was also trying to play for Northampton Saints for a while, so I was in teams more because of his ability than mine.

He was exceptionally talented. In fact, I still believe he is probably more naturally gifted at certain sports than I am. He's powerfully built, an absolute beast when it comes to strength. And he was also good enough to compete in the English Schools' Athletics Championships in the long jump. But, sadly, he could never quite deal with failure. Instead of making him fight even harder to succeed, it often crushed him.

My only other big fight as a kid happened around the same sort of age, outside a pub called the Grebe. Five or six of us were hanging around in the streets in the evening again, when two blokes came out of the pub and gave us a little bit of verbal. A couple of the guys with me decided that was a perfect opportunity to give some back. And so it all kicked off.

One of our lads got thumped quite hard and his eyebrow was split pretty badly, while one of their guys was knocked to the floor and booted in the head. Then it all started to get quite rough. They went to get a load of other guys out of the pub and it ended up being a massive brawl.

This might sound strange, but I remember thinking the whole time, even when I was throwing punches and whatever else, 'I don't want to do this. I don't want to be fighting. This is ridiculous. These two blokes have walked out pissed up, and obviously some of my mates were being a bit mouthy but really, it really wasn't that bad. Just a few kids giving them a load of shit. Now somebody has been booted in the head, somebody has had their eyebrow popped and they are running back to the pub to get a load of other people to join in.'

Some guys really seem to get off on that, just pointlessly turning on other people for their own weird pleasure. I've never got that, and never enjoyed being anywhere near it either. Seeing somebody get in a fight and being beaten up is not something I relish. Luckily, this time, before anyone got badly hurt, we ended up doing one and running off.

As a sports star, it's drummed into you that you should try to be a role model, but I want to be honest about my past. You can be a total dickhead and yet still succeed. If you make one mistake, or even a hundred mistakes, it doesn't mean you have screwed up for good. I am testament to that. It's more about perseverance, accepting that things don't always go your way and learning to bounce back.

CHAPTER 5

Trials with Aston Villa

Throughout the period when I was doing stupid things, I was still playing a lot of sport. Like other lads my age, I tried pretty much everything, including rugby, badminton, basketball, table tennis, track and field, and I picked most of them up very quickly and played them to a decent standard. I have particularly fond memories of my dad putting a piece of chipboard on top of an old writing desk in our garage so we could play table tennis on it. The one exception was football, which I was absolutely shocking at – at least to begin with.

Most young lads dream of becoming a professional footballer. I was no different. As a kid, I loved watching and talking about every match on TV, so naturally I also dreamed of emulating my heroes, Ryan Giggs and Paul Scholes, and playing for Manchester United. When I was nine, my parents took me to my local youth team, Woughton Wanderers, where I was rightly put in H team, the worst of all. Because at that stage I literally couldn't kick a ball straight. I was terrible!

I was so bad, in fact, that my manager soon told me, 'Greg, you need to go in goal now.' He was trying to keep me involved, I guess, and being nice on one level. But all it did was reaffirm just how awful I was. Often we would be put on a pitch out of the way, playing seven-a-side, yet we would still be getting hammered by some other awful team who were nevertheless miles better than us.

Unknown to me at the time, I came from good footballing stock. My great-grandfather, John 'Jock' Rutherford, was a right winger who earned 11 caps for England in the early 1900s and was lauded as the 'The Newcastle Flyer'. Sometimes I wonder whether that is where I got my speed from. Reading the reports from the time, he was obviously a very decent player, who made his debut at Newcastle at 17 and earned three championship titles and five FA Cup final medals. He then moved to Arsenal, where he became the oldest player to represent the club, being 41 and 159 days when he made his last appearance on 20 March 1926. Even when he was 38, *The Times* was referring to him as 'a tower of strength' for Arsenal, so maybe I got my natural power from him too. He's even honoured on the walls along Ashburton Grove, next to their stadium, and in the Arsenal museum.

Jock holds a family record too, in terms of the number of people who have watched him: he performed in front of 101,117 at Crystal Palace in the 1905 Cup final, in which Newcastle lost 2-0 to Aston Villa – over 20,000 more than saw me win gold at the Olympic Stadium in London 2012.

He wasn't the only one who excelled at sport: his son Jack – my grandfather – also played for Arsenal. However I didn't know that side of the family at all back then because, as I've mentioned, Jack had left my grandmother when my dad was just two. The subject is still not broached much within my family even now, and I have never spoken to my grandma about it. Of course, it was devastating for my poor dad, who grew up in real poverty and without a father. At least my London 2012 gold medal had one nice unexpected consequence: the members from great-grandfather Jock's side of the family got in touch, and my dad ended up speaking to his half-sister for the first time.

While I might have inherited Jock's speed and power, if you had seen my early efforts to play football you would never have known I was related to him. Fortunately, there was some level of ability within my genes which came through after a bit more encouragement from my dad, who had been a very good player himself as a lad.

I wasn't doing any extra training; in fact, I was relatively lazy. But I loved playing games and I loved competition. I was always that kid who, if we lost, would be in tears because I took it very badly, especially as a child. I was that kid who would be crying in the corner because I wasn't happy, even when people said things like, 'Oh, well done – we've done well to get this far.' I hated losing.

After a while, I left the Wanderers and moved to Bletchley Colts, who were regarded as one of the strongest teams in Buckinghamshire, as two of my friends played there. Slowly, I improved my touch and I began to dribble better too. But I looked a lot better than I actually was because of my speed. Without question, I was the quickest kid in Milton Keynes at that time. And so, more often than not, when the ball was lobbed over the top I would beat the offside trap and be in on goal. The trouble was I was awful at taking a ball round a keeper. Basically, I would bank on the fact that I'd probably get ten chances a game and I would score three or four of them. Arguably, I would have scored a hell of a lot more if I'd actually taken the time to develop some skills, although, saying that, as I got older I became good at judging where players were around me and bringing them into the game.

What also helped was that my dad started to give me a bonus every time I scored. I still remember the rates now: a quid for a right-foot goal, £1.50 for a header and £2 for a left-foot goal. And because we never got pocket money, the incentive was actually pretty strong. My dad has always kept a pot on the dashboard of his van for his loose change. It's like a million twopenny pieces and a few pounds and whatever else. How good it felt after a football match to get in his van and be given a couple of quid.

Sometimes it was a lot more. When I was 13, Bletchley Colts disbanded and I joined New Bradwell, but the goals kept coming. We won one game 14-0 – I scored seven and was determined to get a triple hat-trick. Unfortunately, the referee ended up blowing the final whistle ten minutes early because it was so one-sided. The whole time I was thinking, 'I don't know if my dad is going to have enough money to pay me!' I made sure I scored a couple of tap-ins with my left foot too, to bump up my winnings. It's amazing how money can motivate you as a child, especially when you never get a chance to see it very often.

Inevitably, people started calling me Little Paul Scholes

because I was ginger, even though I was a striker not a midfielder. It's the same old story: apparently all gingers look the same, and if you were ginger and you played football to a decent level at that time you were always going to be called Scholes.

By the time I was 13, clubs had started to scout me because I was scoring a bag of goals purely because I was quick. And when I was offered the chance to train at Aston Villa I wasn't going to say no.

We trained just outside Birmingham, and myself and a guy called Mark Randall – who went on to play professionally for Arsenal and the MK Dons – would travel up together. Mark loved football even more than I did, and was far better than me too. A few years ago, the Arsenal manager Arsene Wenger said he was one of the most talented youngsters he had seen.

However, training at Villa wasn't what either of us expected. For the most part we would stand around, do some drills and whatever else, and then go home. I wasn't used much at all; I never played a game for the club, it was just training, and more training. I saw how the set-up worked and I simply didn't enjoy it.

It did, however, make me realise that football is a hard world. I remember we would head to the car park afterwards, and the coach would walk up to certain kids and say, 'Don't come back next week,' and that was that: you were gone. I wasn't astute enough at the time to understand that the writing was on the wall for me. I never had that talk, but after a few months of training we went home one day and my dad said to me, 'I don't think we should bother with that any more, they're not using you. You are standing around, and we are wasting our time a little bit.'

He did it in a nice way. He didn't say it like, 'You are wasting my time.' But I think he probably knew that it was never going to happen for me. So, rather than let me suffer the disappointment of being told I wasn't good enough, he sold it to me by saying there was probably no need to go back, and so we didn't. I thank him for that.

Sometimes I am asked whether I had the ability ever to have turned professional. Honestly, I don't think so – at least not at the highest level. Possibly I could have scraped into a League One or League Two side, but I would never have been a top footballer. At the time, I fell by the wayside because I wasn't prepared to put in the time. I don't think I committed to a single tackle during my entire football career and, because of my laziness, my technical development plateaued massively. As I got older, I realised that I possessed nowhere near the ability I have in track and field.

There was one thing I really enjoyed about those trips up to Birmingham and back, though: I got to spend a couple of hours in the car with my dad, who shared the driving with Mark's old man, and we would talk football or whatever else was on our minds. Sometimes my dad was clearly very tired, but he loves sport and, because he didn't have the opportunities when he was growing up, he made sure I would have every chance to get into sport. Later on, my mum was also brilliant at taking me everywhere, especially when I was on the verge of becoming a professional track and field athlete.

Despite their often liberal use of the wooden spoon in

disciplining me, I had no doubt they wanted the best for me when it came to sport. By now, I knew that I wasn't going to make my fame and fortune in football, but I was still convinced there was something else out there at which I could become the best in the world. It was just a question of finding it.

CHAPTER 6

In Search of the Right Sport

My ambition to become a professional footballer might have bitten the dust, but there were plenty of other sports I liked and was good at – including badminton, which I began playing when I was 12. It started when my mum and dad went out for a couple of Sundays, and I remember thinking it was bizarre they were spending time together. Each time, my mum came back really red-faced and sweating quite heavily and I thought, 'What's going on here? Why are you going out and coming back looking like that?' Eventually, I found out there was an innocent explanation: they were playing badminton, and they were more than happy for me to give it a go too.

I had a few rallies with my dad, and while he was significantly better than me, I wasn't bad. Soon, I tried out for my secondary school team, got selected and was quickly named captain. And by Year Ten, when I would have turned 15, I was put forward for county trials at the National Badminton

Centre in Milton Keynes. That was an eye-opener, because I was surrounded by a bunch of posh kids who had a very inflated sense of their status. I'll never forget it – when I went there I felt as if I wasn't deemed to be the right kind of person. Everyone appeared to be looking down at this oik from Bletchley.

I had this Karakal racket which I absolutely loved. It wasn't cheap – it must have cost around £80 and I remember thinking at the time, 'This is unbelievable that my parents are spending this amount of money on me.' But sport was the one thing my parents would loosen their wallets for. If I needed a pair of spikes for the year, my dad would go and get me a pair. If I needed a pair of football boots, I got them – although, of course, they would have to last a very long time. It helped that by this stage my mum was also working full time as a maternity nurse, so they had a little more spare cash. However, my Karakal racket was nothing compared to those of every other kid at the trials: they all seemed to have top-of-the-range Yonex rackets with special sets of strings.

I was paired with this posh lad, who was much better than me. I could handle him beating me. But it was this very dismissive look he gave me every time he won a point that really grated. Looking back, it was no surprise he was better: I played badminton once a week at my secondary school and it was like an after-school club in a way. Nobody had ever taught me technique, or how best to move around the court. My opponent, an arrogant little bastard, to put it nicely, was training all the time at the National Badminton Centre.

But badminton was never the sport I wanted to turn into a

professional career. The truth is, while I loved playing it, I believed I was capable of succeeding in a more high-profile sport.

I have been fairly critical of my parents' behaviour during my childhood, but they loved me playing sport. Whenever I was running, kicking or throwing something, my dad was happy. I loved those times when sport brought us together, and longed for the moments when we could kick a football around or he would come to watch me play on Sunday.

And he was always brilliant at giving me a kick up the arse when I needed it. There were a lot of Sunday mornings when I had to be dragged out of bed for my own good because I was a bit lazy. Sometimes I wouldn't want to go to football and would start arguing. But my dad would just tell me to get in the car. When you are a kid, often you don't appreciate what your parents are doing for you: you just think, 'Well, obviously they should take us everywhere.' But when I look back now I realise that actually almost all of their time was consumed by either working or taking me and my brother to sporting events – and for that I am hugely thankful. Without them, there is no way I would have been an Olympic champion.

And what I perceived at the time to be pushy parenting was nothing compared to what I have seen since. When it came to sport, they struck the right balance between putting a rocket up my arse and an arm around my shoulder.

Sometimes, though, they went too far. Once, some mates called round to ask whether I fancied hanging out, just before I was due to have badminton training. I told my parents I wanted to go out with them, because for me badminton wasn't a sport I wanted to pursue seriously, even though they had bought me a nice racket, and the row quickly escalated.

I don't ever remember using particularly harsh words, but I was arguing quite hard, saying things like, 'You just don't ever let me be normal, do you?' In other words, exactly the sort of thing that kids up and down the land say to their parents when they enter their early teens and their hormones are raging and they start to crave independence. But my mum wasn't going to stand for me arguing with her, especially in front of my mates.

She smacked me across the face and I fell back against the kitchen worktop in surprise. It hurt a lot and later, when the crying had subsided and I looked at my face in the mirror, I could see the marks. As I ran off past the front door, I heard one of my mates tell my mum, 'You shouldn't do that just because he doesn't want to play badminton.'

Despite all the evidence to the contrary, I still believed I could be a professional sportsman. I simply assumed it would happen at some point. I was very blasé because I was naturally gifted at every sport I had tried, apart from football. But gradually I realised that athletics was likely to offer me my best chance of succeeding.

I was always much quicker than anyone else around me as a kid and by Year Four I was picked to be the main sprinter for my middle school in the inter-schools event held every summer. Even though I was running against people in the year above me, I still won.

After that, I was asked to come down to Marshall Milton Keynes Athletics Club. At that point I said, 'No, it's fine, I'll run for my school for a bit and I'll just play football and a bit of rugby and whatever else,' because I just loved football so much.

But when I was 12 or so, I started training twice a week at Milton Keynes. One of the reasons I started going was because there were girls at the track. And, as a hormonal lad suddenly seeing members of the opposite sex running around in tiny shorts and a vest, I thought, 'Well, this is the greatest sport in the world.' I loved the fact that I could also talk to my mates in between doing stuff as well. It meant that while I was very lazy when it came to training for most sports, almost every Tuesday and Thursday I would turn up at the track. True, there were still moments when I felt, 'No, I can't be bothered to go,' and there would be an argument with my parents. But the fact that there were girls at the track made me want to stick at it.

At the time, I was the fastest kid in Milton Keynes, which might not sound like much now but back then I was really proud of it – and the fact that I could run 12.8 seconds for the 100m and 26.1 seconds for the 200m. A year later, though, I was no longer top dog, as I found myself being beaten by half a second by this young lad called Craig Pickering. Craig turned out to be a hugely talented sprinter, who was good enough to run for Great Britain and win a 4×100m bronze medal in the 2007 World Championships. At the time, though, he was nobody. It sounds bad but a year earlier I had raced him and beaten him so easily that when we met again he didn't register as a dangerous opponent. I certainly didn't take that view when he thrashed me by half a second, which is a long way in a 100m race even when you are 13!

That was a wake-up call. Being beaten that much by a guy

from my own town pretty much told me I was never going to make it as a top sprinter. Milton Keynes has never been a hotbed of sprinting talent like London, Manchester or Birmingham – it's just not big enough.

That said, it was a weird period in the town's history because we had a fantastic crop of young athletes all coming up at the same time, including myself, Craig, Mervyn Luckwell, who represented Britain in the javelin in London 2012, and Andy Whetstone, who competed for England in the 800m. Female athletes like Joey Duck and Kadi-Ann Thomas were also extremely talented, and at the time were considered stars of the future.

I certainly didn't stand out in this crowded field. But there was a moment when I thought I might have the ability to do something in this sport. It came when I was 14 and I went to the 2001 English Schools' in Exeter to compete in the long jump. There was a guy called Seamus Cassidy, who everyone thought would be the next big thing at the event, and I was up against him. We stayed overnight in this dormitory, and I remember at one point Seamus started flexing his muscles in the mirror while he looked on approvingly at his body. I recall thinking, 'What the hell are you doing? This is the weirdest thing I have ever seen.' To make matters worse, he then started kissing his biceps.

I looked at my own body. I was then just this quite small and pasty kid – a pathetic creature who was standing there thinking, 'This is really odd and very uncomfortable.' However, the next day I ended up finishing fifth, having jumped a big personal best of 6.16m. Some half-decent athletes had beaten me, but I didn't care: I'd gone from being the number two sprinter in Milton Keynes for my age to being the fifth best in the country in the long jump. Nobody could see it yet – not even me. But I had found the event that would change my life.

CHAPTER 7

All-nighters and GCSEs

If I'd had more sense, I would have knuckled down after that English Schools' result. Instead, I was enjoying more all-nighters. In the summer months we would head to fields on the outskirts of the Crownhill industrial estate, and drink and stay out until dawn. Merlin, the company that makes Premier League stickers, is based there, so we would jump the fences and plunder their bins for the stickers and cards that had been thrown out. Then we'd raid the huge skips, grabbing some cardboard boxes, and whatever else we could find, and lug them to a nearby underpass or park.

That park has been developed now, but back then it was just grass and field. We'd build a massive den out of cardboard, get rather drunk, and then wake up the following morning around 5am. Once we'd stirred, groggy and stinking of booze, fags and sweat, we'd go out and find the milkman doing his round. We'd nick a crate of milk off the back of the float and return to the park to drink it. I hated milk but we were all so thirsty and hungry by that point, and needing to sober up, that we'd down the lot.

These days, of course, if I went to the park and some kids had created a filthy can-strewn den which my son Milo wanted to go in and play, I would be thinking, 'What a bunch of little dickheads. Who do they think they are?' And yet that was exactly what we ended up doing most weekends during the summer. Drinking, smoking, trespassing. Getting into a little bit of trouble here and there; getting chased by the police every so often.

When I look back at all that now, I know much of it was stupid and wrong. But I couldn't stop myself. I had a conscience, but somehow I always convinced myself it was OK to hit the override button.

If those all-nighters weren't bad enough, I also started turning up hungover for school while I was in Year Ten – exactly when I should have been knuckling down in preparation for my GCSEs. I wasn't quite stupid enough to make it a regular thing – that came later, during my A-levels – but again, it showed my reckless side. If there was a door to be pushed, I pushed it until it flew off its hinges. One particular incident, when I was 15, sticks in my mind. I'd left a bottle of Malibu at my brother's friend's house one night, and the next day his girlfriend brought it into school. I remember being a little bit annoyed at first because, well, it was my Malibu. But during our lunch break we went to the school fields and shared whatever was left of the bottle.

Before long I was swaying into our humanities class, merry on the delights of life and coconut rum. Unfortunately, our teacher had decided not only to have a class debate, but to put the pupils in a circle. Inevitably, I couldn't help becoming more animated and boisterous than normal.

I guess I was a bit of a Jack-the-lad, someone who was loud and noisy, without ever intending to be malicious. Most of the time I was simply trying to make people laugh. School wasn't so much about how much I could learn, but about how many people I could make laugh that day. But in that lesson it obviously went a step further. Eventually, the teacher started looking at me. 'You are being very strange this afternoon, Greg, what is going on?' he said. At that point I froze. I knew if they found out that I'd been drinking I'd be in real trouble, so I said something like, 'Oh no, I'm just really enjoying the debate.' Somehow, I managed to get away with it.

In hindsight, I was sabotaging myself and others. There were too many times when I would talk non-stop in class and prevent my classmates from learning. But you never see it like that when you are a teenager; all you think is that you are being a bit funny. The reality was different: drip by drip, I was ruining any chance of getting ahead, let alone going to university.

My secondary school, Denbigh, was highly regarded, so perhaps they assumed that most students – especially ones like me, who played a lot of sport and were considered relatively clever – would scarcely be drinking in the middle of the school day. You could hardly blame them.

I suppose some people might have thought I was a bit chavvy, but really it was just what kids were wearing back then: tracksuit and a T-shirt most of the time. I remember Kappa trousers being very popular, especially the ones with the poppers on the side, but my mum would never let me get a pair because the logo featured two naked people leaning against each other, and she thought that was too rude.

But there were other rules set by my parents that I took delight in getting round. When my brother and I were growing up, we were told we weren't allowed girlfriends – it was drilled into us, in fact. My mum, in particular, got angry at the idea because she saw it as religiously quite dangerous. However, that was a red rag to a bull for me. In typical fashion, I took her warnings as a challenge. To be honest, any time anybody tells me I'm not allowed to do something, the first question is always: why? In the early years, it was just sweet and a little silly: you hold hands with a girl at school and she's your girlfriend, that sort of thing.

But as I got older I started having more serious relationships. They didn't always go to plan, though. Once, I ended up dating an athlete for a short period of time, but it wasn't working out so I dumped her by text message while I was sitting in my mate Ross's bedroom next door – very classy. I know this doesn't sound good, but in my defence, I was too scared to do it in person because I had just heard the story that she had taken a knife to her mum and dad's brand-new leather sofas and spat milkshake all over the walls. I remember thinking, 'I don't know why she has done that, but I have got to get out of this relationship – fast!'

Another time, I really liked a girl called Emma, who had a mate named Laura. One day, I was hanging out with Laura – who, funnily enough, now works with my brother as a teacher at his school – when she told me that if I wanted to appear more attractive to Emma, I should think about not always wearing sports clothes. I was so clueless that I went down to JJB Sports, where I always shopped anyway, and bought a brown fleecy top and a pair of really bad-fitting boot-cut jeans. I thought I looked smart, and I wore them all the time because they were the nicest clothes I owned. However, looking now at old photographs of me, I really don't know what I was thinking. I was dressed like some sort of lumberjack.

Subsequently, I started going out drinking with my older brother, often at the Empire nightclub in Milton Keynes, but I'd also go roller-skating at Rollers in Bletchley with my school friends, which was the cool thing to do back then. Rollers also hosted foam parties for under-18s to dance and rave and have a hell of a lot of foam thrown at them, and I used to get fully stuck in.

Funnily enough, my dad had a big reputation for being able to dance. He was really into Motown back in the 1970s and '80s and his mates dubbed him Rubber Legs. I don't think anyone ever told me I was a really good dancer when I was growing up, alas ... Now, as I write this, I find myself about to embark on *Strictly Come Dancing*, so I guess we'll find out once and for all whether or not I can dance.

As a teenager, I did, though, create a move of sorts, where I leant back on one hand and gyrated slightly on the floor, like some sort of bad striptease. I guess it was a bit like break dancing, thinking about it. Once, a girl from school, who I didn't fancy, tried to dance with me and it became really awkward, so I ran off and hid in the toilet and didn't come out again. Ever the gentleman ...

By then I was already a working lad, too. On my 16th birthday, I began work as a slope patroller at the indoor ski zone in Milton Keynes, where my brother worked. It was four hours on a Friday night with a few hours more on Saturday, and the occasional shift to cover on a Sunday as well. I was on minimum wage, and my bosses weren't great either, so we'd sometimes sneak away and have a cigarette, but I loved skiing whenever I got the chance to give it a go.

My next job, at Dexter's Grill, was a bit grim as my sole task was to clean up tables for the other waiters and waitresses. I got no tips and I think I was on £3.24 an hour, plus a fiver at the end of the night when the senior staff would cash up. Unsurprisingly, it wasn't much fun being constantly on my feet cleaning tables for no tips . . .

Up until that point, I actually had vague notions of becoming a chef. When I was a kid, my mum would bake these amazing cakes – her sponges were absolutely delicious and she would make a mean rock cake too. I would often help out and, so I thought, got reasonably good at it. The 1990s marked the height of the national obsession with TV chefs, so the prospect of becoming the next Gordon Ramsay seemed quite a glamorous idea. However, working at Dexter's quickly disabused me of such a notion.

That said, I much preferred it when, after a few months, I was promoted to be a waiter. That suited me a lot better because I really enjoyed interacting with the customers. I would always be chatty and nice to them anyway, because that is how I am, but I was keen to earn my tips too as it was the only chance of making a reasonable wage.

Like most waiters, therefore, I kept a special circle of hell for anyone who spent their meal being horrible or rude – people who applied the final insult by not leaving anything for service. That is why I always tip generously when I go to restaurants. I remember how painful it was to return to a table where a large group had just eaten to find they'd not even left a couple of quid to say thanks. While I was there, I also fell hopelessly in love with a fellow waitress for about six months, which ended in complete disaster. However, soon afterwards I met someone I did really fancy – a girl called Liz, who was also from Milton Keynes – and we began a long-term relationship.

About this time I gave up cigarettes. Most people smoke more when they are stressed, but in my adolescent wisdom, just before my GCSEs, I went the other way. It wasn't deliberate, but down to circumstance: because I was stuck at home supposedly revising for my exams, I had nowhere to smoke. I say 'revising', but I was terrible at it and I never particularly bothered. Everyone says they didn't do any revision, but I really mean I did absolutely none. My mum would shout from downstairs to ask whether I was working – I'd pretend to do so for a bit, then go and play on my computer. Essentially, like everything else I was doing in my life at that time, I was just trying to wing it.

When my results came out, I was half happy, half nervous. There was one grade A in PE – anything less would have been a bit embarrassing – and a B in history, my favourite subject. There were also two Cs in English language and literature, which I was thrilled with because I'd worked hard for the teacher, who I genuinely liked and respected, along with another couple of Cs in biology and the humanities class I'd taken the year before.

I honestly can't remember the rest. I took on way too many subjects at GCSE, including things like cookery and woodwork, because I felt I had to and, if I didn't like the teacher, I didn't do the work I was supposed to. If you couldn't engage me in the classroom, you lost me entirely.

My brother is dyslexic, and didn't take too many GCSEs, but when he got his results they were decent given the problems he had faced, so my parents took us out for a meal at Fatty Arbuckles to celebrate. Before I got my results, I had been hoping for a similar treat. My friends had all been offered money to get good grades – 20 quid for every A to C and so on – and I was thinking, 'Well, I've not been offered anything,' but I was still hoping my parents would be pleased enough to take me for a slap-up meal. Instead, I just got a slap. Looking back now at the effectiveness of financial incentives when it came to my footballing skills, perhaps all my mum needed to do was offer me the same bonus scheme and I would have achieved straight As!

Personally, I thought I'd done OK – but it wasn't nearly good enough for either of them. When I showed my grades to my parents, my poor mum was so disappointed that she smacked me around the face, while my dad wouldn't speak to me for days. I was really upset, as I'd done much better than my brother. However, my parents always held on to the strange view that I was somehow a straight-A student – despite the evidence to the contrary. None of my teachers ever told them I was that good, and I never showed any inclination to want to be top of the class. It's as though, from the moment I was born, the bar my parents set for satisfaction with me was much higher than everyone else in the family; and, for some reason, to them anything less than perfect was my fault, not simply the way things worked out.

Of course, my teachers always said, 'If you work hard, you could do well' – but is there a student anywhere who hasn't been told that? Especially anyone who, like me, was playing the idiot and being disruptive to others in the class. In hindsight, it's clear that I was always going to fall short because I couldn't deal with the concentration required or the workload. I think I knew that, and I stopped caring. I also knew deep down that I just didn't have the ability to excel in education. I wasn't academically inclined, or indeed clever enough. Thank God I was good at sport.

CHAPTER 8

Car Surfing in Country Lanes

Going into my first year of A-levels in September 2003, I should have been knuckling down as a student and an athlete. After all, my GCSE results, while not as good as my parents had wished for, showed I was at least reasonably intelligent. And my performances for Milton Keynes suggested that I was one of the better teenage long jumpers in the country. However, I still wasn't applying myself much at all.

This will sound strange, but even as I was sinking another turbo shandy (Smirnoff and beer) a few days before an important competition, I kept telling myself that it didn't matter: I would still end up making it in sport. I might not have had anything resembling a workable plan, but having a dream was enough.

But drinking wasn't the only stupid thing I was enjoying. Around this time, one of my brother's friends, Dan, had learned to drive. He had a Renault 5, and Rob and I would often accompany him in the lanes near Milton Keynes. But this was a drive through the countryside with a difference, for my mate Ross and I would dare each other to climb into the car boot and be driven up and down Sandy Lane with it open. We'd be thrown around, having a laugh, and while it was a little bit dangerous, we soon decided it wasn't dangerous enough. Which is when we started car surfing, clinging on to the roof as we whizzed around Buckinghamshire at speeds of up to 50mph. Yes, this is a very dumb thing to do.

Dan would be driving and my brother would be in the passenger seat, while Ross and I would be on the car roof. We managed to work it so that I would hold on first and then Ross would lie next to me before placing one arm over me. With us both holding on to each side, Dan would then push the accelerator down and we'd start car surfing. We tended to drive around Woburn Sands because it was so quiet and there were rarely any police or other people around. Looking back, it was probably a good thing that Dan was a bit wet and I'm sure he would never have taken it to the point where his speeds were going to potentially kill us, especially with my brother there as well, but it was still hugely dangerous and spectacularly irresponsible.

Yet – and I know this sounds completely mad – I always did things that were risky; it's that reckless streak I've already mentioned. What's more, I still do it now. I will go downhill mountain biking in the middle of the athletics season, and I absolutely love downhill skiing. The faster the better, I don't mess about. I see it as a way of pushing myself to the point where there is danger. In fact, I crave it. I love the idea of being right on the edge.

Earlier in the summer of 2003, I jumped a club record of 7.04m just as I was finishing my GCSEs. I also had my first serious coach, Tom McNab, who was considered to be a bit of an athletics legend. In the previous autumn, I'd actually stopped training for a few months, but when my dad got a call asking whether I would return to Milton Keynes because Tom had arrived, I agreed to give it another go.

Tom's CV was impressive. Not only had he been a Scottish triple jump champion, but he had gone on to coach loads of athletes. On top of that, he'd been a technical director on the set of *Chariots of Fire*, helping the actors train, had whipped some of England's World Cup rugby players into shape before the first Rugby World Cup – and, for good measure, he was a novelist too.

He had so many anecdotes about athletes, and so much experience, that it was hard not to be impressed. For a 16-year-old kid, he was a hugely inspirational figure, because he was somebody who'd been there, done it, and knew what he was talking about. I was probably a little bit in awe of him, at least at first.

Sometimes, we'd go to Tom's house and he would always have really nice pork pies and other high-quality foods. I remember once he held a barbecue and it was all fillet steaks. At that point, I had never had one of those in my life and I thought it was incredible.

Shortly after meeting Tom, he asked me to join a separate training group. I was certainly up for it – I was the only guy in the group and the girls, who were around my age, were all attractive, which was obviously a massive pull. Thankfully, my parents agreed to pay Tom his fee of £200 a month to coach me three times a week. As you will have guessed, that was a hell of a lot of money for them, but they always did everything they could to make sure that my sporting career had a chance, and this stretch was indeed instrumental. It also meant driving me to either Eton or Bedford and back – something they were always happy to do.

I remember Tom used to get me to do a lot of jumping off what we called a 'beat board', which was basically a raised wooden platform. Often, Tom would be talking to an acquaintance, telling them one of his many stories. He was a man who loved chatting away, but when he saw me by the board he'd say to his friend, 'Oh, watch this guy now, watch him' – and then he'd ask me to jump. I would run down, leap off the board and almost fly over the pit. Tom, acknowledging his friend's approval, would nod his head sagely and say, 'He is my guy!' I wasn't convinced that his showing me off like that was the best approach, but at least I felt I was making progress.

Yet I was still happy to sabotage my ability by going out all the time, drinking and clubbing. By now my older brother was playing rugby with mates who were bouncers, which meant I could get into all the clubs. And I didn't need a second invitation to get stuck in.

It was the same with the car surfing. I do wonder, though, whether being a bit of an idiot runs in our family. I say this because, unlike most of my bad behaviour as a kid, I have talked about car surfing with my dad. He thought it was stupid, of course, but he has a mate called Keith who used to perform a stunt that was not unlike the stuff you see on shows such as

Daredevils. Keith and his friends would be driving down a main road, and then someone would clamber over from the passenger side into the driver's seat as the original driver climbed out of the window on to the bonnet and back around the other side.

I know Keith, so it doesn't surprise me that he might attempt such outrageous feats. And I also have a feeling that my dad was involved, because Keith is one of the main people he used to hang out with as a lad. But so far all I have are suspicions – my dad won't confirm whether he did or not. Perhaps it's the fact he saw so much of his past in me that made him so strict.

The following summer, however, something made me stop car surfing altogether: I had a panic attack in the midst of the best season of my young career so far.

At the time I wasn't doing any proper weight training, but I was naturally filling out and getting stronger as I approached by 18th birthday. And it was starting to show in my results. At the end of June 2004, I entered the AAA Men's Under-20 Championships – a competition for the best junior athletes in Britain – and won it with a leap of 7.24m. The nominal prize for the winning jump was a small trophy. But the much bigger carrot was automatic selection to compete for Great Britain against Australia in an international match in Manchester the following weekend.

You can imagine how excited I was to be representing my country for the first time. My team-mates at Milton Keynes, Craig and Joey, had made international teams before and they would sometimes come to training wearing their GB kit, but until now I was a rung or two down from them on the ladder. Now it was my time to wear a British vest on my chest. It became my pride and joy – it still is today. It was such a massive deal for me, not only because I was representing my country, but because it showed I had achieved something.

There were plenty of household names in the British team, including Jessica Ennis, who came second in the 100m hurdles, and Hannah England, who went on to win a silver medal in the 1500m at the World Championships in 2011. I also remember the likes of Martyn Rooney, Eilidh Doyle, James Ellington and Michael Rimmer, all of whom were in the Team GB squad with me in the Rio Olympics, being there too. Looking back at the results of the meeting, most of these future international stars either won or came second in their events. Me? I had an absolute shocker. I finished seventh out of eight competitors with a leap of 6.82m, nearly a metre behind the winner, John Thornell of Australia, who jumped 7.65m.

Afterwards I felt incredibly embarrassed. I'd had an opportunity to show my ability, to do myself justice, and I had let myself down. When you're a teenager, you tend to magnify everything by a thousand times, and I was sure that one bad performance meant I would never be selected for my country again. Sport is sometimes of this nature – you often feel you are only as good as your last competition.

Occasionally – and I see it now – when certain people come into a team they have this aura about them. They are the big guys on campus. I was just this new kid who nobody knew. I made no impression on the team because I was awful. I went home and I half-accepted that this might possibly be the pinnacle of my athletics career: one solitary appearance competing for Great Britain.

I knew I was a pretty good long jumper on a national level. But I'd gone straight from nationals to competing internationally, and I'd been shown up as second-rate. What made it worse was that the family all came up to Manchester to watch me. I still had this enormous belief that I would be a professional athlete, but I began to wonder whether I was just kidding myself. This was a fragile moment in my progression as a sportsperson, and it could very easily have been the end.

However, I will never forget how immensely proud my parents were. In particular, I remember my dad being incredibly kind and supportive. Despite all the other stuff that had gone on when I was growing up, when it came to sport he was always ready to help me, and I loved the fact that I could make him really happy. We would talk sport all the time – in fact, we still do – and he's very knowledgeable about athletics because he watches everything and comes to as many meets as he can.

When I got that GB vest, he told me just to go out and enjoy it – and not to put any pressure on myself: 'This is your first time, there will be more opportunities – relax.' Afterwards, when I was devastated and sobbing away, he picked me up. 'Don't worry about it,' he said. 'You'll be back.'

I wasn't so sure. At the time, I was a complete nobody. If I'm being honest, I had probably won the AAAs only because a few others had pulled out, and I didn't particularly deserve to have anybody's respect at that point.

Knowing my dad, he was probably hurting as much as I was after a bad jump, but he was fantastic at encouraging me. As he put it to me whenever I did badly, 'Losing doesn't mean that you are not a good jumper – it just means that you had a bad day.' That was something he would always say to me. And it was such good advice. Because that's the horrible thing about sport – even winners usually have plenty more bad days than good.

My dad was also brilliant at keeping my feet on the ground. He never let me get ahead of myself or above my station. Even now, if he ever thought I was being arrogant he would be the first to check me on it. I hate it when people say they are 'keeping grounded' and all that rubbish, but that's what my dad did for me.

Even though I was embarrassed about my performance, I would wear my GB kit when I went down to train at Milton Keynes. The first time I did so, I remember wearing the long tights and I had undone the zips at the bottom because it was a little warm – and I got laughed at for doing so. As one of my mates pointed out, 'People don't wear their tights with the zips open at the bottom!' I also wondered what people at the club were privately thinking. Was it, 'How has Greg managed to fluke his way into getting a GB kit?', or something like, 'You have qualified for one small event and you've blown it for Great Britain – yet you still have the cheek to wear your kit'? In reality, they probably couldn't care less.

That setback didn't last long, for in August I put in a couple of big performances. That summer I had started running 100m and in Haringey I not only went under the 11-second barrier but absolutely smashed it, running 10.69. I was standing at the back of the track when the time was announced and I began running around like crazy because I was so excited. My team-mate Craig Pickering ran 10.41 that year so I wasn't a million miles away from him either. At the time, a friend and fellow long jumper at Milton Keynes, Kershel St Helene, worked at Pizza Hut, so I celebrated that performance with an absolute ton of pizza!

Six days earlier I had jumped 7.28m in Abingdon, which was also a personal best. And yet I was living a dangerous existence, competing hard while doing stupid things. And suddenly something hit me at the back end of those summer holidays, during a car surfing episode.

I remember the sunroof was open and we were driving along relatively fast at about 40 or 50mph and suddenly I froze. I've done so many crazy things in my life, without ever really considering the consequences, but all of a sudden I had this terrifying image of Dan having to swerve, me coming off the top of the car, hitting a tree and being paralysed. I don't know why, but I remember vividly to this day that horrible sensation of thinking, 'If I come off tonight then that could be the end of everything – my athletics career and maybe even my life.' I froze.

My brother looked up at me and said, 'Are you all right?' and I answered, 'Stop the car! Stop the car! Now!' Dan pulled up and I got off, and I think I semi-laughed. But then and there I told everyone: 'I am not doing that again. I'm done.'

Mind you, there were plenty of other foolhardy things I kept doing around that period, but this was one promise I kept. Subconsciously, I wonder if my athletics ability had finally given me reason to tip the balance towards being the best I could be on the track.

CHAPTER 9

Chasing My Dream

Milton Keynes is a busy enough place that you used to be able to go out on Monday, Thursday, Friday, Saturday and Sunday nights and find the pubs and clubs rammed – I can vouch for that, having had plenty of first-hand experience in my late teens. In my first year of A-levels especially, we would often go out on all those nights and hit it pretty hard. This was a period in which my drinking got a bit out of control and it meant I turned up to school nowhere near as often as I should have. In a sporting context, I think the ages of 16 to 18 are where so much talent is lost, mainly due to late nights and alcohol, and I could have ended up the same way.

When I did attend lessons, I would sometimes be half-cut or even still drunk. On one occasion, I turned up for a business studies class very drunk, having walked to school from my mate Sam's house after a very late-night session. My teacher was a guy called Mr Fitzgerald, who I never got on with and who certainly didn't like me. So you can imagine the scene, as I crashed noisily through the classroom door. Even in my intoxicated state I realised everyone was staring at me, and I saw in their expressions the silent question: 'What is this guy doing?' Then I nonchalantly went to the back of the class and slumped over my desk, head resting on arms.

It probably wouldn't have taken me long to fall asleep. Yet a few seconds later I heard Fitzgerald shouting angrily: 'What on earth do you think you are doing, Rutherford?' I waved my hand dismissively at him before replying, 'Oh, just shut up, Fitz.' He chose to ignore me, but after five minutes I decided that was enough business studies for one day and I walked out of the class.

When I look back at incidents like these, I think what a complete dick I was. I had gone in and disturbed a class full of people trying to better themselves, been insolent to the teacher and then just walked out again. If I saw that sort of behaviour nowadays I would be very angry.

But it was just another example of my skewed thinking because, weirdly, while I had it in my head that I was going to be an athletics star, I was doing nothing that would make anyone think I had a cat in hell's chance of succeeding. I was drinking too much, hanging out and acting up, and I wasn't training particularly hard either. Basically, I was in that classic late-teens rebellious stage. But the strangest part is that I don't think my parents really cottoned on. I guess I managed to hide it incredibly well, because I knew how disappointed they would have been.

Another time, I was sitting in the ICT room and there was a guy called Ed Slater, a seriously good rugby player who went on to captain Leicester Tigers and whose brother happened to be in my year. And he said to me: 'Do you really think you are going to be in the Olympics one day?' I replied: 'Yeah, of course,' and he laughed, before saying, 'Yeah, right, you've got no chance,' and giving me a bit of shit. I could hardly blame him. In my head there was no doubt I was going to go to the Olympics, but everyone else thought I was living in la-la land.

The lack of time and attention I was devoting to my studies hit home when I got my AS results, which were as bad as I had feared. I did well in one subject – product design – which was odd because I can't draw. It was one of the most frustrating subjects for me because, while I really enjoyed it and thought I had some pretty good ideas, I couldn't get them across as well as I would have liked. Even so, I still ended up with a B despite not turning up for the exam at the end of the year, to go with a C in PE, a D in history and an F in business studies. I was particularly frustrated with my history grade, but at AS level we had started learning about the rise of the Labour Party and Bolshevik Russia – subjects I find very interesting now, but back then all I wanted to learn about was medieval England from the latter Dark Ages through to the rise of Tudor Britain. I was obsessed with it. So, because I was not as interested in what I was being taught, I half-switched off.

Because my AS grades weren't great, I spoke to the school and asked whether I could resit the year. When they said yes, I told myself, 'Right, I am going to take everything more seriously now.' But my new-found resolve didn't last long. I decided to give A-level biology a go because I'd got a C in GCSE science, but within ten minutes I was so lost I had no idea what was going on. All I can recall from that class is the word 'lipid', and for some reason I spent several days calling my mates 'lipids' as a term of mild abuse.

As the autumn term wore on, my attendance grew worse. By February, I was hardly there at all. It got to the point where, if I did ever turn up, my teachers would remark, 'Oh, you decided to come in today, then?', to which I'd reply, 'Oh, probably.' But at least I was now training more regularly again and on 13 February 2005, in front of the TV cameras, I had a breakthrough of sorts, jumping 7.64m to finish third in the AAA Indoor Championships in Sheffield behind Nathan Morgan, who won with a jump of 7.96m. Chris Tomlinson, who I was in awe of at the time, was second with a leap of 7.91m. At 18, I was the youngest in the field. Yet I had actually held my own.

Of course, I knew that jumping 7.64m wouldn't get me anywhere on the world scene, but that moment ended up being a massive turning point for me, because the following week the head of the sixth form department called me in for a chat. 'We saw you on TV, and we were very impressed,' she said. 'But you are in the last-chance saloon here. We've already let you resit your first year and we're not going to let you do it again, so we really need you to start turning up to classes again now.'

I thought this is it: time to decide, Greg. And so I very politely replied: 'Actually, I am going to become a professional athlete in the next year or two, so I am going to leave school and focus on that.'

She looked at me like I was an idiot. I knew she thought I had no chance of succeeding. But having appeared on TV once I was convinced I would prove her – and everyone else – wrong.

I knew I was capable of being one of the best long jumpers in the world if I just knuckled down and sorted out my life.

For the past decade or so I have worked incredibly hard to become an Olympic gold medallist and world champion, but when I left school all I had was natural ability and pig ignorance. But they weren't bad attributes to have, because I soon got over poor jumps and bitter losses, however painful they were at the time.

I was just as pig-headed when it came to joining the world of work. During the previous Christmas, I'd done temporary work on the shop floor at Gap, and shortly after the British Indoors they offered me a full-time contract. But I told the manager: 'I feel I need time to be able to train and focus on athletics and so I am going to turn the job down.' Thanks, but no thanks.

It was March 2005. I was 18 and had no job and no money. Not much, in fact, but my ability to jump reasonably far into a sandpit. Like a poker player who throws in his last chips on the table, I really was going all in on my athletics career.

CHAPTER 10

Breakthrough

The 2005 European Junior Championships in Kaunus, Lithuania, were a huge game changer for me, for two very good reasons. First, I broke the eight-metre barrier for the first time – which is a good indication that a young long jumper might make it at world level. Second, and perhaps just as memorably, I was exposed to, and involved in, the hedonistic and promiscuous behaviour that is a familiar theme at the end of major championships. Sometimes I found myself, and more than one other couple, going at it in the same room. I guess it's not surprising that many athletes let their hair – and their inhibitions – down after months of hard training.

Two weeks earlier, on 6 July 2005, I had been at my coach Tom's house when it was announced that London would be hosting the 2012 Olympics. There was an almighty cheer and Tom turned to me and Lucy Boggis, a hugely talented heptathlete until she picked up lots of injuries, and said with a twinkle in his eye, 'Let's see if we can get you there.' I wasn't so confident. After all, I was still pretty much a complete nobody – an 18-year-old who had yet to go over eight metres.

But then in Lithuania, I suddenly jumped 8.14m – a new junior British record and the best by a British jumper, junior or senior, that year. In fact, even today I think it counts as one of my greatest ever performances, because very few people have ever jumped that far at 18. Even Carl Lewis, who has won numerous Olympic and World Championship gold medals and whom I subsequently discovered is one of the world's biggest arseholes when in 2016 he denounced the long jump as 'the worst event in the world right now', never jumped that distance at that age.

Suddenly, it wasn't just those obstinate voices in my head telling me I was going to be a contender. Other people – often wise old heads in athletics – were starting to do the same. It was a watershed moment. I'd wanted to be a professional athlete before, but now it seemed that I actually could be one, as though somehow I'd pulled it off.

Admittedly, I was a bit surprised to jump that far given the poor weather conditions and the fact that the long jump runway wasn't particularly quick – two key factors affecting performance. I wasn't sure how particularly safe it was either, as the German athlete Sebastian Bayer, who later set the European indoor record with a leap of 8.71m, did a run through the pit before the competition, slipped and snapped his ankle.

But I was jumping so well that I had already won gold before my final attempt, which was also the last jump of the competition. The pressure was off, so I gave it everything, attacking the board like my life depended on it, and kicking my legs forward way past the eight-metre marker.

I knew it was big, but even so, I wasn't prepared for what I was about to see on the stadium scoreboard. When 8.14m flashed up, I briefly wondered whether my eyes had tricked me. Then, when I was sure they hadn't, I ran up and down the runway screaming until I was blue in the face. I went completely berserk.

Just before the competition, my team-mate Craig Pickering had won the 100m title. When he saw me, he held up his gold medal and said, 'Win yourself one of these, Greg.' I really don't know whether or not he was mocking me – maybe I was being oversensitive because he was the big star from Milton Keynes and I wasn't – but I thought: 'All right, mate, that's what I'm going to do.' And I did.

It was my first taste of winning something important, and to become the national junior record holder made it even more special. There were some really good athletes on that team, including Jessica Ennis and the high jumper Robbie Grabarz, who both won medals at London 2012, as well as the European 400m champion and 4×400m relay legend Martyn Rooney. The pole vaulter Steve Lewis, who then became a really close friend of mine, was there too.

On the night of the closing ceremony, there was a big party – and I found what went on absolutely unreal. Nowadays, I know that madness is par for the course at the end of a major championship.

At the time, though, I was new to it, and was staggered by just how many people got absolutely smashed and the bedroom-hopping that took place left, right and centre. It was a total free-for-all, with truly unbelievable scenes. It's not often talked about, but after a big competition things do get quite hedonistic among a large number of the athletes.

But what you have to understand is that everyone is extremely serious before a major championship – and for months, not just days. Most athletes are probably on a very strict diet and not drinking very much, if at all. They are training incredibly hard, and are under a huge amount of stress. It's not just about winning or losing, or personal bests – it's knowing that a bad performance could mean losing funding and sponsors either ditching or downgrading your contracts. Imagine if you were in an office job, and for months in advance you knew how your performance on one day, and one day alone, could dramatically change your salary for the next year, or indeed mean you lose your job altogether. Wouldn't you want to let off steam, too, after whatever happened that day?

Athletes' minds are no different – even if their bodies certainly are. As I found out in subsequent Olympics and World Championships, most of them, wherever they come from in the world, are more than happy to finally get a chance to switch off. Some of them do so by getting an early sleep; others, myself included, can get a bit debauched.

That night in Kaunus there weren't many who weren't getting involved, especially in the drinking. Not everybody was shagging, although there was a fair bit of that going on. Obviously, I can't name names, but this was a side of athletics that I had heard whispers about and now I was suddenly experiencing them up close and very personal. Though one person who definitely wasn't out that night at all was Jessica Ennis. Even back then she was more mature and more focused than the rest of us. However, I was just 18 years old and had produced the performance of my life. Of course I was going to celebrate.

What made my performance in Lithuania more satisfying was that three weeks earlier I had competed in the AAA Under-23 and Under-20 Championships and jumped just 7.31m to finish a disappointing third. I was so terrible that day, and found myself running up to one of the British selectors and actually begging him to take me to Kaunus: 'I am so sorry, please still take me – I promise I won't be as bad!' He laughed and told me not to worry, as I had already jumped the qualifying distance.

However, there had definitely been a feeling that I was ready to make a great leap forward. After quitting school five months before, I had made the conscious effort to distance myself from many of the people I had grown up with, and become a bit more responsible. I wasn't exactly living like a monk – if there were a couple of weeks to go before an event I'd have a night out – but I was training a lot more seriously, no longer going on the lash five nights a week, and it was beginning to show in my results.

The month before, in June, I had gone to Mannheim in Germany to take part in the long jump and won with what then was a personal best leap of 7.90m, beating Michel Torneus, the Swedish athlete who later finished fourth in the London 2012 final. I had also entered the 100m, which made me incredibly nervous as I hadn't done much running, at least in races, in a while. But in the final I beat a good field to win in 10.38, which was pretty quick – especially as, with ten metres remaining, I had my hand in the air and was celebrating like I was Usain Bolt and I'd just won the Olympics.

I followed that up by winning my first senior national long jump title with a leap of 7.79m at the senior AAA Championship in Manchester.

On paper, this made me the top dog in Britain, although neither Nathan Morgan nor Chris Tomlinson, who had beaten me in the AAA Indoor Championships, was there. What made my victory perhaps a little more impressive, though, was that I was also simultaneously trying to run three rounds of the men's 100m against the best sprinters in the country, including Christian Malcolm, Darren Campbell, Jason Gardener, Mark Lewis-Francis and Marlon Devonish – these last four making up Britain's gold medal-winning 4x100m relay quartet at the Athens Olympics in 2004.

I had entered the 100m competition for a bit of fun, but I ended up getting through my heat and then running 10.39 to finish third in my semi-final – knocking out Darren Campbell, who finished fifth. My dad told me later that he had been standing by the warm-up area when the results came through, and there was one official who looked really downbeat. When he asked her what the matter was, she replied: 'Oh, Darren Campbell has been knocked out, and he's my hero!' So my dad said, 'You know who knocked him out? My son!' My dad is not at all boastful or unkind, and he definitely didn't mean it in a horrible way, but he was so happy I'd made the final that he just blurted it out.

Trying to win the long jump while also attempting to do well in the 100m was pretty tricky, physically and logistically. As I finished my long jump competition I saw the sprinters coming out for the 100m final – and I needed to be on the start line. So I went to the nearest official and told them I would be making my way right over. Alas, being a typical British Athletics official he was a real jobsworth, and told me I had to register first.

'But the 100m final is about to start!' I pointed out.

'I'm sorry, but according to subsection 29.2.1 of our rules you have to check your name against the list first,' he replied, or words to that effect.

This meant I had to sprint from the sandpit to some random squash courts inside the stadium to register, before begging with officials to let me run after they had originally told me that I'd missed the cut-off and it was too late. When I finally got their permission, I then had to pelt back to the start line, scraping it just in time. In fact, in the unlikely event you ever watch a recording of that event on YouTube, you'll hear the commentators say, 'And it's Greg Rutherford in lane one, oh wait no, he's not here, actually it looks like he is still long jumping so he won't be in the final . . . oh no, hang on, he's made it!'

By this point I was exhausted: that day I'd already run two heats of the 100m, won the long jump and felt like I'd sprinted halfway round Manchester just to compete in the final – so it was no surprise I trundled home in last place.

That race didn't end in glory. But it was around this time that sponsors were starting to become more interested in me. Many people outside track and field don't realise perhaps that sponsorship is a huge thing for athletes. It's important not only because of the kudos but because it allows athletes to actually make a living, as they will often earn far more for exclusively wearing a certain brand than they ever will for winning major races or competitions. Though, having said that, despite there being a bit more interest, there wasn't exactly a desperate clamour for my signature.

My coach Tom McNab used to receive a box of kit from adidas a couple of times a year, so he asked them to send me some stuff too. When it arrived, there were some trainers, a pair of sprint and jump spikes, and a couple of pairs of shorts and tops in a small box. I tried on the trainers, which were horrible big clumpy things that looked more like fell-running shoes – hardly ideal. Then I gave the sprint spikes a go and a plate cracked on them. I remember my dad phoned the adidas rep Joe Rafferty to tell him and he seemed indifferent, so it was clear they had no great interest in signing me.

But shortly after the European Juniors, I got a call from my dad: 'We've just had Nike on the phone and they want to offer you a contract for £3,000 a year.' It doesn't sound like a lot, but I nearly crashed through the roof in joy. I had seen plenty of athletes my age – like Craig Pickering with adidas – getting lots of nice gear, and I wanted the same. I'd also spoken to Julian Thomas, a really good junior 200m runner at the time, who told me he had 50 pairs of Nike trainers because he was one of the main juniors they sponsored. And I was thinking, '50 pairs of trainers – you're kidding me, right? Who needs 50 pairs of trainers?' I was absolutely in awe of these people.

Julian also told me that Nike were known for giving more kit than everyone else, and for really looking after you, so I was happy to sign on the dotted line, and grateful to have money in the bank to start being able to buy things.

Contract duly signed with Nike, seven enormous boxes arrived at our house. I had never experienced Christmas like most kids do, but this was how I imagined it must feel. There was just so much stuff! I had more hoodies, trainers, T-shirts and other gear in that one moment than I had ever had in the rest of my life put together. My granddad was there when I opened the boxes and he couldn't believe it either. At one point he said, 'That is a lovely hoodie.' I was sure it would really suit him – it was a very cool, grey number with orange toggles, not exactly your average granddad attire. I really wanted him to take it. 'You have it, Granddad,' I said. But he laughed and replied, 'Don't be silly – this is your stuff now.'

As I have since learned, receiving large amounts of kit is pretty much standard for most professional athletes. These days, I put most of it in a storage unit in my house; and whatever I don't wear, I make sure I give to charity.

However, not everything was entirely rosy. Through this period, while I was setting personal bests and attracting interest from sponsors, I had also been running and jumping through a pain in my ankle, which had needed strapping for most of the season. By the time I jumped that 8.14m, I couldn't really bend the ankle properly at all, and shortly afterwards it was decided I needed surgery to remove a large bone growth.

That snapped me right back down to earth. I was fearless and on a roll, and I had total belief that I could have jumped even further. I also had a 'B' standard qualifier for the World Championships in Helsinki, which meant that British selectors could have used their discretion to pick me alongside incredible athletes like Paula Radcliffe and Jonathan Edwards. Instead,

Chris Tomlinson, who had been jumping terribly that year, ended up going. I was pretty down about it at the time, which shows how much my mentality had changed. A year earlier, athletics had been only a part of my life, fitting in around drinking, partying, car surfing and occasional studies. Now I was absolutely gutted that I wasn't going to be competing at a World Championships – which arguably I had no right to be in anyway – against the best jumpers in the world.

I watched the Helsinki championships from my hotel room in Spain, where I had gone on holiday with my then girlfriend, Liz, and her family. In fact, relations became a bit fraught, because I spent most of the time in my room watching athletics on the telly, rather than spending any time with Liz or her family. That, as you can imagine, wasn't a popular move. But I was glued to the screen, desperate to see what I was missing out on. Torturing myself a little, I suppose.

At least there was a silver lining to cheer me up. The 8.14m I had jumped in Lithuania meant I'd qualified for the Commonwealth Games in March 2006 – which gave me enough time to recover.

Before then, though, I had to find a new coach, because Tom and I had gone our separate ways. I'd had no inclination to end our relationship, but one day, as we were heading down to the track in Eton in his car, he suggested increasing his monthly fee to £400, and in addition he wanted to take a cut of my future earnings.

My first reaction was one of bewilderment. He can't have had any idea what my finances were, and wouldn't have realised how impossible this was. My contract with Nike would bring in

£3,000 a year, and was then my only source of income. It wasn't till the end of 2005 that I was put on the British Athletics world-class performance programme and allocated £10,800 a year of lottery funding. So he was effectively asking for more than I was actually making. Up till then, I'd also never been paid for an event, which becomes normal when you are a better established athlete. All of a sudden, it felt as though the man I'd seen as quite an important figure in my life was asking for everything I had – well, more than I had. I was really shocked, and could only mutter something like, 'OK, well, we will have to figure it all out with my mum and dad and everything.' But it felt incredibly weird. When I told my parents, my dad was appalled by what had happened and couldn't understand Tom's demands.

I should stress here, though, that I am definitely not against the idea of paying coaches what they are worth. I am lucky enough to work with the best coach in the world in Dan Pfaff, and I pay $12,000 a year to Altis in Phoenix for the right to see him. On top of that, I then pay around $15,000 a year to fly him around the world to coach me when I compete. Paying people what they deserve is a hugely important principle to me. But the situation with Tom was very different, because he was asking for money from somebody who didn't have much, and I wasn't equipped then to deal with it in a professional manner and negotiate or ask for an explanation.

At this point, I had also just joined a management company, Stellar Athletics. Such organisations help athletes find sponsors, book you into competitions, do everything it takes to make your life easier in exchange for a percentage of your earnings, normally between 15 and 20 per cent. I wouldn't recommend

Stellar now, based on my subsequent dealings with the company's president John Regis, who in my opinion seems to spend too much time up in the VIP area, but one of Stellar's other founder members, Ayo Falola, was an absolute legend. He played a key role in my life and was a tremendous influence on me, especially in the early days. He taught me so much about the world of athletics, and always tried his best to take the stress away from me during his time at Stellar, before he was fired in 2011. He had been an athlete himself as well as a coach, so he really knew what he was talking about. Tragically, he died in 2015, aged just 47, and was a huge loss to his family and everyone who knew him.

When I told Ayo what had happened with Tom, he told me not to worry about it, and that the best thing to do was to agree a contract between Tom and myself which set out terms that I considered fair. So, one day we all met at Brunel University, and when Ayo gave me the nod I left them together to discuss the detail. However, the idea of a contract didn't go down well with Tom, and so it became inevitable that we would part company.

Later, Tom wrote to *Athletics Weekly* suggesting that I had ditched him for no good reason, which I felt was unfair. As my father pointed out in a very good response, that simply wasn't the case. I hope my dad's letter changed people's perceptions at the time, but I was still very hurt. I felt let down by someone I'd thought was on my side, who had not only demanded a ton of cash but then written things that I believed were untrue – and in a magazine which I thought everybody in the world was reading – making me out to be a terrible person.

The reality was somewhat different. I had enjoyed most of my time with Tom and had learned a lot, although there were some signs that it wasn't a completely ideal relationship. He couldn't coach me on Mondays, for instance, because he had tennis practice. And during a competition, if something started to go slightly wrong, he would sometimes tell me, 'Oh, you are rubbish,' before walking off in disgust. I think he was doing it to try to get a reaction – and to make me even more determined to succeed. But I'm not sure it was the best approach for a young athlete. Instead of getting technical advice on what I was doing wrong, all I would see was a very frustrated man. Yet he had been my first proper coach and had taught me a great deal about jumping, so I was completely gutted that our relationship had ended.

CHAPTER 11

Silver Lining

The 2006 Commonwealth Games were a massive deal for me. I was barely 19 and had never set foot outside Europe, nor competed in a major championship for my country. Yet here I was, standing in front of a packed Melbourne Cricket Ground, wearing my first senior England vest, about to compete in the long jump final. As I stood on the runway, I was pretty confident my heart was beating louder than it had ever done before, but such were the Mexican waves of noise from the 100,000 people in the stadium that I couldn't tell you for sure.

The trip had already changed my life. Six weeks earlier, when I had flown out as part of the England team, I hardly knew anyone else on the plane. Yet soon I found myself in the team holding camp on Australia's Gold Coast – and later in Melbourne – drinking hot chocolate with athletes I had looked up to, and who had already had Olympic medals around their necks, and slowly feeling like I might belong.

There was something more profound about that trip too. I realised that I didn't want to be one of those athletes – and there are a great many of them – who find themselves lucky enough to travel the world, yet scarcely see outside their hotel rooms, where they spend all their time, often playing big FIFA tournaments on PlayStation against their team-mates. I found I had an urge to explore places, to learn more about different cultures and environments and – although I would never have expressed it in such terms – a desire to better myself. Effectively, I wanted to break out of the small-town lifestyle of my upbringing.

It helped that I was sharing a room with Andrew Steele, the 400m runner, who was to become one of my best friends. He was far more cultured than I was – admittedly not hard back then. For a start, he could speak Spanish. He also wanted to explore places. Alas, my uncouthness often got the better of me. Once, in the early days, Andrew was driving us around and this guy cut him up. It was the most minor incident you could imagine, and Andrew wasn't fazed in the slightest, but I suddenly blurted out, 'You should have got out of the car and smacked him!' – because I was a bit of a wide boy and trying to be funny, and also because that's what most people I hung around with in Bletchley at the time would have said. But Andrew just replied, 'Why on earth would I do something like that?', cutting me down and leaving me thinking, 'You're such an idiot, Greg.' He was right too.

It turned out that Andrew was far more interested in the wider world than most people I associated with. I was so impressed that he would mark words or passages in a book he was reading, if they were particularly interesting or he wanted to remember them, and that he could speak another language. The idea of being able to chat away to people in a foreign language seemed incredible to me.

It wasn't that I thought I was any better than other athletes on those camps, but it did seem to me that some of them were just wasting their time, whereas I wanted – like Andrew – to get something more from the sport than simply saying I'd been in a hotel room in a foreign city. And just by hanging around with him I found myself getting into and enjoying new things, coffee shop culture for example, which was far removed from anything I'd experienced growing up in Bletchley. There were other benefits too. One coffee place we frequented had several attractive girls working there and during one visit I shared a jokey and mildly flirtatious conversation with a waitress. I had pretty much forgotten about it, when a day or two later I received a heavily scented letter, which appeared to have been doused with a whole bottle of perfume, asking whether I'd like to hang out with her. Of course, I took her up on the offer – what would you do if you were 19?

It was my first experience of the pulling power of the accreditation we all wore around our necks. As I subsequently learned, the older members of our team referred to it as a 'pussy pass' because, well, it unlocked a few doors. English athletes were heavily criticised after the Commonwealth Games for not winning enough medals or appearing to work hard enough to succeed, and I could see why: some of them seemed more intent on having fun and being a bit naughty than trying to set personal bests. I'm not sure the culture has changed that much since, sadly.

By then I had a new coach in Frank Attoh, a former Great Britain international triple jumper who had guided the Jamaican Trecia Smith to triple jump gold at the World Championships in 2005; and, with my ankle healing steadily from the operation I'd undergone the previous autumn, I had a renewed sense of optimism. Before I left for Australia, I was desperately hoping I could win a medal, even though deep down I knew that both mentally – with my change in coaches – and physically I was short of my peak.

The rules of the camp specified that we weren't allowed to tell the press about any injury problems. This led to a farcical situation when, ten days before the competition, I went jet skiing with pole vaulter Steve Lewis and a few Australian friends and burnt my legs. Unbeknown to most people, I was suffering really badly with shin splints at the time, and I was having my legs taped up because of it. Anyway, the medical team told me to claim that the Kinesio tape on my legs was, in actual fact, rehydration strips because I had got sunburnt, which sounded absolutely ridiculous. Fortunately – perhaps because this was in the early days of Kinesio tape use – no one questioned it too much.

Despite my injury problems, I managed to get into the final, which was my first experience of a truly amazing crowd. That night, the Australian John Steffensen won a surprise gold medal in the men's 400m and everyone in the MCG appeared to be screaming for him. It was so loud I felt the noise reverberating round my chest. It was absolutely unreal. The only crowd I've heard since then that has been louder was the one for Super Saturday during the London 2012 Olympics.

Unfortunately, it wasn't able to inspire me to victory – nothing like it. My first attempt was a foul. The second, a modest leap of 7.85m. Then, as I was hammering down the runway on my third attempt, about five or six strides to the board, my hamstring went – bang! I'd badly ripped it and, in a split second, my first major championships were over.

Not that I was ready to accept it just yet. I grabbed my hamstring and called for a trackside doctor, who made a very quick assessment and told me it was torn and I had to get treatment. But I wasn't having any of it. 'No, no, it will be fine, just give me some tape,' I told him. Part of me was thinking this might be my only shot at a major championship, so I wrapped a compression bandage around my hamstring as tightly as I possibly could. Then I stood up and I thought, 'Do you know what? This actually feels fine. I can keep going.' So I stepped forward with my left leg, and put down my right leg. And the second I did that, I collapsed into a heap. It was a suitable metaphor for how I was feeling: having built the Commonwealth Games up to be something so big, I had the overriding sense that I had wasted my time being away from my friends and family for so long. I just wanted the ground to swallow me up.

To compound this absolute thunderstorm of pain, devastation and self-pity, knowing that my Commonwealth Games were over, I then had to be taken off the track in a wheelchair. And to make matters worse, I was then left in the mixed zone, the area where athletes speak to journalists, as my team-mate Martyn Rooney came through having finished a very creditable fifth in the 400m final. He was roughly the same age as me and was one of the few other athletes from the European Juniors team who had been selected for the Commonwealths, and now he was being praised by all the journalists there. To my shame, I experienced stinging pangs of jealousy – why him and not me? – and then started to feel even more sorry for myself. I put a towel over my face and began to cry. I had finished eighth in my first major competition as an international athlete, yet it still felt like an absolute disaster. As I've since discovered, no matter what you achieve in sport, the goalposts keep moving, however high you go.

For the next few days, every time I moved or did anything, I had these horrible grabbing sensations, which anybody who has ever torn a hamstring will recognise. It was just a brutal way to finish my first major championships. And it was a catalyst for me to revert to some of my former ways for the rest of that trip. I ended up in and out of clubs, getting very drunk and roaming the streets despite suffering from an excruciatingly painful ripped hamstring. I was so devastated that I went absolutely mad. Part of getting rid of both the physical and mental pain was to just forget everything and go on a bender.

About five weeks after my return from Melbourne, my hamstring was judged to have healed enough for me to go on a training trip to Cuba, which was very different from what I'd been used to. We stayed in this bleak apartment in Havana with an outdoor shower, shutters instead of glass on the windows which meant bugs were always in my room, and horribly uncomfortable beds which meant I hardly slept. But what really hit home was that we didn't get to train at the sports college where the Cubans take all the promising athletes and have their national trials, but at a local track that had seen better days.

And that is putting it kindly. On lanes four, five and six on the back straight there was a dirty great crater where the track had been ripped away. Yet it was hard not to be impressed with the Cuban athletes. They were working incredibly hard, probably eating only one meal a day, but killing themselves day in, day out in the hope of making it to the next level. Cuba has a proud history, especially in the technical events, and this tough training environment must have its benefits. Some of them make it and get super, super-strong. But I'd be willing to place a substantial bet that many more ultimately break down prematurely.

One day early on in the trip we did a jumps session and the pit hadn't been raked particularly well, so when I landed I twisted my ankle on a chunk of hard sand. I had to return home. Upon closer inspection, UK Athletics said, 'Don't worry, you will never need surgery for this – we will be able to manage it.' But although I got through the season with my right ankle still hurting a lot, I was jumping in pain for the rest of the year and eventually had to go under the surgeon's knife in early 2007.

I am sure my ankle problems contributed to one of the worst performances of my career. In late June, I was selected to represent Britain in the European Cup in Malaga in Spain – a big honour for me. The competition pitted country against country, with each athlete's performance in an event determining how many points they won for their team. So the winner of the long jump would be awarded nine points, the second-placed athlete eight and so on, down to the athlete in last place, who scored just one. Unfortunately, I had an absolutely torrid time, with 5.98m being the best I could produce from my four jumps. I didn't take off. I ran through each round, getting very stressed as the competition went on. As one scathing newspaper report noted, that was less than a modestly talented female long jumper would have achieved. Needless to say, I finished last.

Afterwards, I was so gutted that I walked round the back of the stadium to an area of scrubland, found a bin and punched it as hard as I could. I didn't realise that Spanish bins are made of solid metal, not plastic, so I cut open all my knuckles. To make matters worse, a UK Athletics press official was behind me, wanting quotes on my performance. Even with my mind in turmoil, I thought surely this was not quite the right moment to be trying to interview a young man who has just had a crushing failure. She made me realise that by finishing last, we as a team missed out on the top spot. I took that very badly. Looking at the points totals, I would have had to jump 8.30m to win the competition and put Britain first overall – further than I had ever jumped in my life at the time.

Yet, in a massive turnaround, three weeks later I won the UK national trials with a leap of 8.26m, the equal second longest jump in British history and only one centimetre behind Chris Tomlinson's record. I was absolutely delighted, of course, but there was also a part of me that thought, 'Flipping heck, what is going on?' In Malaga, I was all over the place. Now I had defended my AAAs title and booked a place in the British team for the 2006 European Championships in Gothenburg the following month.

Obviously, the ankle issue wasn't helping matters. But it was only after I joined Dan Pfaff later that I realised that neither of my early coaches, Tom or Frank, was actually teaching me the fundamentals of the event. They were good coaches at British level, but compared to the best US coaches, in my opinion they were way behind. Neither was able to get my technique honed to a level where I would consistently produce excellent performances. And that, as I learned from Dan, is the key to winning major championships.

If I'm being honest, the reason I'd go from jumping 7.60m to 8.20m in the space of a few weeks was because I really felt like I had no idea what I was doing. I simply ran as hard as I could, took off and jumped – and hoped for the best. Within the first year I was coached by Frank, I realised he wasn't right for me and that actually I wasn't learning a great deal. But he kept saying, 'Well, it takes at least 18 months or so until the new programme kicks in.' And, being young, I thought, 'I'll stick it out, I'll be fine.' Sadly, I stuck it out for far too many years and looking back now, I wish I had found Dan Pfaff sooner.

Luckily, those European Championships in Gothenburg happened to coincide with one of my good nights. To say the event had started badly for Britain is almost as big an understatement as pointing out that the North Pole gets a bit chilly. Everything was going wrong. It began the night before the competition when Christine Ohuruogu, who later became one of Britain's most decorated athletes, was sent home after missing three doping tests. Then our performance director Dave Collins, the man in charge of the team, quickly upset most of our athletes by deciding to give everyone marks out of ten for how they did – and then telling the media what those scores were.

If that wasn't bad enough, the BBC TV commentator Brendan Foster then told millions of viewers that British athletes were heading towards a 'doomsday scenario' where we would be humiliated in front of the world at the 2012 London Olympics because most of us weren't good enough, while two key members of our 4×100m men's relay team were at loggerheads. Darren Campbell did not want Dwain Chambers to be in the squad with him because he had just served a two-year ban for taking the designer steroid THG.

By the time I competed in the men's long jump final on the second night, Britain had yet to win a medal, after Kelly Sotherton and Jessica Ennis had missed out in the heptathlon and Mark Lewis-Francis and Dwain Chambers had also fallen short in the men's 100m final. Not many people were giving me a hope of breaking that duck. For, although I had a new coach in Frank, I was still hugely inconsistent. The ongoing ankle injury had also been making life difficult going into Gothenburg.

The final started badly, as I ran through the sandpit on my first attempt, which was measured at 5.34m. But then I got one to click, and jumped into second place with 8.03m, behind the Italian Andrew Howe on 8.20m. My ankle was so painful at that point that I didn't take my third-round jump and was overtaken in the standings by the Ukrainian Oleksiy Lukashevych. My fourth- and fifth-round attempts weren't any good either – but I still thought I could claim gold.

So I gritted my teeth and gave it everything. I produced my best leap of the night – 8.13m. It was not quite enough to surpass Howe, but I didn't care: despite being the youngest individual member of the team at 19 years and 263 days I now had a European Championship silver medal around my neck. As I told journalists afterwards: 'There were people who thought I couldn't hack the pressure but it doesn't matter how young I am – I've shown I can go out there and win medals.' For good measure, I suggested that I would be jumping 8.40m within a year and should be regarded as a contender to win Olympic gold in Beijing in 2008. The confidence and arrogance of youth! But I knew I had plenty of promise: I had grown to a gangly 6ft 2in and was one of the quickest on the runway, yet I still hadn't started lifting weights, so I felt I had great potential to get stronger and faster.

To make the night even more special, I was presented with my medal by Lynn Davies, the last British long jumper to win a European Championship silver medal, in 1969. Lynn, a lovely man who has always been incredibly supportive, had a wide grin on his face as he told me in his deep Welsh brogue, 'How fantastic to see a British long jumper on the podium again and I hope you win many more medals!'

Afterwards, I enjoyed regaling the media with tales of my great-grandfather playing 11 times for England and my brief period training with Aston Villa, and the next day I got my first real exposure in the national press. One paper called me 'the ginger-topped teenager who has arrested Britain's calamitous start at the European Championships'. Another hailed me as 'Superkid'. I guess the British media wanted any good-news story they could get their hands on, given that it ended up being Britain's worst medal tally at the Europeans since 1978, with just one gold in the relay plus five silver and five bronze medals. It was also the first time ever that our athletes hadn't won a single individual European title, and as you can imagine there were calls for Dave Collins to resign. But the performance director of UK Athletics remained defiant. 'You think I'm going to retire, go to Bexhill and grow tulips? No, I don't think so. It's not me,' he told the press. 'Absolutely, I'll battle on.'

I can't recall what Collins gave me for my performance – hopefully it was at least a nine out of ten – but others were very publicly chastised. The hammer throwers Shirley Webb and Zoe Derham were each awarded just two marks. Paula Radcliffe spoke for many at the time, telling reporters: 'I have to say that I absolutely hate it.' It hadn't been a happy trip for most British athletes, yet for me the experience couldn't have been sweeter.

CHAPTER 12

(Not So) Bulletproof

If 2006 had been an almost dream-like introduction to professional athletics, then the following year was a recurring nightmare. I was constantly being injured, recovering from injury, or trying to stop myself getting injured. Nothing seemed to break the spell. I seemed to tear a hamstring every couple of months and I was only fit enough to compete twice all year. To add to my misery, I was forced by UK Athletics to leave home and move to London – and ended up having a psycho flatmate who nicked my stuff and didn't pay the rent.

After the success of my silver medal in the 2006 European Championships, I had been hoping to receive a little more lottery funding. Another British athlete, Nathan Douglas, who had also won a silver medal but in the triple jump, saw his funding increased and I remember thinking it was ridiculous that I had not been treated the same. It's this inconsistency that really bothers athletes when it comes to support from our governing body; it's never about the money itself. Well, at minimum wage it certainly wouldn't be about the money, but the fact that some seem to be shown favour over others is what drives athletes mad. If the federation just had a transparent policy for how it awarded funding, their lives would be so much easier.

If it wasn't bad enough being left on my luxurious £10,800 salary, the decision came with an ultimatum from Dave Collins, the performance director of UK Athletics: if I wanted to keep receiving that money, I had to move from Milton Keynes, where I was living with my parents, to London to train more closely with my coach Frank at Brunel University.

In truth, I wasn't Dave Collins' biggest fan. He was someone who I found hard to trust. I thought he didn't know athletics well enough, and in my opinion he made a number of poor decisions – and this was a classic example, which ended up causing me no end of problems. In hindsight, I should have challenged it with greater force, but I had just turned 20 and was new to the system. At that age, you tend not to question or push back; there is a sort of 'don't want to annoy the boss' mentality that scares you into going along with whatever they say. So, without any help – financial or otherwise – from UK Athletics, I found a three-bedroom flat in Northwood which cost £1,500 month to rent. Given that I was making peanuts, I was relieved when I found another athlete to move in with me. I don't want to give him the pleasure of naming him in this book, but he turned out to be a nasty piece of work.

To give just one example from many: I had been away on a training camp for three weeks and there was nothing in the house when I got back. So, I dropped my bags, went out and bought some food to eat. And in the hour or so that took, my PSP hand-held games console disappeared. We had only just started to live together so I didn't want to point the finger, but when I raised it with him, saying I was sure I had left it on top of my bag, he somehow managed to convince me that I must have lost it in South Africa. I was pretty certain I hadn't, but I let it go, partly because I couldn't be one hundred per cent sure, but also because he was much bigger than me. Other things had a habit of disappearing too, and he stopped paying the rent. Unsurprisingly, I soon felt uneasy living with him.

It didn't help my state of mind that I was injured almost all the time. Some of this, admittedly, was my fault. Winning that European silver and jumping 8.26m in 2006 changed my mentality to the point where I nearly ruined my career. Because I'd reached the podium in Gothenburg without much training, I began to wonder what I could achieve if I actually went at it hammer and tongs. This is a mistake that young athletes commonly make: 'If I train twice as much, then I'll be twice as good.' I needed someone to tell me that it was quality not quantity that mattered, but Frank's and UK Athletics' coaching ethos at the time actively encouraged athletes to push themselves far harder. In fact, they had a buzzword for it: becoming 'bulletproof'. The idea was that we now had to do two or three hours of warm-up, drills and various exercises in the morning to make our bodies more resilient – or 'bulletproof' – and then train hard again on our specific sport in the afternoon. So while UK Athletics appeared absolutely sold on imposing this regime on everyone, no one seemed to work out that it was completely wrong for me. I was physically exhausted and constantly breaking down and getting injured.

Their approach, for example, would be something like, 'Greg, you've had some hamstring injuries, so let's do yet more intensive hamstring strength.' Often, I felt it was basically a case of people giving themselves work in order to justify their jobs. And for me it just led to a terrible breaking down of the body, which was always blamed on the athlete. What I found strange was that if an athlete got injured, it was always their fault, never the physio's, never the coach's. Either they were not strong enough, or they had done something wrong.

I've come to really hate the term bulletproof – and I'm not alone. My coach Dan Pfaff, who most people in track and field would agree is one of the world's best, doesn't like it either. Unfortunately, back then it enjoyed almost cult status in UK Athletics circles, with many physiotherapists, doctors and coaches totally won over. However, instead of becoming bulletproof I was breaking down. The idea was so flawed, because it involved building up muscular strength through a selection of exercises that were not actually geared to the actions I was trying to perform. Instead of conditioning myself to running and jumping, I was better primed to do a hamstring curl.

My year started with warm-weather training in Potchefstroom, a 90-minute drive from Johannesburg in South Africa. Or rather it tried to start, before sputtering to a frustrating halt. When I arrived, my ankle was hurting a lot, the legacy from my hard 2006 season. Apparently, I was not yet bulletproof. At the end of the previous summer, I'd been told by UK Athletics doctors that I wouldn't need surgery, that some rest and painkillers would do the trick.

I tried desperately hard to believe them, and committed to their mantra of building up my physical resilience. But there was something else too: I slightly feared Frank. I think that's the way he works as a coach – deliberately making athletes a little scared of him so that he can dictate everything they do. It was a strange relationship. I remember missing a few calls from him once and him telling me off. Perhaps the tactic works for others, but for me it was counterproductive. You may have deduced by now that my relationship with authority is a difficult one.

That said, Frank and I worked incredibly hard together – far too hard, in fact – but the improvement he had promised didn't happen, even though I went from training three days a week to double sessions six days a week. Knowing what I do now, the technical input I received was very poor, and because I was doing double sessions most days I was knackered. Yet I was young and still very naive. After all, his other athletes did what he told them, and went along with the 'bulletproofing' strategy as well. But a few weeks into that South Africa trip it was clear that no matter how many drills I did each morning, my ankle wasn't getting any better and it was agreed that I needed an operation.

The surgery itself went OK but the rehab was a disaster. Unfortunately, I just didn't think that the physio who was looking after me, coming in once or twice a week to treat me, got it right. The physio gave me exercises like leg presses – and bear in mind that at that stage I'd never even lifted weights – on the side of the leg that had been operated on, and my body reacted so badly that I got a huge inflammatory response, including weeping from the wound itself.

It seemed clear to me that what he was doing was setting me back massively, and I wasn't healing from the surgery as fast as I could have done. I distinctly remember him saying to me that he didn't understand why this wasn't working – as it had been more successful with another athlete Again, I thought, 'This guy has no idea. He's just part of a system, and just because it worked for someone else, doesn't mean it will work for everybody.' This thinking very much informed the British approach to sport rehabilitation at the time. When you were injured, you were handed over to a physiotherapist and your coach didn't really play any part until you were deemed clear to compete. This is in stark contrast to the system I later joined under Dan Pfaff, where the coach is effectively the manager of all other staff, and all rehabilitation is completely functional to your event.

At this point, I was staying in the Olympic Medical Institute, the live-in medical centre in west London created by the British Olympic Association and consisting entirely of Portakabins, and becoming very depressed. That was one of the reasons why I went up to Manchester to do an event for Sainsbury's with Daley Thompson – to get out and about and to earn some money. You have to remember that, if you aren't competing, if you are injured, you aren't earning any money. You still have funding – touch wood – which in my case was enough to buy some food each month and pay the rent, but that was it. So this day trip to work with some kids in Manchester was a big deal. I think I was paid something like £1,000 or £1,500 – and that is a hell of a lot of money to somebody who is not earning on the track, equivalent to about six weeks' 'wages' from my funding.

I particularly recall this trip because the medical team were not keen for me to go, I don't know on what basis. But I was desperate for the money. Then, when I got back, Frank and I sat down with them to discuss the fact that my foot wasn't getting any better, and they tried to say that it was because I'd gone to Manchester for the day when they'd told me not to. I was incredibly frustrated by this stance. Instead of admitting that what they were doing wasn't working, and that they didn't know how to fix me, they were making out that it was my own fault. Athletes never want to be injured, but the prevailing attitude among UK Athletics staff seemed to be that it must be, at least in part, the athlete's fault.

Something more significant came out of the Manchester visit, though. I had got to know the 400m runner Andrew Steele at the previous year's Commonwealth Games, but had not seen him for a while, so when I knew I was going to be in town for the day I suggested meeting up. We went for a coffee, and it struck me how Andrew was even more cultured than I remembered – he was really into his coffee and was even drinking it black. We were in Starbucks, I think, and I ordered something hideously rich like a Banana Java Chip Frappuccino, all 800 calories of it. At the time, I thought I liked coffee; in fact, sometimes I had three of these in a day – and to think I wondered why I put on a bit of weight when I was younger. This was a dessert, not a coffee.

While I was supping this ridiculous drink, Andrew mocked me lightly, suggesting I should be more sophisticated. So I remember trying his black coffee and handing it straight back, saying, 'Ugh, that tastes of ash!' But it set the wheels in motion for what was to become an important thing in my life: my love of proper coffee. Sportspeople, cyclists in particular, seem to be terrible coffee snobs. Maybe it's because it's the only vice we can have – we can't go to the pub, so we drink coffee.

Andrew was to become one of my closest friends from this point. I think I was drawn to him because he represented what I wanted to be. I was still a bit of a mongrel – going out on the lash, being a real lad as well as an athlete, doing stuff that he simply wouldn't contemplate. But as we got to know each other better, he became a role model for me and I stopped some of the wayward behaviour because I had the feeling he would be disappointed.

I had always, as I've said before, been a bit of a follower. But now I was making a conscious effort not to be the scally kid I'd been in my teens, and he became the person I aspired to be. I didn't even like coffee, but it seemed like something a sophisticated person would enjoy. I was never posh – as my trolls and critics would think after London 2012 – but certainly I wanted to be more cultured than I was. I think most of us grow and evolve as we get older; I was no different.

Andrew opened those doors for me. Just by watching him and hanging out with him, I learned about food and drink, and it marked a huge turning point in my life – because it occurred to me that with all the travel that comes with a career in athletics, you can actually taste and try so many new and exciting things.

Outside friendships and coffee, 2007 was a very difficult year on the track. I have a reputation within athletics for being lucky enough to heal incredibly quickly, but when the body constantly breaks down – a strain here, a tear there – it takes a lot out of you, not just physically but mentally. It was a vicious circle, and much of it came down to bad physio and very bad training.

Finally, towards the end of July I was just about fit enough to return to action. It had been nearly a year since my last competition, but sadly the theme of the year rang true. I tore my hamstring on round one, but still managed to land, albeit in a heap at 7.96m. That performance was enough for Dave Collins to say I could go to the World Championships in Osaka, Japan, that August, because I had hit the qualifying standard with my performances the year before. Now I had to rehabilitate and get ready again. Though I was delighted at the time, with hindsight I desperately wish I hadn't gone.

One of my overriding memories of Osaka was that myself, Andrew and a few others – including the 800m runner Michael Rimmer and the high jumper Tom Parsons – formed a sort of group. We considered ourselves a bit more worldly and, ridiculously, called it the Gentlemen's Club. We were at a holding camp in Macau, staying in a palatial resort hotel. It was really grand, very old, and we came across a room that had high-back chairs, pictures on the wall and looked like an old-fashioned smoking room. So we would sit around in it, joke about smoking and wearing velvet jackets and the like, and spend too much time playing the ridiculous children's board game Pass the Pigs.

Looking back, we were obviously being pretentious idiots. Most of us had never even seen that sort of life, let alone been born into it, so it was just mucking around. Even so, other athletes must have thought we were total arseholes.

Macau was actually quite an eye-opening experience for me – the only long-haul destination I'd been to until then was Australia. Macau was on one level very westernised, but then you'd have to look out for the rabid dogs running around and the terrifying gigantic spiders hanging from trees. I always hated spiders, so I struggled with that. But generally I loved it – this glimpse of a world so different from what I was used to.

The World Championships themselves were terrible – not because of Osaka itself, but because my performance was so bad. I felt like I had, once more, been a massive letdown. It was a double-edged sword: on the one hand, I was learning about life, experiencing a lot and having a wonderful time, but on the other I was completely below par when it came to competing. Ultimately, I needed to perform; I needed to come good on the promise I'd shown.

At the holding camp, although I'd only really managed about ten days of proper training due to the hamstring pull, as I tried to manage my various niggles, things seemed to be going better. I was running really fast, and having won a medal the year before I still had the belief that I might somehow be able to make the podium, despite my limited preparation.

But it didn't come together and I took it very badly. This time I distinctly remember punching the concrete wall next to the runway in qualification and feeling utterly devastated. It just seemed like too much after an awful year. I was hating what I was doing at the practice track, hating jumping because I was always injured.

It was almost the beginning of the end. Around that time, I started thinking – or beginning to let myself think – about giving it all up, and getting a 'proper' job.

And back home, what did I have? A flatmate who owed me a ton of money, and who then stopped paying the rent. Given that my family were the guarantors on the contract, it put me in a predicament. He was a big guy so you wouldn't ever have wanted to pick a fight with him, which is perhaps why the situation went on as long as it did – and why he got away with his behaviour.

I ended up breaking the contract early to get away from Northwood. My parents were encouraging me to get a place of my own and, fortunately, with the help of a self-certified mortgage that was backed by my mum and dad, my then girlfriend and I were able to find somewhere near the track in Uxbridge where I trained.

But we didn't want to move in alone. I have always loved dogs. Like my parents, I was distraught when our family dog Franz passed away when I was about 11, and I always promised myself I would have a couple of my own when I bought my first house. So, just before I left for Osaka I went out and got two Labrador puppies.

Harry Aikines-Aryeetey, who has been a mainstay of the British 4×100m relay team for years, came with me to this guy's house and immediately saw a Labrador on its hind legs, yapping along but in a really cute way. I was smitten with that dog, and later named him Dexter. Harry, however, liked another Labrador even more and told me I must get him too. I called him Murphy and he turned out to be a right mischievous little monkey – so I blame Harry for that! But with both of them it was love at first sight and they're still lolloping around my house; eating everything in sight and shedding fur.

But on the very day I picked up the dogs, I had a phone call from the estate agent saying we had been gazumped on the house. And as you may gather, this means I had to ring my mum to tell her that I would have to stay with them for while.

'I don't know if you would mind, but can I bring a couple of friends back with me?' I stammered.

She went really quiet for a moment and then said, 'You haven't bought dogs, have you?' When I arrived back in Bletchley she was standing on the porch with a look that said she wouldn't mind at all. It came at a price for my parents, though. As I had to leave almost immediately for Osaka, she and my dad ended up having to handle the potty training by themselves.

Dexter and Murphy are now nine years old, and through all the ups and downs in my life and career they have always been there for me. I absolutely love them to bits. They are pretty nifty training partners too. Whenever I go training in the woods and hills around Woburn Sands, they eagerly scamper along with me. Following a similarly disappointing World Championships, in 2013 I got a third dog, Gus, who is a Northern Inuit, similar to the ones in *Game of Thrones*, and he too is very lovely and boisterous – and accompanies me on runs and when I go downhill mountain biking. Sometimes I have to shout at all three of them to get out of the way because they become overly excited and run in my path.

Back in 2007 I was too scared to tell my coach Frank about the dogs. He didn't want me to have animals – or a girlfriend, for that matter – because he thought it would affect my training. And while he must have known that these dogs had materialised in my life because I had told everyone else, I had not informed him. One day, I was making idle chat with Frank and a psychologist at Brunel University in between training sessions when she asked me: 'So how are the dogs?' I went into complete panic mode and semi-shook my head as if to say, 'No! Don't talk about them!'

It was such a weird and pathetic reaction on my part, and I wish I'd been more of a man about it. Yet Frank and I never spoke about the fact that I had dogs. I'm not sure why. My guess is that he wanted such a level of control over my life, as he does with all his other athletes, that maybe he chose not to mention it because he'd realised that, in this instance, he had not got his way.

But I clearly wasn't in a good place that year. It took me a while to comprehend this, but your state of mind has a huge impact on your performance. And when a sporting body tries to pull you away from what works for you, I think you are destined for failure. Before I moved to London I had a lifestyle that was conducive to me being happy. Now I didn't.

Almost all of my experiences of being a professional athlete to date were of injuries, dissatisfaction and mild depression. I knew I had so much potential but it was really hard to keep on plugging away, with the body always breaking down. I wasn't unmotivated – I was still too much in fear of Frank to ever just not turn up to training – but I started wondering whether I should look for a way out.

It's worth bearing in mind that the government money athletes receive hardly supports a comfortable lifestyle. Scraping by on the bare minimum we get from funding, I started to wonder why the hell I was putting myself through all this heartache, all this pain – for what, exactly?

I also began to ask myself whether I was doing the right thing. I was probably earning less than guys working in fast-food restaurants, so I went online to see whether I had the qualifications to join the Royal Air Force or the police, and how to apply. I even discussed it with Andrew, who urged me not to do anything too hasty and pointed out that it had only been 15 months since I'd been less than ten centimetres away from winning a European gold medal. But right then I wasn't exactly the easiest person to talk to sensibly.

A moment I remember from the Osaka World Championships might help explain why I kept going.

At all the major championships, the big brands each have their own corporate hospitality. If you are sponsored by the likes of Nike, adidas, Asics and so on, you get to go and hang out there, eat amazing food, sit with the other athletes, see their staff, learn about what they do. I was in the Nike House and there were some incredible ex-athletes walking around – and then the shot putter Reese Hoffa strolled in.

He had just won, and there was a tremendous fanfare for him. Being a shot putter, he was a gigantic, imposing bloke, and he was literally picking up staff in celebration. Everyone was swarming around him because he was the champ – the real world champion. I remember looking at him, and thinking how much I would love to experience that. Instead, I was just some nobody who the people on the door had to check was even on their list in case I wasn't really meant to be there.

When I saw Reese's triumph, it refuelled my desire to succeed. I reminded myself that when I was a kid people would laugh when I told them I was going to be a professional sportsman. And yet I had proved them all wrong. Was I really going to give up now after one bumpy year? I had never been a quitter. And I wasn't about to start.

CHAPTER 13

Doing It for Jim

At the start of 2008, the thoughts of every British athlete turned sharply eastward towards Beijing. And although I'd barely jumped at all in the previous 16 months, I was at least comforted by the knowledge that I only needed to complete two tasks to make it to my first Olympics: get myself fit – and then jump the qualifying mark of 8.20m or beyond.

Physically, it didn't help that I was still trying to recover from that ridiculously pesky ankle injury, or that over the previous 12 months I'd been prone to bouts of tonsillitis as well as an increasing number of hamstring problems. You can have all the talent in the world, but it doesn't do you much good if you're forever stuck on the treatment table. Incidentally, hamstring problems were to become a recurring theme: after my gold at London 2012, Dan Pfaff worked out that I had suffered 17 major hamstring tears in my short career.

At least mentally I was feeling far happier after moving out of my flat in Northwood. Since being gazumped a few months earlier, I'd exchanged contracts on a small place in Woburn Sands, a village just outside Milton Keynes. The house needed work. It had a downstairs bathroom, was very old-fashioned, and it took nine months of dedicated and very kind graft by my dad to make habitable – but it was something I could call my own. While it was being renovated, I was supposed to be staying with the sprinter Christian Malcolm in his place in London, but for the most part I was based in Milton Keynes, travelling down to Brunel University from my parents' house in Bletchley first thing in the morning and then returning in the evening.

Once again, we started the year at a training camp in South Africa, which on the surface had plenty of benefits. It was hot and sunny – a prerequisite for running fast and jumping far – and the facility had a plunge pool, gym and 400m grass track. But that year it felt like a negative place to be because Frank made our group train away from the rest of the British athletes. I guess there was a fear factor at play, because he didn't want people assessing his methods or trying to steal his athletes. But, in fairness to him, he was far from alone in that mindset.

On one occasion in South Africa, I was having dinner with Frank and two other senior coaches, John Herbert and Aston Moore. And I felt all they did during that meal was criticise other British coaches, saying how terrible they were, and asking how on earth they had ever trained anybody. But the minute John got up from the table, they started on him. There is such a tricky culture among British coaches.

In my experience, most mistrust their peers. And too many of them – especially the old-timers – believe that they know everything and refuse to accept that they can learn from others. It really hit home later, when Dan Pfaff came over from the United States. Despite the multiple Olympic medallists he had worked with in a 25-year career, including Carl Lewis and the 1996 Atlanta gold medallist Donovan Bailey, some of our coaches wouldn't give him the time of day.

Initially, I had gone along with everything Frank told me. But the longer I stayed with him, the greater my concerns became. He would say things like, 'Sprinting is the easiest event in the world to coach – all you're doing is running as fast as you can in a straight line.' I didn't believe it then, and I certainly don't now. If I had been taught to sprint properly when I was growing up, it would have saved me a lot of time and heartbreak.

However, during 2008 I began to train much less with Frank's group. It wasn't deliberate on my part, but rather because my grandfather Jim became desperately unwell with stomach cancer and I wanted to spend as much time as possible with him before he passed away. I was particularly close to Jim, who was an elder in the Jehovah's Witnesses. I remember once going to Kingdom Hall in Hemel Hempstead with him and my grandma, and one of the older boys asked me, 'What do you want to do when you're older?' And I replied: 'I want to be a professional football player.' 'Well,' he said, chastising me, 'that's not very good for a religious boy to do.' That was quite a common view in my faith, but conversely my granddad was never anything but incredibly supportive and always encouraged me.

Around January 2008, Jim was diagnosed with a tumour and they had to remove his stomach. The doctors performed an operation in which they stretched and expanded his oesophagus and then attempted to turn it into a kind of mini-stomach. We had hoped he was going to get better, but a few months later he went in for further tests and they found that the cancer had spread. It ripped my world apart.

My days consisted of training in Milton Keynes and then going to Hemel Hempstead to visit my granddad in hospital. Despite working out by myself, and feeling emotionally wrecked by my poor granddad's illness, I began to notice that I was getting fitter and stronger – even though I wasn't doing much more than sprinting up the steep hills near my home.

I finally returned to competition at the end of May, jumping an encouraging 8.04m in Zaragoza in Spain, before a less convincing 7.82m in Prague in June. Time was slipping away. To qualify for the Beijing Olympics, I would have to jump 8.20m at the Aviva national trials on 22 July.

But just ten days beforehand, we got the news I had been dreading. Granddad's cancer was terminal. I was devastated and seriously contemplated pulling out of the trials. I honestly thought that even if I went to Birmingham I wouldn't jump well anyway, and why waste a day that could be far better spent with Jim?

However, two nights before the competition, I went to Hemel general hospital to see to my granddad and he wasn't having any of it. 'Go out and get it done,' he told me, in no uncertain terms. He was so brave, even though by now he was beginning to weaken, that I didn't want to let him down.

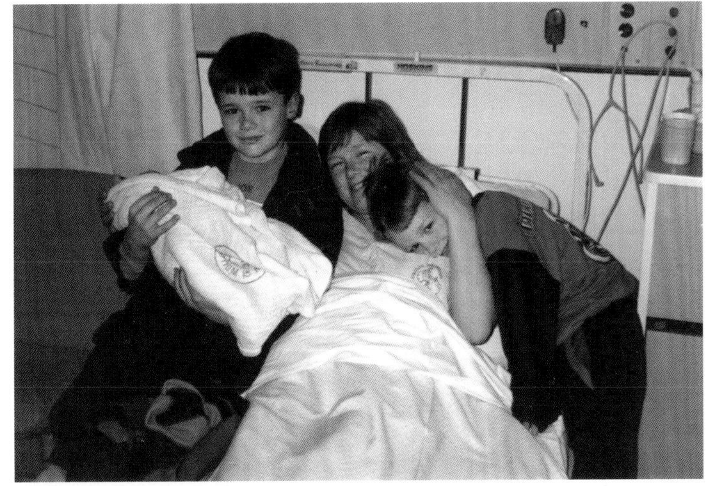

Robert holds our newborn baby sister Natalie, while Mum gives me a cuddle.

With my dad and Natalie at an adventure playground.

When in a hole – stop digging. A lesson I didn't immediately learn.

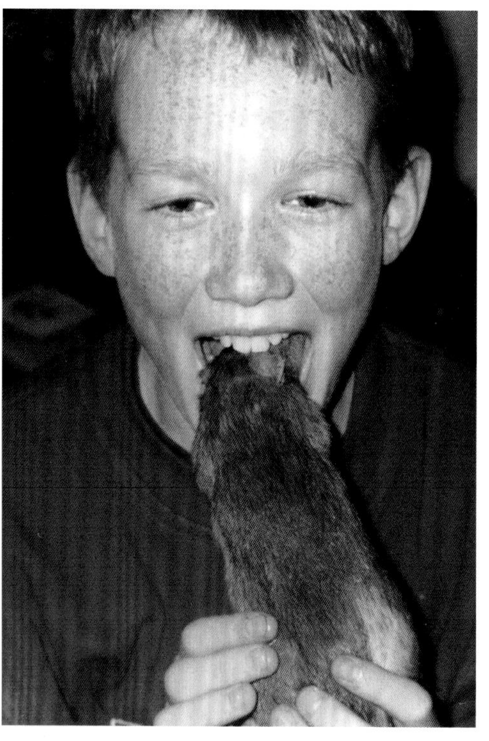

I always wanted to push my boundaries, but I'm not sure this was the best way to do so.

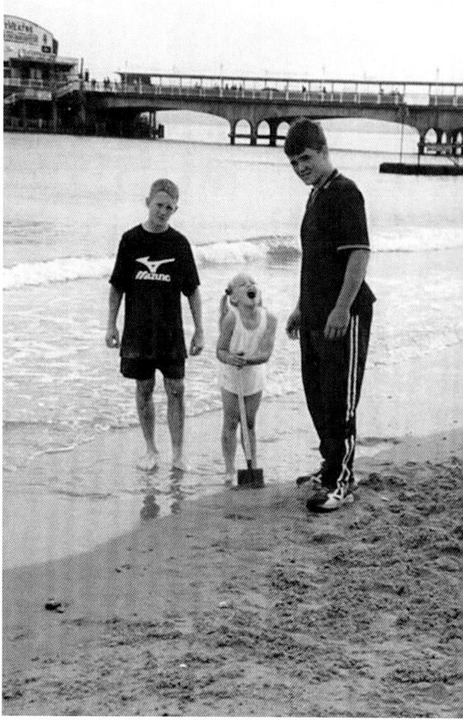

Holiday time with Natalie and Robert.

Me, Granddad Jim, Grandma Carol, Robert and Natalie at a family wedding.

few days after London was chosen to host
e 2012 Olympics, I was in action at the AA
hampionships in Manchester, in both the
)0m and the long jump. Trying to compete
two events proved really tricky. *(PA)*

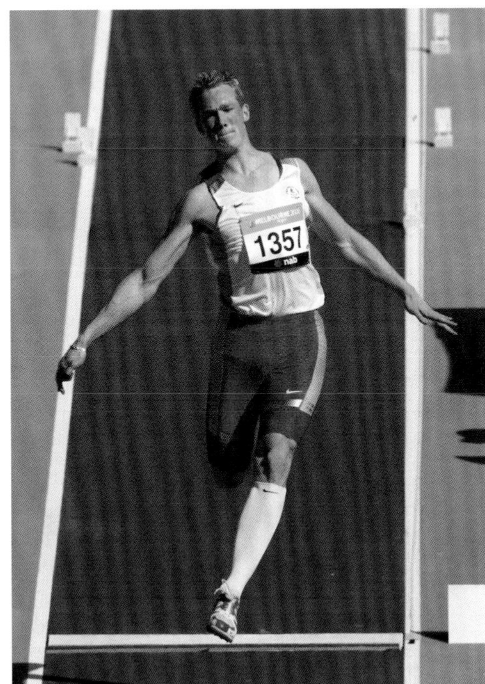

Jumping during the qualifiers at the 2006 Melbourne Commonwealth Games – at the age of 19, it was my first trip outside Europe, but sadly it all ended in a bad hamstring injury. *(Getty Images)*

There was better news that August when I won silver at the European Championships in Gothenburg, even though the GB team was struggling. *(Getty Images)*

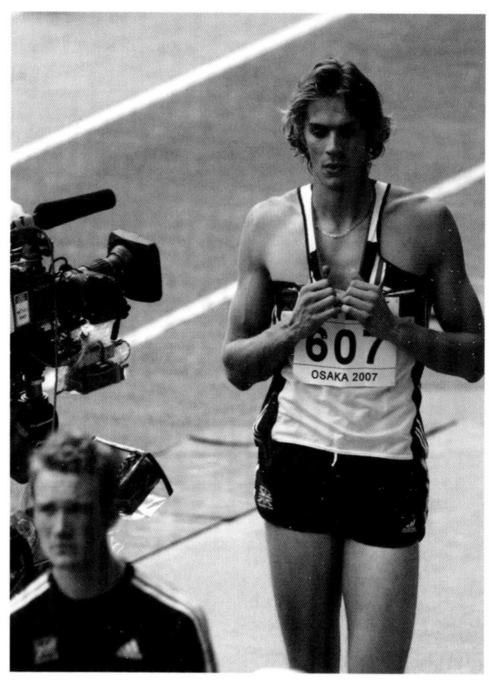

The World Championships in Osaka in 2007 were not a great success for me, or for my long-term rival Chris Tomlinson. *(Getty Images)*

The pressure was on at the Aviva National Trials in July 2008 to qualify for the Beijing Olympics, but my mind was on my granddad, who was fighting terminal cancer. *(PA)*

Battling with tonsillitis, bronchitis and a severe kidney infection, I finished in a disappointing tenth place in Beijing and ended up in hospital the day after. *(PA)*

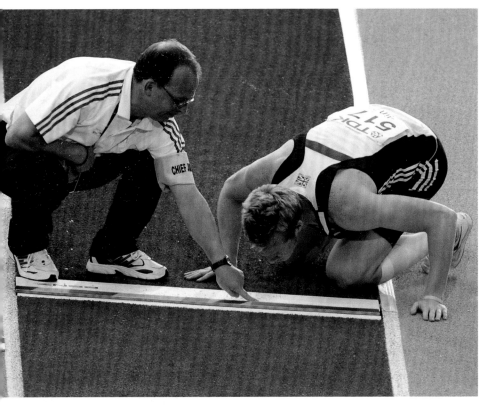

After I'd nailed a jump in the 2009 World Championships in Berlin, I was furious to have it red flagged – especially when I was sure it should have been called good. *(PA)*

remember the New Delhi Commonwealth Games of 2010 more for the extreme levels of poverty I saw around the city than for my silver medal. *(Getty Images)*

When my hamstring popped just as I took off during the qualification round of the Daeg World Championships in 2011, my tournament was over. *(Getty Images)*

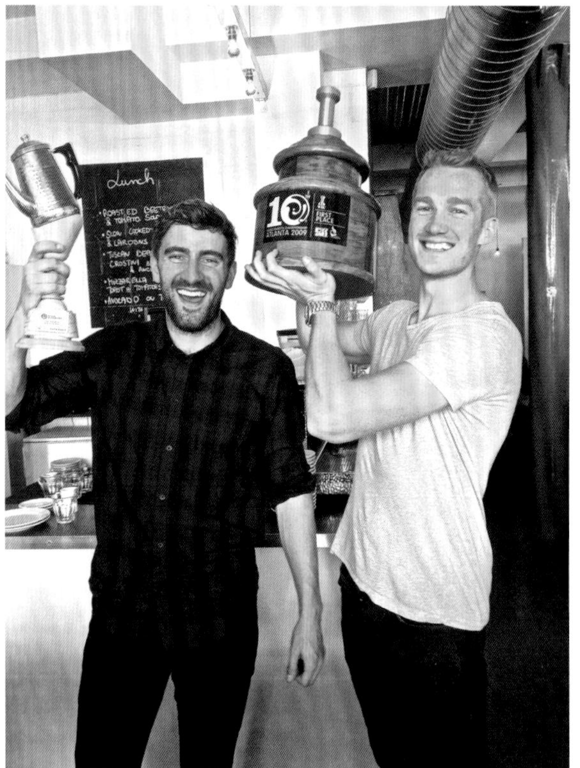

Andrew Steele has introduced me to some of the finer things in life, including the importance of a goo cup of coffee. Here we show off our barista trophies.

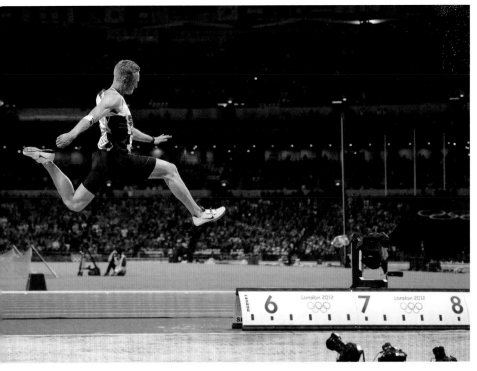

The best evening of my sporting life: leaping to gold on Super Saturday during the London Olympics. *(Getty Images)*

Carrying the flag during my lap of honour, which is all a bit of a blur – but I tried to savour every moment of it. *(Getty Images)*

During the medal ceremony the following day, the emotion of it all became almost too much. *(Getty Images)*

So I went. But it was a highly emotional time, and it didn't help that during the warm-up before the competition got underway, one of my rivals, Jonathan Moore, was being really aggressive, trying to psych me out. At one point he even shouted at me that he was going to beat me up. Part of me found it almost amusing – he was trying to get into my head, an approach that's never worked – but at the same time, I did feel that I already had enough stress in my life. As Moore started going off on one, I thought, 'I'm not in the mood for this', and just focused on the task in hand.

As I stepped on the runway that evening, I also had my dad's words from earlier that day ringing in my ears: 'Go out and make him proud, son.' Simultaneously, those words brought a tear to my eye and added six inches to my chest. I wasn't about to let either of them down.

Slowly, in the first three rounds, I became aware that some of the old jumping sensations were flickering back into life. My speed on the runway was good and I felt better than I had for a while. And then in the fourth round I uncorked a big one – 8.19m. No wonder I jumped around screaming, 'I'm back! I'm back!' I'd had so many injuries and issues and now I'd put together my biggest jump for two years – and the second longest in my career to date.

Not that everyone was impressed. As I heading to my seat, Moore said something to me in passing and I smiled back. His reaction was blunt: 'Don't you fucking smile at me.' Some people like to keep their focus, and don't even want to see someone smiling at them when they are preparing to compete.

Unfortunately, that 8.19m jump was still one centimetre short of what I needed to guarantee selection for Beijing. But now my confidence was up. I could do this.

On the runway I took a deep breath and thought about Jim, something that became part of my routine in the years ahead. And then I unleashed every last ounce of energy in my body, on the runway, on the board, in the air . . . and I did it! Exactly 8.20m – and at a wind speed of plus 2.0 metres per second, right on the limit of what constituted a legal jump.

I briefly celebrated and then I started to cry. I was so highly charged because of what was happening to my granddad, and now me, that I couldn't deal with the thousand emotions crashing around my body all at once.

As soon as I stepped down from the podium, having won the competition, I jumped straight into the car with my father and shot back down to Hemel general hospital to spend the rest of the day with my granddad. His first words were, 'I'm very proud of you.' Whether I had made it to Beijing or not that day, that is all I'd wanted to do. Make Jim proud.

As it turned out, my poor granddad had only a few more weeks to live.

CHAPTER 14

A Bad Couple of Nights in Beijing

Most athletes spend the night before an Olympic final trying to enter a yogic-like state of calm so that they can produce the best performance of their lives the following day. Me? I was in the athletes' village in Beijing, obsessively clicking around the property website Rightmove – my form of meditation.

In my head, one thought kept swimming around like a mantra: 'If I can just win an Olympic medal, I'll be able to get a nicer house.' I became particularly fixated on a place around the corner from the one I then owned in Woburn Sands, on sale at £250,000. If I won a medal, I resolved I would trade up. Given my working-class background – and the sorry state of my finances – it was perhaps not surprising that I was more money-minded than some. After the UK trials, I'd found out that first prize in the Aviva Grand Prix at Crystal Palace later that month was $10,000. So I asked my dad what I'd be able to do with my new house if I came away with a victory. Being a builder, he rattled through the various options – and then I went out and won.

Yet, despite this good run of form, by the time I stepped on to the Bird's Nest track in front of 80,000 people, I was a mental wreck. Shortly before I flew to the British holding camp in Macau, my granddad Jim died. I had desperately wanted to stay at home for a few more days so that I could go to the funeral, but Frank urged me to put the team first. 'You're going to the Olympics now, and if you arrive a few days late it will impact on your performance,' he said. Looking back, I really wish I had told him where to go – I think any reasonable coach, knowing what my granddad meant to me, would have advised me to delay my departure and attend the funeral – but I duly fell into line.

On the day of Jim's funeral I was thousands of miles away, and it was absolutely devastating. Christine Ohuruogu, who is an incredibly kind and thoughtful person, came up to me and said, 'Frank has told me that your granddad's funeral is today, so if you want to do a service with us, we can talk about it.' Of course, it was a lovely gesture. But part of me also thought, 'Why is Frank doing this? Why the hell is he getting somebody who – however nice they are – I don't know particularly well and is not even from the same religious background, to approach me, when he had insisted I miss the funeral in the first place?' Instead I called my mum, who was too distressed by the loss of her dad to attend the service, and we sat in silence on the phone together.

To this day, I hate the fact I didn't say goodbye properly, and put chasing medals before my family. Nowadays, I would do whatever I felt was right, regardless of what anyone told me.

That wasn't the only misjudgement we made before those Olympics. At that stage in my career, lifting heavy weights was not part of my programme, yet when we were in Macau Frank took us to a gym and we pounded the iron. I did some squats and other exercises, along with everyone else, and of course I ended up with stiffness in my body – delayed onset muscle soreness (DOMS) as it's called – for about a week afterwards. Like anyone blasting out a new routine in the gym, I was sore because I wasn't used to it. Looking back, it was a bizarre decision to try something so different just a fortnight before I was due to compete in an Olympics. I think Frank's thought process went along the lines of: 'We're at the Olympics, we've got to work harder than ever before.' But I think it was misguided.

Despite my agitated state, I was still excited. How could I not be? I was 21 years old and representing my country at my first Olympics. We flew into Beijing from the holding camp and got the team bus to the athletes' village. I'll never forget the moment we turned a corner and the Bird's Nest stadium appeared – we all just screamed in excitement and delight.

We had been given these little Panasonic camcorders and most people started recording. Then the Water Cube, venue for the swimming and diving events, came into view as well. The entire Olympic complex looked unreal. It's a bit like when you go to the Grand Canyon and you ask yourself: 'Am I really seeing this?', because the whole place appears so vast and unimaginable, the brain can't process it.

Then, just before I was due to jump in my qualifying round, I had an incredible and hugely welcome surprise – my parents turned up! I wasn't expecting it at all, but they had decided right at the last minute to come and watch because, after all, it might be the only time I ever got to compete at an Olympics. For them to show up like that was a really amazing thing to do, especially since they'd had so much on their plate with granddad's funeral. I was delighted to see them there and it's a memory which I hold dear.

I was happier still when I leapt 8.16m to qualify for the final. It was a horrible jump technically, but I couldn't have cared less. I went over to my parents and gave them a massive hug, before we all watched Usain Bolt destroy the world 100m record, claim his first Olympic gold and change athletics forever.

By now I was feeling a bit more confident that I might win a medal, but on the morning of the final, two days later, I woke up with a scratchy throat and feeling rough as old boots. I ran down to our medical team, searching for a doctor to tell them I thought I had tonsillitis. The long jumper Jade Johnson was there and when she heard me she said, 'Get away from me then – I don't want to catch it!' Part of me thought it was a bit harsh, but the athlete in me totally understood – I wouldn't have wanted to be near me either.

After being checked out, the doctors confirmed that my throat was swollen and the tonsillitis that had plagued me on and off for months had returned with a vengeance. The stress I had accumulated over the previous few weeks surely can't have helped and had probably lowered my immune system.

I hoped that a combination of paracetamol and adrenaline would carry me through, but by the time of the final that evening I really didn't feel well. Before I got on the bus to the Bird's Nest stadium, the 110m hurdler Andy Turner, a really good friend over the years, gave me a pep talk. 'You could break the British record today,' he said, which was really nice of him.

But instead of smiling and thanking him, I tensed up and muttered, 'Oh yeah,' as waves of stress flooded my body. I had my serious face on, because that is how I thought you had to be before a major event. I was too uptight, telling myself that I had to succeed or else – and my illness, coupled with what had gone in the previous few weeks – made me feel spent.

The whole final was a disaster. I had a foul in the first round, jumped 5.20m in the second, and could manage only 7.84m in the third, which was not enough to put me among the top eight places to guarantee me another three jumps. Instead, I finished tenth, a very long way behind Saladino of Panama, who jumped 8.34m to win gold.

Looking back, I think part of the problem was that I had never been taught well enough to be consistently good, whatever the conditions or my state of mind. After running through the pit on my first attempt, I told myself, 'OK, it's fine, I can deal with this.' But I wasn't fine. Not really. I didn't allow myself to sit down. My brain was in hyper-drive, a voice in my head telling me, 'This is an Olympic final so you have now got to pace up and down until your next round and then you're gonna go and get it done.' Essentially, I was telling myself off, and consequently making myself more tense.

To make matters worse, for the first time ever in my career, I started obsessing about random numbers on the scoreboard, taking them as possible indicators of what I was going to do next. While I was jumping, the women's 400m hurdles and men's 200m semi-finals were going on – so if I saw someone run a time of 20.14, I'd say to myself, 'Right, I'm now going to jump 8.14m.'

I know it makes no sense whatsoever. But it shows where my mind was at the time – or rather, where it wasn't. It didn't help that I wasn't getting any feedback from my coaching team, no guidance on what I needed to adjust or what I should be doing. My brain was just not thinking straight. Instead it was lurching off at unwelcome right angles.

I ran through on my second attempt because I was very out

of sync and didn't have the technical aspects of my jumping nailed down. With the benefit of hindsight, I only wish I'd joined my current coach, Dan Pfaff, three or four years earlier, because I believe that without question I'd have won more major medals, including in Beijing. Remember, I had jumped 8.26m as a 19-year-old. So another nine centimetres, which would have been enough for gold in 2008, would have been perfectly feasible with two years of expert guidance.

But in Beijing, having messed up my second jump, I was now in a very stressful position. I went over to Frank at the side of the runway and he said to me, 'You need 8.10m to qualify for the last three jumps.' These days, I would be confident of doing that: my body's been there so many times, and I've won plenty of major championships with those sorts of distances. Back then, however, I had jumped over 8.10m only a handful of times in my entire career.

I can now see what Frank was trying to do: amp me up for a big one. Two days earlier I had qualified with 8.16m, so why couldn't I do 8.10m?

But as things transpired, he hadn't been paying sufficient attention to the scoreboard, as a much easier jump of 7.92m would have been enough to put me in eighth position, and thus given me three more jumps in the final. So, unwittingly, he had actually put extra pressure on me, and I was already dealing with the stress very poorly. Mentally, I was all over the place – pulling numbers from the scoreboard, constantly looking at the wind gauges, unable to jump properly. I didn't know what I was doing, but I was gone.

I tried my hardest to spur myself on: 'Come on, do it for Granddad.' I even comforted myself with the thought that so much had gone wrong in 2008 that if I could win an Olympic medal it would be the ultimate fairytale ending to a rubbish year. But even then I knew that fairytales rarely happen in real life. My final jump of 7.84m was closer – but not enough. I went over to my mum and dad in the crowd. They hugged me tight and were clearly as gutted as I was. Then my Nike rep at the time, the guy who was responsible for determining how much I was sponsored and how much kit I received, spoke to me. 'Make sure you never do that again,' he said. And then he walked away.

I found that particularly brutal, the verbal equivalent of giving me a flying kick to the groin just when I was at my most vulnerable. I was embarrassed: with myself, with my performance, and everything that had happened. But I didn't deserve that.

The next day I woke up feeling terrible, but still planned to head to Beijing's famous silk market with a couple of other athletes, hoping to buy some cheap but realistic-looking fake goods. But when I got off the train I was in a bad way, and so I turned around and headed straight back to the village. By the time I slumped into bed I was feeling truly awful, the most ill I could ever remember. It felt like my body was shutting down. The worst catastrophe in the world could have been taking place, and I wouldn't have been able to move. Eventually, my room-mates came back and they tried to get me to wake up, but I was slow to come round. As I later found out, not only did I have tonsillitis but bronchitis and a serious kidney infection too.

When the UK Athletics team doctor, Bruce Hamilton, arrived, I was shivering convulsively. He took one look and said, 'We need to get you to hospital – can you get out of bed?' It took all the effort in the world to do that, and to climb into a wheelchair to be taken to hospital. When I got there, the Chinese doctors were brilliant: it was one of the most efficient hospitals I've ever been to in my life, and I've been to a few. They did everything incredibly well and quickly, including chest and torso scans and blood tests. I was given antibiotics and was soon put on a plane home to recover. I remember watching the rest of the Olympic Games from the sofa at my mum and dad's house, feeling like absolute death.

After the Beijing Olympics had passed, I was fortunate enough to meet Ian Bullerwell, who became one of my biggest helps in the lead up to 2012, both financially and mentally. Ian is a prominent businessman in the Bedfordshire area, and we met at the annual SportsAid lunch in Milton Keynes. Like many businessmen you meet, he offered me his card and said he'd love to help. If I remember correctly, I was late to the event as the exhaust had fallen off my car en route, so I felt as if I could do with some assistance.

At those sorts of occasions, you tend to see businesspeople bid for the odd piece of sporting memorabilia to raise money for whichever charity or organisation is involved, but I didn't hold my breath expecting much else to come of it. However, Ian had been a professional rugby referee and the chairman at Bedford rugby club, so clearly loved sport, but more than that he loved helping people. He took me under his wing straightaway and became a hugely important influence.

When the little things, which can often be the most important things, are taken care of, it gives you the freedom to crack on. Ian helped with a car, initially a Saab 93 (which I loved) and then a Ford Mondeo which I had until the end of 2012. He also covered my flights and paid for my warm-weather training in 2011. I honestly do not think I would have been as successful in 2012 if I had not had his support.

CHAPTER 15

A Local Rivalry

For years Chris Tomlinson and I had been considered rivals, which was no great surprise given we were both doing the same event, were from the same country, and clearly had the potential to challenge for the podium at major championships. Chris was five years older than me, and I'm sure he considered himself the better athlete, and he was relatively well known in the British athletics community. So when he joined Frank's group to train alongside me, some expected sparks to fly.

Part of me could see why. Chris and I have always had what you might euphemistically call an interesting relationship. At one stage, he was one of the bigger names in UK athletics – he broke the British record, and came fifth in the 2004 Athens Olympics when he was only 22, although he unluckily ended his career with only a couple of minor championship medals, which must be hugely frustrating for him considering the potential he had.

But the thing with me – and I think he never understood this – is that I don't really care much who I'm training with, or even who I'm competing against. In fact, I believe the way to get the best out of yourself is to compete against the best – you learn from that, after all. But in training, you just take it as it comes, whoever you are with.

I think Chris probably struggled with that, and let what other people did bother him too much. I used to take a little time before launching myself down the runway. Once, during training, I was focused on my preparation, rocking back and forth at the start, getting ready to go, when all of a sudden I heard Chris behind me: 'Oh, for crying out loud, just get on with it!' But that's training: everyone can do what they want when it's their turn, and you can't let that sort of thing upset you in the slightest. After all, if little things like that bother you in training, then it doesn't bode well for competition, when you really need to be able to tune out distractions.

In 2009, I went to the South African training camp in January as usual. Frank was coaching, and I was one of a small group of long jumpers, including Chris, Jonathan Moore and some younger boys coming through.

It was an odd set-up, as far as I was concerned. Most of the time, the long jumpers would be training on the 'far' side of the track, away from everyone else. But there were still the same conversations going on, over and over again – how so-and-so was a bad coach, so-and-so wasn't a good athlete. The atmosphere was quite negative, with people complaining and grousing about others all the time. Sadly, this was – and is – a common theme within British athletics.

That trip was the longest I spent with Frank's group all year – and it marked what was, really, the beginning of the end of my relationship with him. Being a sociable person, I wanted to hang out with others in the team, integrate with them. But our group seemed to want to be on its own. It was quite segregated, and I didn't like that. Yes, we compete in individual sports, but I wanted to get to know people. As someone who loves the sport of athletics, and is a bit of a fanboy, I will always want to meet fellow athletes who are really good at what they do, whatever event they compete in. I had good friends like the hurdler Andy Turner, who went on to win a World Championship bronze in the 110m hurdles and become a top bodybuilder, and other mates I'd want to relax and have fun with. We'd even go out drinking because it was early in the year – though admittedly we'd have to sneak out because not many people in the camp would have approved.

But Frank wasn't happy with any socialising outside the group. In some ways, he acted more like a dictator than a mentor, and I've never responded well to people like that. I'd had a conversation previously with the 400m runner Tim Benjamin, a fantastic athlete whose career sadly ended prematurely due to illness and injuries. He'd mentioned a coach to me, someone training out in California, who he said was brilliant. That person turned out to be Dan Pfaff. Tim was in semi-regular contact with him, and told me about the other athletes Dan had coached. At the end of 2008 I'd even looked into Dan's coaching and his own career, and I'd started to wonder what it would be like to work with someone like that. But at that point, making a move overseas was no more than a pipe dream. I was living with my girlfriend and had two dogs, a house – a whole life in the UK.

Just upping and leaving all this didn't seem remotely possible, so I buried the idea and carried on as before. But during that camp in South Africa, the more I spoke to my friends, the more I realised how unhappy I was with my situation. I could see major flaws in the training methods, and I didn't like the way Frank seemed to be playing Chris Tomlinson and me off against each other. Maybe he saw it as a way of motivating us, trying to build a rivalry to push us, and better us. And maybe that would work for some people, but not for me. I am confident enough in my ability to understand that, as long as I have a good day, then I have a chance of winning. I don't need to get in anyone's face – or slag them off – to do that.

I was running fast again that year, and feeling good. I didn't much like the atmosphere in the camp, but in performance terms I was doing OK, and got some good jumps out. But the overriding memory of that trip will always be what happened to my old rival Jonathan Moore, who climbed naked on to the roof of a house in Potchefstroom, spread his arms and jumped six or seven metres on to some guy's Ford Bantam pick-up truck.

For a while Moore had been considered the next big thing in British long jumping, having won a European junior silver medal and been World youth champion, although at 24 he had not yet fulfilled that early promise. He didn't really like me, as events at the Olympic trials the year before had shown, and he always wanted to beat me. We were hardly best mates. But I certainly wasn't expecting to see someone with such a bright future end up in the situation he did at a training camp.

The first sign that something was up was during a competition that took place in Potch, where we were actually training the day before he jumped off the roof. I went to watch, because there were a few jumpers there, and Jonathan was the main British guy. It was a relatively small-time meet, mostly involving locals, although Potch does attract athletes from all over Europe.

I noticed with envy how some of the other athletes were chatting with friends from other countries. I also realised that quite a few people were staring at Jonathan, who was behaving very oddly. He kept taking a few paces, opening his arms wide and looking up at the sky, and then sort of muttering to himself, and then doing it repeatedly. He'd always been pretty intense when it came to competing, but this was different: I remember thinking, 'Something isn't right here.' Nevertheless, he competed, although he didn't jump that well, and then that was that, we went home.

Then, the following day, a call went out that Jonathan had disappeared. No one knew where he was. Everybody spent some time looking for him, in the fields around the track and all the open land. He was nowhere to be found, and there was a real sense of unease in the camp. Finally, there was a call from the police station to say they had found him. Of course, we all thought, 'Oh flipping heck, what sort of stupid thing has he done to land himself in trouble with the police?'

Sadly, though, it wasn't trouble, but some kind of breakdown. He had climbed on top of someone's house and then jumped off completely naked when the owner had come outside and seen him. Really, he was very lucky. This was South Africa, at a time when a young black guy standing naked on top of a house ... well, he could have been shot.

The next time I saw Jonathan was on the flight home. It was so odd – this was a man who at times had been incredibly hostile towards me, but he was sitting on a bench in the airport with his dad, arms linked like you would with a child or your girlfriend. And the look on his face was that of a child. Even the way he said hello to us was in a sort of child's voice. We said, 'Hope you're OK?' and he simply replied, 'Yeah,' then went back to hugging his dad. It was an odd moment. There were times when he'd said bad things to everyone, but then here was this guy for whom things had clearly gone monumentally wrong.

I guess that experience in South Africa shook me a little, because shortly after returning was also the last time I missed a drugs test – one of two missed testing slots in my 11-year career. People may not know, but as a drug-tested athlete you are required to provide the authorities with your whereabouts every day of the year; details of where they can find you and turn up unannounced at any time to take a blood and urine sample. There is a system which allows you to update your information if for any reason you change your plans, but – and this is especially so when you are a young athlete – very occasionally you might forget.

Now, I'm not an organised person by nature, and on this occasion I'd decided pretty much at the last minute to go directly to a meeting in Glasgow, to try to qualify for the European Athletics Indoor Championships in Turin. I woke the next morning to a phone call from my dad, who said, 'The testers are here!' My heart skipped a beat. I couldn't believe it – I'd forgotten to update my whereabouts with the testing authorities. Missing a test is obviously stupid and not good at all – and it stays on your record as a kind of 'first strike' for 18 months. Naturally, I was even more careful after that and for some time I was in constant dread of forgetting to update my whereabouts. The worry ends up dictating your life. Even nowadays, whenever we go anywhere it's something I make sure I do the second I arrive.

It may seem impatient, seeing as it was only the winter after I'd appeared in an Olympics, but I felt like my career was stalling somewhat. However, after Glasgow, things changed a bit. I jumped decently there, achieving the qualifying mark for Turin with a leap of 7.91m, which was one of my best openings to an indoor season. I wasn't going to training as much, just doing stuff as and when I could, often with my dad. And perhaps because of that I actually started to enjoy the sport a little more again.

It felt as if I'd developed a new mindset, deciding that, in actual fact, I needed to do things my own way. I'd moved into my own house with my girlfriend, and it felt like a kind of freedom after being miserable in London with that awful flat-mate. I wanted to train more in Milton Keynes, as well as in the woods near my home in Woburn Sands. And I was working hard, running up and down hills and doing steps sessions. I really enjoyed that, and was starting to notice the benefits.

So in March I went to Turin, an amazing experience because I got to watch the German Sebastian Bayer put in one of the longest jumps in history – an astonishing 8.71m. It's still to this day the second longest indoor jump ever, and I was completely blown away by it. Eight metres and 71 centimetres!

I'd felt pretty confident going into that competition. I knew I was a contender, but by no means expected to do anything spectacular. And I would probably have said the same for Sebastian, given that we had often jumped together since we were juniors and I'd usually beaten him. Yet in Turin there was something about him. Even in the warm-up, before he'd done a single jump, I thought, 'He's won this.' His presence had changed, completely. He had an air of confidence, even cockiness, about him that I'd never seen before. It didn't disconcert me, because to me he was a friend, but it just seemed weird that he was so assured.

I have no idea how he knew it was going to be his day. Sometimes, I guess, as a sportsperson you just sense it. But when he jumped 8.29m in the first round, I thought, 'OK, he must be right! But how is he doing that, how is he making it look so easy? Here I am, giving it everything I've got, and just about managing eight metres.' It was a really 'sprung' runway and a very bouncy board, which has never suited me. Being quite a heavy guy, the springiness just absorbs all my effort, and I can't utilise the skills I've got, so I pretty much knew that was all I had that day. I did a couple of 8.00m flat jumps, then a shorter one. It felt like a decent series, but really frustrating as I couldn't get any further.

So then Sebastian, having passed a few rounds – almost as if he was thinking, 'I've won this, I'll let them battle it out for silver' – got up again. He was the last to jump. I was sat on the benches watching him, and as he ran past and took off I knew it was big. But when the distance flashed up, I could hardly believe it. Someone I knew, and who had never beaten me before, jumped 8.71m right in front of me. It blew my mind.

Sebastian has never come close to that distance again. But that jump made me understand something: every jumper at this level has the ability, once they catch their perfect day, to do something special. Without wanting to belittle his stunning performance, I believed that actually I was a better athlete than him. I was faster and stronger, so clearly I must be capable of jumping a lot further too. Then again, it was also a wake-up call – because it showed that you can never write anyone off, that anyone can have their day. It was just that I hadn't had mine yet. I finished sixth, with a distance of exactly eight metres.

After that competition, I decided I needed a break, so I went skiing with my dad and my brother. We drove direct from Turin to the French Alps, to Les Arcs, where my parents had a little one-bedroom apartment. They had both been working solidly since I was little, and had started to think about the future. Since they had no pension arrangements, my dad had decided to take out another mortgage in order to buy this place, which they'd had for a couple of years. I'd never seen it, so I was really keen to go.

My dad really, really adores skiing. Sometimes I reckon he loves the sport more than anything, particularly the feeling of freedom. It wasn't an obvious choice for someone from his background but once he'd got the bug, there was no looking back. Of course, working as an instructor at the dry ski slope in Hemel earned him a bit of extra cash but, really, I think he did it because he loved it.

That skiing trip was odd. My brother and my dad fought constantly. My dad has a very different work ethic and outlook to my brother and I think he gets easily frustrated with him. Rob was really great at sport, but if he ever made a mistake it really discouraged him. I guess we are sort of opposites in that sense; for me, my response to a cock-up would be, 'OK, I've got to improve, I've got to get better, I've got to win.' My brother, who arguably was more physically gifted than me, just really hated losing, so he shied away from putting himself in the position to do so – and my dad has always found that incredibly frustrating. I think there was a period of about nine months when my dad and my brother didn't say a word to each other, although they were living in the same house.

Of course, my dad loves him to bits, but, like many blokes, he can just be terrible at expressing his emotions. On that trip, they had a huge row that became really heated, then both of them got quite upset. And in the end, my brother just sort of shouted, 'What's the point in anything? I will never be as good as him' – referring to me. My heart sank. Naturally, when you are kids you always want to outdo your older brother – because he's your older brother. But he had his niche – he was brilliant at rugby – and I had mine in athletics. Yet suddenly, for the first time, I realised that on one level I was a weight around my brother's neck. I know he was proud of me and always has been, but I also felt as if I was partly responsible for the fact that he felt fed up about the way his life was going.

My brother and I have always got on brilliantly, but we responded very differently to our upbringing. In typical Greg style, I reacted against the strict rules imposed by my parents, such as absolutely no girlfriends allowed, but my brother was always more loyal, so he really listened. I was the rebel; he was more sensitive and obedient. It'll happen with Milo and other children who come later; just because they're siblings, it won't mean they approach life the same. Bert is now working a steady job and routine is perfect for him. I don't even know what I'd be good at if I didn't have my athletics career.

That row shook me a bit, and, as we were all staying in a tiny one-room apartment, I was quite glad when it was time to leave and start training again. I was actually feeling quite positive about things. So, of course, with my typical luck, I ended up falling ill. Very ill, in fact.

I'd always been prone to tonsillitis and had suffered seven or eight bouts of it in a relatively short period up to this point. Now I came down with it again, so the doctors decided it was time to whip my tonsils out. I was desperate to get back into training; instead, I had to undergo further surgery. It was frustrating but, equally, I wanted to get rid of these wretched tonsils that were the bane of my life.

I had them taken out at a hospital near where I lived, and usually it's a fairly routine operation. I went to stay at my parents' house afterwards, so they could keep an eye on me, as the hospital had said you can get a little bit of post-op bleeding. Generally, though, it was expected that I'd be back in training pretty quickly.

But it turned out to be far from routine. For about five days after the operation, I was still in a ridiculous amount of pain. I was so sore I could barely stand it. I took all the painkillers I could just to try to take the edge off, but nothing worked. I was hardly sleeping, which didn't help. What I didn't realise at that point was that I had a severe infection. I remember waking up one morning at about 3am and sitting on the edge of the bed in tears with the pain.

Then, the following day, I woke up to the usual household sounds – my sister getting ready for school, my brother and parents for work. I had this weird sense that I should keep my mouth closed. I went straight to the bathroom, opened it up and blood just poured out. 'God, that's disgusting,' I thought, and spat it out. But within seconds it was full of blood again. It was like a tap that couldn't be turned off.

I began to feel horribly queasy, and the trickle of blood was getting faster, too. I started banging on the floor with my foot until my brother came and asked if I was OK. He immediately fetched my mum – by this point there was a steady stream of blood coming out of my mouth – and she rang for an ambulance. I was starting to feel very weak now. It was the first time I'd ever been blue-lighted to hospital.

Although my mum actually worked in the hospital, it was the only time I'd seen that real emergency part of it, with people on stretchers and ambulances coming and going. The doctors checked me and said they would have to re-cauterise the wound, as it had split open. They put my head back to look, and as soon as it moved forward my throat filled with blood again. I remember thinking, 'Flipping heck, this is not good.'

People were wiping blood off my face, and my mum was standing beside me. I was whimpering to her, 'I feel so sick. I feel really, really sick.' She said, 'You've lost a lot of blood. You are going to be feeling rough, don't worry.' And I said, 'No, no, I'm going to be sick!' And all of a sudden I started throwing up, screaming as I did so because the pain from my stomach was like nothing I had experienced before. I was puking blood. Essentially, all the blood that had been seeping from the wound in the night had been going in places it shouldn't. I was lucky I hadn't choked on it, or 'drowned' in it during the night.

I looked around while this was happening, searching in desperation for help because it was by far the most horrific experience of my life. I felt exceptionally weak and tired, my head started to droop and I had the sensation that I was about to pass out. They had given me a bucket to puke into, and I remember looking down into it and I swear the gross stuff in there had made the shape of a gory skull. It sounds a bit melodramatic but at that moment I genuinely thought it was a sign and I was going to die.

The doctors went into action mode, giving me anti-sickness drugs and putting me on a drip to rehydrate me. It worked: I stopped being sick and just felt awful. I had lost about a quarter of my body's blood. No wonder I was feeling like utter rubbish. They examined me and said, 'Well, the wound is open, and you've had a serious infection, but it's not bleeding as heavily now.' So they then shipped me up to a ward, and I was on a drip for a couple of days and monitored to see if they needed to re-operate.

It was an open ward, and I was bored out of my mind. As I was extremely tired, I slept a lot, but I was also thinking, 'Bloody hell, it's not long before the summer season. I have just puked up a large proportion of my blood, and I am in bloody hospital again. This is so typical – something always seems to go wrong.'

A few days later I was allowed home, and my mum came and picked me up. We walked to the car and, despite having just competed in the European Indoor Championships and been skiing, I could barely even manage the five stairs up to the car park. It felt like climbing Everest. My body was so depleted that every stair was a battle, and I had to have a break after each one.

When I finally got home, the recovery began, and it took a long while for me to feel good again. The experience did have a positive side effect: the freedom not to have to travel into London to train with Frank's group, in the environment that I didn't enjoy any more. So by the time I was ready to train again a few weeks later, the natural way to get fit again was to attack my favourite hills in the local woods.

The first time, I managed one single hill. I got to the top and was nearly puking because my body was so tired. But it was a great barometer for my recovery because my dad timed this particular run at 57 seconds. Five weeks later, it was down to 37 seconds. It was a marker of my progress and an indication that I was coming back again.

My dad was brilliant during this time, not only because he would come to the woods to time me and count my reps, but because he was keen I didn't push myself too stupidly hard, as I was inclined to do. It was working. I was enjoying training again, getting fit, getting strong and rebuilding. Doing all the things that worked for me, and not the stuff that didn't. In fact, in that whole year of 2009, I probably went to London to see Frank and the group perhaps ten times.

I knew my relationship with Frank was on its last legs. I used to avoid his calls, and barely spoke to him. There was one time he caught up with me and started saying, 'Well, you've seen how well Chris is jumping this year, right? That's because he listened to everything I have said, and done everything I've told him to.' He almost seemed pleased that Chris was doing better than me.

I just thought, 'Fine. I'll keep doing what I'm doing, and I will jump well too.'

Around this time, I also looked into Dan Pfaff again. In fact, I'd even heard a rumour that he was coming to the UK, to work with British Athletics. So I asked for a meeting with Charles van Commenee, the new performance director at British Athletics. I had to be a bit careful because officially I was still being coached by Frank, even though I was basically training myself. So I asked Charles if it was true that Dan was coming to the UK.

'Yes, he is,' said Charles.

'Well, I'd really like to work with him,' I replied.

'Absolutely no way,' said Charles, in that typically blunt Dutch way of his. 'I am not bringing in one of the best coaches in the world to coach people like you – you aren't good enough. You've not won anything, you are never going to win anything; you just about make the team.'

'But I believe I can!' I said. 'I think I can do much better and he is the guy who can help me.'

'No, no, no!'

And that was that. I pleaded with Charles, but he wasn't having any of it. I was exceptionally hurt because from my point of view I was trying to do something positive by working with one of the best track and field coaches in the world. Eventually, he muttered something vague about Dan perhaps working with me in the future, but not as things stood right then.

This was all in the run-up to the 2009 World Championships in Berlin. The first time I actually saw Dan he was coming out of a lift in a hotel in Berlin. There he was, a quite small guy, not intimidating at all, just a very American-looking man with a massive cowboy moustache. But to me, he was this terrifying guru of the sport who I was unworthy of even speaking to. As he walked past, I managed to say, 'Hi, Dan, I'm Greg, nice to meet you,' and he just nodded at me and walked on. 'Oh well,' I thought, 'he probably has no idea whatsoever who I am.' But then I became paranoid that Charles might have mentioned me to him, almost like a joke, and maybe that's why he'd walked off.

In a way, that spurred me on during the World Championships. I felt like I had something to prove. Sebastian Bayer was there, one of the favourites after his amazing jump in Turin. But he was at his home games and possibly feeling the pressure, because he sat there with a towel over his head, hiding from the cameras. And it made me think, 'Hang on, this is just Sebastian, the guy I've beaten a million times before – I can beat him again.'

So when it came to the qualifying round, I stood on the runway, revving myself up, ready to blast off three years of frustration. As I was standing there, some other athlete came and moved his marker – this is really not the done thing as it's off-putting if someone suddenly appears a metre away from you on the runway, potentially in the way. I don't know if it was deliberate or not, I didn't even know the guy, but I smiled to myself and set off, not even caring if I hit him on the way down. Luckily he moved in time.

I ran, hit the board, and began to soar. I knew it was good. Really good. In fact, it was the best jump of my life. When the distance of 8.30m came up, I jumped around, screaming with joy. Not only had I broken the British record, but I'd proved to the guy who was then boss of British Athletics – and who had just told me I'd never do anything – that I could be a legitimate contender. What's more, I'd shown Frank, who had been telling me everything I was doing was wrong, that I could thrive and fly outside his control. It felt so good.

Charles actually came over to say, 'Well done, I knew you could do it.' And I just thought, 'You arsehole, you didn't think that at all.' At that time I didn't like him one bit, as you can tell. But, funnily enough, nowadays I get on really well with him, and hugely respect him as a coach. I wish he was still running things in Britain.

Weirder still, Frank came over, waving a piece of paper at me. It had the initials 'GR' on it, and next to them, 'BR'. 'Look!' he said. 'I knew you were going to break the British record, I wrote it down!' I thought to myself, 'You had no idea! You've hardly seen me all year, and you've been saying that Chris is far better than me because he has been doing everything you tell him.' Maybe he'd seen the writing on the wall, and knew deep down I was going to leave him, and was feeling a bit unsure.

This was only the qualifying stage, of course. But it was a good feeling, thinking that for the first time in my career I really had a chance of winning a big medal, and doing it on my own terms. So I went to the final – and, as always seems to happen, something went slightly wrong.

The underlying problem that hampered the early part of my career was that, while I was fast and strong, I was neglecting the technical side of jumping, the skills needed to achieve greater consistency. I could jump 8.30m off the back of my natural ability and a training regime and lifestyle that made me happy, but technically I was still all over the place.

In the final, I improved in every round of the competition, starting with a leap of 7.83m and finishing with 8.17m to end up in fifth place. But in the third round there was one that got away. I thought I had nailed it, but the judges pulled up the red flag to say it was a foul. I was absolutely certain it wasn't, and asked them to show me. The official pointed to a mark, and I said, 'No, that's not mine!' He then indicated another one, and I said, 'Hang on, you can't claim that two different marks are mine and say that I fouled!' So I argued and argued, and probably held things up and pissed off the other competitors, but it felt like this was my chance. I'd put myself in a position where I could maybe even win a medal and I wasn't going to give that up for what I saw as an appalling injustice. I felt like those officials were taking it away from me. I was furious.

Eventually, they called over the head judge and he said, 'OK, we need to go to video analysis. Come with me.' So he led me from the competition to a room up in the stadium, where there were two other officials. They pulled up the footage and showed the image, with my foot possibly over the line, possibly not – it was the kind of 'foul' that sometimes gets called, sometimes doesn't. One of the judges then announced that he agreed with me, the other said, 'No, it's a foul.' This argument went on for a couple of minutes, at which point they got a call on their radio, asking them to bring me back to the track because I had to jump.

I had no idea what was actually going on but the competition was still underway, of course, so the judges said, 'OK, look, leave it as a foul but your second-round jump of 7.96m has put you into the top eight, so you've got to go down and jump again.' My head was spinning. I knew I'd jumped far, but I don't know how far, because although they measured it, they never told me the distance as it remained a foul.

It probably says a lot about my bloody-mindedness that I went back down and pulled out probably the three best jumps I'd ever done in a major championships – 8.05m, 8.15m, then 8.17m – having dashed back to the pit from that weird tiny room in the middle of the stadium. And while I wanted more, of course, I was pretty pleased with fifth position. The American Dwight Phillips won with 8.54m, while Godfrey Mokoena from South Africa finished second on 8.47m – which I'd expected – and a new Australian star called Mitchell Watt finished third with 8.37m.

For once, I left a major championship with a smile on my face. I had given it my all and come up smelling if not of roses then of something far sweeter than I had been used to. Fifth in a World Championships was good for sponsorship and invitations to big events. Myself and my room-mate, the pole vaulter Steve Lewis – he was always my roomie at championships – had a really good time. He finished seventh, and we both felt we deserved the bit of fun we had afterwards.

It was at those championships, too, that Usain Bolt ran a world record in both the 100m and the 200m. I had gone to doping control to be tested after my competition, feeling pretty happy with the way things had gone. I really wanted to watch him run, so I had to lean out of a window about two storeys up to see him come around the bend in the 200m, my head hanging out as he stormed to a world record of 19.19 seconds.

Berlin was a great experience. As usual, there was an awful lot of partying afterwards and the customary shenanigans. I loved the city, and my parents came out to watch me, too, which was wonderful. My dad really loved Berlin, which surprised me as he usually only enjoys mountains – and there aren't many of them in the German capital.

I finished my season a month later at the Great North CityGames in Newcastle, where I somehow managed to jump 8.17m despite being really quite hungover, if not still a little drunk. Back then, the competition was spread over a Friday night and Saturday afternoon, so when my mate Steve had finished vaulting on the Friday night he invited me out for a few drinks with four of his fellow competitors. I told him I was jumping the next day, so would pop along for a quick one. Instead, I ended up getting absolutely destroyed.

At one point, I ordered 12 shots of tequila for the six of us. As the barman started pouring out the shots, the bottle emptied, so he had to look for another one. While he did that, I leant over the bar, grabbed one of the open bottles and poured a load of whatever alcohol it was in my mouth, drank it, then put the bottle back without him noticing.

The night then went quickly downhill for me. When I took the tequila back over to the table, I said, 'Right guys, two shots of tequila each.' But Steve said he hated tequila and the rest of them didn't want it either. I thought, 'You are kidding me – I just brought you all a drink!' So, not wanting to waste anything I then necked every single one.

It all got very blurry after that, but apparently I went to bed at 2.30am. The following lunchtime I woke up and got in the lift, where by chance I bumped into Chris Tomlinson. I must have reeked of alcohol as he looked at me and said, 'Are you drunk?', to which I replied, 'Nah, I'm fine,' even though I was swaying all over the place.

I went downstairs and grabbed something quick to eat, then headed to the track feeling awful. A couple of Australian throwers who had seen me the night before were there, and they started making 'Blurgh! Blurgh!' noises because they thought I was going to throw up after my heavy session the night before.

I was thinking to myself, 'You have no chance today. If you can get over seven metres you're doing well.' But in the first round I went 7.67m and I thought, 'That's pretty good considering: I've jumped worse than that in actual competitions before.' Then, incredibly, I ended up catching one and jumping 8.17m. I couldn't help thinking, 'Flipping heck, I've jumped one of the best jumps of the year and about 12 hours earlier I was literally crawling over the Tyne Bridge back to my hotel.'

How did I celebrate? With a few more drinks, of course.

CHAPTER 16

The Meeting that Changed My Life

In early November 2009 I made the best decision of my life. I finally broke ties with Frank Attoh and joined the revered American coach Dan Pfaff, who had agreed a contract with UK Athletics to coach in Britain until after the London 2012 Olympics. Once again, I had my friend and agent at the time, the late Ayo Falola, to thank for sorting it out. I was a bit nervous about talking to Frank directly, so it was Ayo who told him it was over, just as he had done with Tom McNab. Although I am sometimes referred to as outspoken, I don't seek out confrontation, and did so even less as a young athlete. Without Ayo, things would have been much trickier for me, and he was also the one who then brokered my first meeting with Dan, at Lee Valley, where we sat down over orange juice and sparkling water and got to know each other a little better.

At the time I was completely in awe of Dan – his reputation preceded him. He had worked with Tom Tellez in the early 1980s when Tellez coached Carl Lewis – who was not only a multi gold-medal-winning sprinter, but a four-time Olympic gold medallist in the long jump – and then gone on to coach eight more Olympic medallists and five world record holders in a 30-year career.

I was still just 22, but I was actively trying to be more mature and professional, so I told him I would love to hear his philosophy on training, and how he would help take me to the next level. Within 20 seconds, I had a huge smile on my face. Dan spoke with such precision and sense that I knew instantly that he was the coach for me. Along with the technical aspects, he stressed the importance of rest, of feeling happy with your surroundings, and not killing yourself in order to succeed. All points that resonated so strongly with my own beliefs.

We spoke for about 90 minutes and at the end I asked him, 'When do we start?' It was a Friday and he said he'd see me on Monday morning. And that was it. I went away and couldn't have been happier.

Finally, I had the right path for me with a coach who, in my eyes, is the greatest in the world. I know that sounds like some statement, but I have had conversations with a lot of coaches and none of them quite gets it like Dan does – from understanding the science and art of coaching to the complex interplay between the two, Dan is unrivalled in his expertise. This was the start of what became the relationship we have to this day, a relationship that changed my life.

The first session I had with Dan was bloody hilarious, and highlighted the gulf in coaching competency between my new setup and those that went before. With Frank, drills weren't particularly important. Our warm-up consisted of a jog, a stretch, a few other quick moves, and then you'd start training. With Dan, however, there was a full and extensive list of drills and exercises to work through before you even began the session. In my first few sessions with Dan that November I was a bit fat. I'd enjoyed my month-long break a lot; I'd eaten and drunk too much and lived it to the max. In his words, I looked a bit like the Michelin Man.

We did something called 'Warm-up A', which is basically a series of around 15 drills up and back over 30 metres. These days I do them every day and they feel just like a warm-up. But, in the beginning, this routine was actually a hard workout in itself, and I ended up lying on the floor looking like death.

After recovering, I got up and went over to Dan, who is often a man of few words. 'Thank you so much for today,' I said, 'what an incredible first session – I already feel like I've learned so much.' And he replied, 'What do you mean? That was the warm-up – let's get to work.' I'd thought it was the entire session . . .

I quickly discovered that his approach was drastically different from what I'd known. He wasn't trying to kill me; he was attempting to teach me, to empower me. I was learning about new movement patterns, and my body was moving in a way that it had never done before. It was as if I was starting athletics all over again. I finished that first week dead on my feet but as happy as I've ever been in training because it was different, challenging and interesting every day. Dan, who has a scientific background, also took on the role of physiotherapist or masseur himself, which was a bizarre and alien concept for me – a coach who was actually involved in the physical therapy. But again, it worked. This approach makes so much sense. Rather than seeing a physiotherapist once or twice a week for a massive session in a clinic away from training, Dan brought treatment to the trackside, in small doses, to keep his athletes moving and training well and to try to prevent problems from occurring. It seems so obvious I cannot believe it wasn't the norm already.

It is not my job to speak for him, but I know he wasn't a big fan of most of the coaching set-ups that were in place in British athletics. What basically ended up being his downfall in Britain was the fact that he saw so much wrong with the system – which sadly we've reverted to in many cases – that he was inevitably going to butt heads with a lot of people. Dan's understanding of how the athlete's body works, and how to coach the best from an individual, is so vast that he can't help but intimidate people just by his very presence.

Dan is not an arrogant man at all. He will never say, 'You are doing this wrong, you must do it like this.' He understands the importance of language, of effective communication. Instead, he will be constructive, and try to make the process as collaborative as possible. When we flew back to South Africa for our early-year training camp in January 2010, he held a Warm-up A session for every single athlete on the camp. By then, I had been training with Dan for a couple of months so I was fitter, stronger and loving it. But some of the athletes couldn't finish it – indeed one or two were claiming they were having asthma attacks. I quite enjoyed watching athletes and coaches who had always called me lazy and whatever else struggling to keep up, especially as I was showing them that I could handle it straight off a 12-hour flight.

Initially, I would see Dan at Lee Valley six days a week, with just Sundays off, but I wasn't smashing myself to bits like I had done with previous coaches. Rather, I saw a new side to being a professional athlete – some days I might go to the track facility just to do a few drills and for treatment. Dan actually wanted me to work on fixing my body. He would explain everything: why you do certain types of training and what response to expect; he didn't just bark orders. That might sound obvious, but so many coaches resort to telling you what to do – without giving the reason for doing it. Dan goes into not only the physiology of training, but also the psychology; he has a thorough grasp of the whole package and empowers his athletes to understand this too. This is imperative, because it means you never question why you are doing something; you never feel you are doing a particular workout simply for the sake of it, so you believe in it, and commit.

When I was first working with him, I was a bit nervous about mentioning the hill sprinting work I was doing at home. I felt that it really worked for me, but what if he didn't like it, and wanted me to change it all? I needn't have worried. He listened, and said, 'Fine, absolutely – let's do that as your Tuesday session from now on. So you can do that at home, and you don't need to come all the way to the track – you can just run in the woods near your house that you enjoy so much.'

This seemed so incredibly refreshing to me: here was someone who was clearly a genius at what he was doing, yet he was happy to take on board something I wanted or suggested, rather than instinctively saying no, or questioning it because it wasn't 'standard'. Here was a true coach, not a lecturer.

Another element of Dan's programme that I found brilliant was that from the beginning he emphasised to me the importance of being happy away from training. I was obviously expected to work really hard at times, and I was always up for that. But he understood the bigger picture. He was also the first person I'd worked with who noticed that my body was really sensitive to training, and to turn around and say that the key was to hone what I had, not smash myself to pieces: 'We need to keep you fit and healthy, so your natural ability can thrive.'

So for the first few months, Dan watched how my body responded, teaching me new movement patterns, and even making me unlearn some of the things that had been injuring me all the time. I was thrilled. Everything seemed to be getting better, and I felt that finally I had found someone who I hugely respected, but who also listened to me. So therefore I was happy to listen to him in return.

However, the results didn't come immediately. In March 2010, we went to the World Indoor Championships in Doha, Qatar, which was my first major event with Dan as my coach. I had won the British trials with a modest jump of 7.94m, but in Doha I was even worse and I didn't even make the final. What was amazing, though, was that Dan was simply smiling at me, and his response was not, 'That was rubbish,' but, 'No, no, it's great, you are getting it; you are starting to figure things out.' So even though I was disappointed with my performance, he was happy, and seemed to have such faith in me. Maybe in his own head he was thinking, 'Oh Lord, what have I taken on here?' – but he never showed it, and that is such an important skill in a coach.

Soon after that, I went to a training camp in San Diego. It was the first time I'd ever been to America and I absolutely loved it. I was hanging out with Andrew Steele; we hired a car and were travelling around, visiting lots of coffee shops, of course. And gorging on all the unhealthy American food.

That period was the first time I'd really started thinking about nutrition. Now, I've alluded to the fact that I can put on weight easily, and I'm not exaggerating. Even with all the training I do, I have to be conscious of my diet, otherwise I pile on the kilograms at the drop of a hat. I had some daft ideas at the time: based on absolutely no evidence whatsoever, I had decided that mixing four cereals in a bowl for breakfast was healthier than just having one. Andrew and I nicknamed it the 'Breakfast Quartet'.

The thing is that I was always considered on the heavy side for an athlete. Then all of a sudden, here I was, in a country that considered Reese's peanut butter puffs or Lucky Charms – packed full of sugar – to be a perfectly normal breakfast. And I loved all that stuff; I was like a kid in a sweet shop.

I guess it might seem strange for a professional athlete to talk about this, but I'd actually always had major body-image issues through my career. People would call me a 'fat athlete' and I never once took off my top in training. Even in places like South Africa, where everyone else would be wearing the bare minimum, strutting around with their chiselled abdominal muscles on display, I'd keep my top on in 40-degree heat. I never wanted to get my body out, and never looked as good as the other athletes. I never had a six-pack or anything close to that, so I was always painfully body-conscious, and I think it's an issue that is more common in sportspeople than you might expect. Plus, with the palest skin known to humanity, it's even harder for me to show any definition.

Dan also started looking into my diet. He decided I was eating way too many carbohydrates, so I really cut back on bread, rice and pasta. And, lo and behold, over the next year I lost weight and became a lot leaner. When we then reintroduced carbs into my diet, he advised me to try gluten-free foods – and I noticed a difference. If I eat something with lots of gluten, I'll probably still feel it the next day. Before this, I hadn't put two and two together. I'd eat a sandwich, or a big bowl of pasta, and maybe get bloating or stomach upsets. I'd always been prone to IBS, with awful constipation and sharp spasms in my gut. It hasn't gone away, and I still have a very sensitive stomach and get acidity problems, but cutting down on gluten has helped hugely.

After learning about all this, I made sure I took gluten-free porridge or protein powders with me when I was away, just to make sure I had something I could fall back on. Meat and veg in restaurants are always fine, but breakfast can be the tricky meal. This new knowledge was a big discovery for me. The last time I had really bad tummy problems was when I was competing in 2010, when I was trying to qualify for the

Commonwealth Games. I was doubled up for a while with the pain, but luckily it passed and I managed to jump enough to qualify.

Dan had also started me on strength training and core exercises – lots of medicine ball work and lifting weights, in a very intuitive and focused manner. I'd never done this before, but I was already in better shape than ever, so it was a good time to start. By the time we got to America, I was feeling far more confident about how I looked for a change. One day at the track, we were doing a medicine ball workout; it was hot, and for the first time ever in my life I took off my top. This may sound silly, but it felt like a really big deal for me. I was convinced that I didn't look half as good as 99 per cent of the athletes there, but finally I felt comfortable in my own skin.

Of course, while I was still pretty clueless about nutrition, and trying to resist all those tempting American junk foods, Andrew proved once again to be something of a guide. He actually knew a bit about the subject, and he told me about ketosis, which is a way of making your body burn fat – mainly by totally avoiding carbohydrates and eating a quite high-fat diet. He had with him some of the little dipsticks that you pee on to measure the presence of ketones. Basically, if your body is using fat as fuel, the ketones start to show up in your urine.

So I went from eating sugary cereals to drastically cutting carbs and it was a real eye-opener. I didn't even know that fruit especially and veg contain carbs, so I asked Andrew, 'Flipping heck, what *can* I eat?' As I recall, the answer, as far as snacks go, was basically beef jerky. And not just any kind of beef jerky, because after checking the packet information Andrew and I realised some of them contained a few grams of carbs too, thanks to their sugary marinade.

Looking back on this now, my reaction seems crazy, as these days I live on a very low-carb diet by default. But at the time, of course, the outcome of this change in my eating habits was that I became an extremely grumpy, angry man. I had an old laptop with me that had a game called *Diablo Two* on it. I started playing it incessantly, to try to take my mind off the fact that I was ravenous and hated everybody and everything at that moment. I managed about four days of this, and even when Liz, my girlfriend at the time, came all the way to the States to visit me, I was miserable. After that Andrew said, 'Oi, it's time to stop this now – no matter if you might lose some body fat, it's not worth it if you're going to be like this!' So that was my first attempt at changing my diet, and it ended very badly. It's a stark contrast to me nowadays. Of course, I do sometimes go off the rails and eat to excess, but I have a relaxed, balanced approach, and it's made my life a lot easier.

Most of that trip was great, outside my disastrous food experiment. We experienced a couple of earthquakes while we were out there, which was quite something. We were staying in a crappy apartment by the naval base in San Diego, and an earthquake hit during the middle of the night. Everything was moving around madly. I opened my bedroom door, feeling somewhat blasé about the whole thing, and to my surprise there was Andrew in the doorway, fully dressed, ready to leg it. For some bizarre reason, his instinct when the quake struck had been to put his clothes on, and he was standing there saying, 'Oh shit, oh shit, there's an earthquake!' I was just quite laid-back and said, 'You all right there, mate?' and started laughing. Although he was always one up on me when it came to coffee and culture, I guess I'd been in a lot more dangerous situations than him – albeit most of them entirely self-inflicted . . .

Even the track where we trained was a pretty incredible location for us. We were at the Olympic training centre in Chula Vista, which is right on the border with Mexico, and there was a bit of a Wild West feel to it. Of course, at this stage I didn't know Dan all that well, and was hanging on his every word. I believed everything he told me. So there he was, in this wild area, regaling us with stories in his deep growl. One thing he instructed us was that if we saw a swarm of bees, we should hit the ground at once, because they are killer bees. Well, even I thought that was a bit over the top. Then one day an alarm went off – yes, a special bee alarm – and there really was a massive swarm. I ran, at Usain Bolt speed, into the weights room by the track; Andrew was on the phone and just dropped to the ground. It actually reminded me of a cartoon swarm of bees, one big ball moving across the track. I couldn't believe it was really happening.

Occasionally, there would also be coyotes prowling around the track, and once a helicopter flew over, ridiculously low, trying to usher a group of wild horses back to wherever they were supposed to be. On top of that, you'd hear the odd gun-shot from the Mexican penitentiary across the border. It was an incredible experience. We were training but having fun too, spending time in this beautiful part of the world, right by the beach. It was so different from my previous experiences of camps. South Africa had its moments – one time we actually saw and got to touch some cheetahs – but generally you didn't go anywhere except the hotel or the track. This trip showed me what a training camp could be, and from that point on I have striven to make every camp an enjoyable experience in itself.

But here in San Diego, Andrew and I, along with the high jumper Martyn Bernard, were determined to explore and enjoy what the country had to offer, going to the beach and into LA too – which has now become my favourite city in the world. Having that balance of work and play worked incredibly well for all of us.

The whole atmosphere was so different. And the interesting thing was that our new head coach, Charles van Commenee – with whom I'd initially clashed – along with Dan, really encouraged this. I even have video footage of me playing table tennis against Charles and having a real laugh. Whereas there is absolutely no way that would have happened under Dave Collins, our previous boss. In fact, he had, ridiculously enough, banned table tennis back in 2008. That says a lot about him and the culture at the time. Allowing athletes to actually enjoy themselves along the way is something I feel should play its part in training, and it was short-sighted of the federation not to realise the huge impact a happy life outside of competition has on performance.

When I returned to the UK after that US camp I was feeling positive and on a bit of a high with the way things were working out. My first outdoor meeting of 2010 was the CAU

Inter-Counties Championships in Bedford in late May, and I was confident I would show everyone – including my parents, who travelled up from just down the road – how much I had improved. I just knew I was going to jump well. And, of course, it turned out I couldn't jump to save my life.

In fact, I had one of the worst days of competition I've ever had in my career. I finished fourth, scraping 7.39m. I've never been so embarrassed. The year before, I'd jumped almost a metre further than that. I'd been telling anybody who would listen how incredible Dan's training was, how amazing he was, how it was the best thing I've ever done to go and work with him. And then this! How could I be working with this fabulous coach, who I respect and believe in, and be that bad? I felt I was an absolute disgrace. I never questioned Dan, though. Not for a single moment did I think, 'The training must be rubbish.' But I was confused and so, so embarrassed.

Part of the problem was the legacy of a chronic stress injury. Years and years of bad foot planting – the way your foot hits the board when you take off – had taken their toll and I'd even developed a kind of growth on the outside of my foot. Basically, the abuse to which I'd subjected my body had created an injury to the ligament between two of my metatarsals, which had then calcified. That, in turn, restricted the movement. I was having painkilling injections into that area because it was reacting badly. And, though I tried to ignore it, I had to admit that even with Dan's training and the good therapy I was having, it was still getting worse.

I didn't compete again for another five weeks until, in the run-up to the European Championships in Barcelona, I went to La Chaux-de-Fonds in Switzerland, which is known as the Magic Mountain. Before I left, Charles van Commenee said to me, 'Greg, you need to jump over 7.90m here, or you can't go to the Europeans.' So I went there and jumped 7.92m, and got picked for the team. But the day before the British team was due to leave for Spain, I knew I couldn't do it. I wasn't in shape; I felt there was no way I could win, so I rang up Charles and asked him to take me off the list.

This shows how my mindset was evolving. I didn't want to be a 'nearly guy' any more – one of those people who go to championships with no hope of winning, but just to be there. I had a long chat with Dan, and he was fine with it. He said, 'OK, if that's how you feel we'll go back to work and try to get you ready for the Commonwealth Games in October.'

Watching the Europeans on TV was hard for me, because it was the first time I'd been mature enough to make the decision to pull myself out of an event. And there was one very interesting moment. Chris Tomlinson was there, jumping well, and ended up getting a bronze medal. But at one point the cameras cut to him live on TV, and Frank – who was still his coach – was caught saying, 'Right, break that British record – take Greg's record from him!' It was immediately all over Twitter, people saying, 'Can you believe what Frank just said!' What it showed me, of course, was that Frank hadn't taken it at all well when I'd left him. Instead of coaching Chris to win medals and jump further for his own achievement, it seemed to be about beating me. There was a bit of bad blood between us at that point, but I wasn't the one they should have been looking at. They should have been striving to beat the best, not the guy who couldn't even make it to Barcelona because he was injured and out of shape.

Still, Frank's reaction only strengthened my determination to succeed. I knew that, if I could get my fitness back for the Commonwealth Games, I could win a medal – and prove to everyone that my faith in Dan was justified.

CHAPTER 17

Another Silver in Delhi

My build-up to the Commonwealth Games didn't get off to the smoothest of starts. In July, after jumping in Gateshead, I had a minor kerfuffle with UK Athletics when they messed me about and I missed my flight home. Ayo also ended up having a go at an official because they were really mucking me around, but it wasn't a huge deal. I left, flew to Gothenburg for another competition and was absolutely delighted to jump 8.10m to win it.

When I got home, I rang Ayo to ask whether I could then jump at the British Grand Prix at Crystal Palace, which was the big home domestic meeting of the year. He rang back and said: 'No, they won't let you in.'

'What? But I've just jumped 8.10m!' I replied.

'No, you made somebody in UK Athletics cry.'

'What? No, I haven't! What do you mean? I didn't make anyone cry!'

'Well, I've been told they think you are a bad person.'

I couldn't believe it. I sat there, racking my brains and trying to work out who on earth I could have upset, and coming up with nothing. Then I realised, eventually, that it was probably Ayo himself who'd been arguing with someone. But they wouldn't have any of it: I wasn't allowed to jump, and that was that.

It was utterly ridiculous, and I felt completely abandoned by the people who were supposed to support me, just because somebody thought I'd made someone cry – which I genuinely hadn't. It was a clear example of the kind of power event organisers have, and my own powerlessness in that situation. It also gives an insight into how British athletes are sometimes treated in British meets – there is endemic pettiness and small-mindedness at our flagship competitions, where British talent should be nurtured and achievements celebrated. It feels as though there is a kind of cronyism in the professional athletics meets, which are overseen by a small group of organisers and agents, some of whom have been in their positions for decades and who maintain an unhealthy control of the sport.

I was frustrated because I saw it as an opportunity to kick-start my year and also to earn some good money in a major competition, but I had to regroup. So, in early September I went to Holland and I ran a 100m race in a reasonable 10.56, as well as putting in a modest long jump. I knew if I worked on my start I could run much faster, and in Newcastle two weeks later I proved it, charging to a personal best of 10.26. I even beat Christian Malcolm, which was a really big deal for me. I thought that might earn me a slot in the England 4x100m relay squad for the Commonwealth Games, as I was on paper one of the fastest guys in the country that year. Yet, the way the team worked, selection was based not purely on ability, but on who was mates with who.

Still, I went off to Delhi for the Commonwealth Games knowing I was in shape for a long jump medal – and I then went on to prove it, for once. However, my abiding memory of those championships was not the competition, but the extreme levels of poverty in the city. I particularly remember seeing people with severe disabilities right outside the athletes' village, crawling and pulling themselves across the road – no aid, no wheelchairs, nothing. It was shocking. In 2006, I'd done some charity work in Sierra Leone, a country that has had its problems, but this seemed different: so much dirt and poverty in such a busy city, and no one seemed to be trying to help – here, just outside a major championships, were people who couldn't feed themselves.

There had been some doubts about the athletes' village beforehand, but the accommodation was largely fine: there were some truly disgusting loos when we arrived, and some people did get sick – perhaps from the water. But I still wondered why on earth the authorities were spending £150m alone on the buildings we were staying in, when there were clearly so many more important things to be dealing with, like feeding people and building infrastructure. It wasn't even as if the crowds were great – it felt like it didn't benefit anybody in India to have the Games there. This is where major sporting events need to improve drastically, as was shown at Rio 2016. Sport has a duty to inspire and support the communities in the host city, otherwise it's simply a bunch of people turning up to parade their physical talents.

I qualified for the final without too many problems, but as I was doing my warm-up I managed to tweak my quad. It was when I was doing some bum kicks – where you flick your legs up behind – and I went a little too fast. I headed to the medical room to see the physio, and there was Chris Tomlinson, holding his dad's hand as he had an injection directly into his heel pad because he was in so much pain from bruising. He was struggling, and it looked incredibly painful. And, as much as we've never exactly hit it off, I couldn't help but feel really sorry for him at that moment.

The physio on duty examined me and said, 'Yes, there's a tight spot forming,' so she gave me some treatment to loosen it and taped me up, then I went out again. Luckily, the adrenaline took over, and I managed to start jumping OK.

Actually, more than OK . In the end, I registered my best ever set of jumps in a major championship up to that point, despite the fact that my quad was so painful and so tight that it kept going into cramp. I had been absolutely determined to beat Fabrice Lapierre, the Australian jumper who had won the World Indoors that year, but in the end I had to settle for silver after a leap of 8.22m, with Fabrice winning gold with 8.30m. Five years later, at the 2015 World Championships in Beijing, Fabrice and I would share another one-two – only this time I would emerge triumphant.

Still, I could take finishing second. After so many frustrating years since my last medal at the 2006 European Championships, I was ecstatic as I stood on that podium. I had come a long way in the 12 months since meeting Dan, and with London 2012 still nearly two years away, I knew I had plenty of time to get even better.

CHAPTER 18

A Brawl and a Fall

It would be somewhat of an understatement to say that 2011 began in the worst way possible. Instead of jetting off as usual to a UK Athletics warm-weather training camp in South Africa, I was in court giving evidence about a mass brawl that took place outside a Kentucky Fried Chicken on my birthday in November 2009.

It had all kicked off after an evening spent having a few drinks with mates, followed by some hard partying in Oceana nightclub, which was the place to go in Milton Keynes at the time, to celebrate my 23rd. As the evening ended, I craved the salty-fat hit of a KFC, but when we arrived there was a gang of lads oozing trouble.

Our group was quite large, including my friend Timmy from Sweden. He plays rugby now, but he used to be a good-level ice hockey enforcer. My girlfriend was already in the queue at KFC, so I walked over to give her some money. And as I did so, someone in the gang shouted out, 'Don't jump the queue, you ginger cunt.'

'Don't worry, I'm just handing over some money,' I said, but then gave them some shit back – not just because I was drunk and a little cocky, but also because I really did think his comments were totally unnecessary. Of course, being a late-night fast-food confrontation, that led to them squaring up to me, and I continued to argue with the guy who'd given me abuse.

As we spilled out of KFC, the discussion got more and more spiky and heated. Noticing what was going on, my brother, who is a gentle giant, stood ever so slightly in front of me, while Timmy also moved in to guard me. There was all sorts of male energy flying around.

And then, out of nowhere, this huge fist came flying across my face and smashed my brother hard in the head. Rob just stood there and took it without reacting. But I am more fiery than him, so I immediately lashed out hard towards person who had hit him. I connected quite well, and managed to knock the guy over the taxi rank fence and lay him out in the road.

At the time, what followed felt like a frenetic blur of punches and pain, the potent combination of too much alcohol and adrenaline making it hard to tell precisely what was going on. But later, I watched CCTV images showing clearly what happened next.

My brother, perhaps bizarrely, just grabbed the bloke in front of him to stop him from moving. Robert is exceptionally strong, but he doesn't have an aggressive side at all. So he simply stood there, holding this guy immobile, as other members of their gang smashed punches to my brother's face.

Then Timmy, who has a fist the size of a bloody great sledgehammer, hit somebody else and laid the guy out completely. Meanwhile, I grabbed the bloke in front of me and rabbit-punched him very quickly, multiple times, and dazed him. I have no recollection of this whatsoever, but the CCTV images showed that I pulled him in, said something in his ear and then moved him back a little bit – at which point Timmy's arm appeared over my shoulder, hitting the guy very hard and dropping him.

So by now we'd dispatched three guys, but with my brother doing his passive hold thing, there were still two of us fighting more of them.

Timmy then got caught in the eye and staggered back. I distinctly remember three of them coming straight for me and my brother at that point. I covered up, dropped my head, and tried to block punch after punch thudding into the back of my head.

But bizarrely, because I was drunk, I was also laughing, which probably made me seem a little bit crazy. All of a sudden, the police came piling in, with pepper spray going all over the place. My girlfriend's sister ended up being sprayed, even though all she was trying to do was stop the whole thing. It turned into an absolutely ridiculous, crazy scenario.

I got out of the way for a second, but I was so drunk I then took off my top and tried to go running back in. I have no idea why, but I do remember being very angry that I had just had three blokes punching me, because I saw that again as a bit of an unfair advantage.

Eventually, the entire gang was arrested because it was clear that they had started the fight. Meanwhile, my brother had to go to hospital because his face was a picture as did Timmy, whose eye was pretty bad.

When the case finally came to court, the defence attempted to pin everything on me, because they claimed that as an athlete I have strength beyond a normal person so I shouldn't have entered into a fight – which was clearly ridiculous. I'm a long jumper, not a heavyweight boxer. And what was I supposed to do when my brother was being clocked?

It was also perfectly clear from the CCTV images that the other group were all much larger, and that it was one of their guys who had thrown the first punch. Frustratingly, although it turned out they had been involved in other deliberate confrontations in the past year, they ended up being let off with a slap on the wrist.

When the trial was over, it was too late to go to the camp in South Africa, so instead I headed to Florida to train with Kareem Streete-Thompson, who as an athlete was talented enough to make the World Championship final in both the 100m and long jump in 1999 and was now earning a justified reputation as an excellent coach. That I was able to fly out to the States to work with someone other than Dan Pfaff, who was in Africa, only highlighted another of Dan's strengths. Very early on in our relationship he said to me, 'Look, you will always have a place to learn with me, and I will happily coach you, but if at any point you want to go and learn from other people, or even just spend time with them, and then come back, that's always a possibility. I'll never close the door on you and act like I'm the be-all and end-all, because other people might have something that would work for you too. Be free to go and learn.' As a result of that, I've learned a lot from other people too since joining Dan. He was confident enough in his own ability to listen to others, and that made you confident in him – and then yourself.

I spent three weeks with Kareem, who is basically a younger version of Dan, with stricter recovery times and some fascinating and impressive ideas. It wasn't quite the perfect trip. I found Tallahassee pretty boring and, on the first night, I was very tired and misread the traffic signals. I pulled out in front of someone speeding towards me, who was luckily aware enough to swerve past me.

After Florida, I headed to California for some more warm-weather training with Andrew and a few other athletes, including Martyn Rooney and Kate Dennison. We were all staying in a massive, typically Californian house in Laguna Beach, which had a five-metre-deep swimming pool and 1980s playboy mansion decor. The owner, Chet, was quite the character and would turn up unannounced to cook us dinner sometimes. For some reason, every day I would be up at 7.30, diving into the pool as though I was on holiday, and when we weren't training Andrew and I were keen to explore.

We drove up to Los Angeles quite a lot, and in some sort of cliché LA experience, on one occasion in Hollywood this strange bloke came up to me and said, 'Hi, are you a model by chance? I would *love* to photograph you.' This led to a very strange turn of events. I wasn't sure, but I thought, 'Hell, why not?', and went for it. I drove to this place in the Hollywood Hills and his first act was to somehow cajole me into buying some $300 jeans from a house, not even a shop. In my head, I was thinking, 'You cannot spend three hundred dollars on a pair of jeans, that's outrageous,' but I wanted to save face so I went along with it.

Then he brought us to this stupidly ostentatious house, two doors down from where Jimi Hendrix used to live. At this point I was thinking, 'Is he possibly going to murder me?' It was extremely surreal. Luckily, though, I was with my girlfriend, so it was a little less uncomfortable than it might have been had I gone alone. He spent the day taking loads of photographs of me – in various states of undress in the pool, under a shower and in other places. Afterwards, he said, 'Oh, I will send you the photographs' – and I never heard from him again, despite emailing him repeatedly. Somewhere in Los Angeles, there is a man with a private collection of hundreds of photographs of me in very expensive jeans.

Training was going well, and overall the lifestyle I was aiming for was coming to fruition. It was on this trip that I developed a habit that Andrew, who knows my behaviour quite well, christened 'Greg Going Underground'. I've got a fiery temper, and the slightest annoyance can send me into the biggest rage, something I've definitely inherited from my dad. There were just too many people in that house; I needed my own space or I would have lashed out, so I started simply to leave the group and stay in my room to avoid conflict. No matter how close you are as friends, spending such a long time in one big house on a training camp is a difficult balance, and tempers inevitably get frayed.

One of our housemates in California was a 400m runner called Rob Tobin, who had this annoying habit of reaching over me to grab something when I was cooking breakfast. No matter how unlikely the angle, the arm appeared. I became a bit highly strung about it – it kept happening. I'd whisper to Andrew, 'Shall we go for coffee?', and I'd pretend to go to my room, which was on the ground floor and had a side exit. Then I'd literally run out of the door and jump in the car, just to get away and keep my anger in check, keep my mood happy and ultimately keep me performing.

The camp was, nonetheless, a great success. I'd begun to hone the notion of balancing life, and performance, well. On returning to Britain, I made a strong start to the year, jumping 8.20m at a lowly Southern Athletics Division 1 meeting in May, and then a decent 8.18m at Hengelo, in Holland. My plan was to travel next to Rabat in Morocco, but just as I was preparing to do so I got a call from John Regis, the boss at my agency Stellar Management, telling me I had to fly immediately to Eugene, Oregon, instead, to compete in the big Prefontaine Diamond League meeting.

This was a good opportunity, but I told him I didn't want to go. It was now Thursday evening in Britain, and the long jump was due to start after lunch, local time, on Saturday. I would be tired, jet-lagged, and was bound to perform poorly. John cut through my protests with a sharp reminder that Prefontaine was the big Nike meeting and I was a Nike-sponsored athlete. He warned me that Nike had told him that if I didn't fly out they would cut me at the end of the year.

I don't know whether that was true, and in fairness to Nike they did fly me out to Oregon in business class, which was unusual. Still, I didn't have much time to prepare after the 11-hour flight to Portland followed by the 90-minute drive to Eugene, and I was truly knackered.

It showed in my jumping. After three rounds, I was in eighth place and preparing to make a dash for the next plane home, because all it needed for me to be out of the competition was for the 2008 Olympic champion Irving Saladino, who had fouled his first two attempts, to land in excess of 8.03m. Fortunately for me, he fouled out and in the fifth round I jumped 8.32m – which would have been a British record were it not for the fact that the wind was behind me at 2.1m/s, just over the legal limit. Still, I was thrilled because it meant I'd won my first ever Diamond League event, the athletics equivalent of football's Premier League, and it had earned me a nice $10,000 plus another $2,000 bonus from Nike. I was over the moon.

However, I had no time to enjoy it because I was due to compete in Oslo in four days' time. So I headed to the hotel in Portland airport where all the Nike athletes were staying before their flights the next day. But at reception, they couldn't find my details. 'Sorry,' the woman said, 'we have no one here under the name Greg Rutherford.' There was no Nike rep around, and I didn't have my phone on me, so after about 30 minutes going back and forth, I finally said, 'Look, please let me look at the list.' And there I was – sort of. They had spelt my surname as RUTHERSOD. Still, I've been called worse.

When I arrived in Oslo, I got the sense that other long jumpers were looking at me differently because I had just won in Eugene – something had changed. But as we were warming up it was suddenly announced that the long jump had been postponed by 45 minutes. The reason? The organisers were staging a cross-country skiing event on wheels on the track, of course! It was a bitterly cold Nordic night and I jumped only 7.89m, my worst performance of that season; and, more frustrating still, I ended up getting pneumonia and something called a pleural friction rub as a result.

Not for the first time, I felt monumentally sick. Back in the UK, I remember struggling into Lee Valley to see the doctors, feeling like complete death. One of them used his stethoscope to listen to my lungs and, as I breathed in, he said, 'Oh goodness me, right.' He then called all the other doctors and physios over to listen to my chest because apparently a pleural rub is quite rare and they'd only ever heard it on a recording in medical school. They were all fascinated by the fact that my lungs were making this horrible noise. And that, combined with the pneumonia, meant I was knocked for six.

Unfortunately, it was a bit of a pattern. Like a bubble waiting to burst, something would always crop up and ruin things just as I was getting going. At that point, my body was definitely getting much stronger, but I suspect that my immune system hadn't caught up, and didn't like criss-crossing the Atlantic and enduring two hard competitions back to back.

Dan had suggested that I shouldn't go to Oslo, but I talked him into it – after my victory in Eugene, I was convinced I would win again. But then, that is Dan all over: he is not an authoritarian, he doesn't demand you do what he says; he lets athletes figure things out and learn for themselves. He knew it was a bad move. But equally that I needed to find that out by myself – and I did.

It took me a month to get over the pneumonia, and the next time I jumped, in the Paris Diamond League, I had to sit and watch Chris Tomlinson break my British record with a leap of 8.35m. Of course, I was miffed – nobody likes to lose a record, whatever they say – but I had to remind myself that I hadn't done badly, jumping 8.27m, which at that point was the second longest legal jump of my career. As much as it hurt, Chris had beaten me fair and square that night.

I produced a couple more solid jumps that summer, in Lucerne and Crystal Palace, which reinforced my view that I really could win the 2011 World Championships in Daegu, South Korea. After all, I had won in Eugene, beaten many of the best in the world, and also started to realise that all athletes were beatable on the right day.

After a solid training camp, I reached Daegu in really good form. I kicked off qualification with a jump of exactly eight metres. That was good enough, but I knew it wasn't necessarily going to guarantee me one of the 12 spots in the final. In the second round, the guy before me jumped, and I waited – but they didn't raise the flag to say I could go. I walked down to see what the hold-up was and it turned out that the electronic raker for the sandpit had broken. I then had to wait 25 minutes for them to fix it. And, with just my luck, I finally went charging down the runway, planted my leg to take off – and my hamstring popped. I couldn't believe it. I was in the best shape of my life and ready to prove I was one of the best long jumpers in the world. Yet now I was writhing around in agony. As always, my body seemed to have given up on me at a crucial moment.

I hobbled up to Chris Tomlinson and wished him all the best for the final, urging him to win us a medal; he simply nodded back. Then the self-pity kicked in. The year before what I knew would always be the biggest event in my life, London 2012, I was sitting there in tatters, unable to walk. This wasn't one of the small hamstring tears that I always seemed to pick up; this was a big one. I was in a lot of pain and asking myself, 'Just when am I ever going to get a frickin' break?' I was devastated.

I couldn't comprehend why it had happened, but Dan had seen straight away. I had put myself in a bad position on the board, and got my technique all wrong, putting way too much pressure on that hamstring as a result of my penultimate step. This is why technical competence is so important, not just to perform, but to help reduce injury.

I am known for being a super-fast healer. Not this time. It took me nearly three months to repair, during which time I was in a pretty dark place. I had seen other people on the podium in Daegu setting themselves up to be the faces of London 2012, just like I had wanted to do. At that point, it wasn't my hamstring that hurt most, it was my ego.

CHAPTER 19

A Statement of Intent

The first hour of the year that transformed my life was spent hurling spirits down my neck in my house, and being so drunk I accidentally smashed into a table that was then tossed out on to the street. In other words, a vintage Greg Rutherford New Year's Eve party.

The TV was on in the background. I hadn't been paying much attention, but then the BBC showed a trailer for London 2012 – the famous one of the person diving into the pool. It was like a switch that instantly sobered me up. I remember saying to people, 'Right, I'm not going to have another drink tonight. I have the Olympics this year, and 2012 is going to be the most important year of my life.' It was that sudden: I really didn't want to be drunk any more; I wanted to win Olympic gold.

A couple of days later, it was down to business as I was among the party of British athletes that headed off to

Stellenbosch in South Africa for warm-weather training. For the first two weeks, it couldn't have gone better. I was running fast, eating well, and looking forward to posting a big leap in my first competition, on 21 January. And then on my last practice jump, right on the point of take-off, I felt a massive bang and my hamstring went again. I remember crumpling into the pit, crushed and in pain. When I could bear to look up, I saw Dan with a stricken look on his face that said, 'What the hell just happened?'

I'd had no aches, no pains, no tightness in my hamstring before that point. Nothing. Yet I took off and pop, there it went. As I hobbled away from the pit I swear I saw a number of elite long jumpers from other countries, who were also training in Stellenbosch, smirking. They clearly thought my chances of winning gold at London 2012 had been crippled. At that precise moment I agreed with them.

But Dan and my chiropractor, Dr Gerry Ramogida, who would play an integral part in getting me ready for the Olympics, weren't having any of it. Immediately they began an aggressive rehab programme to get me back in shape within a couple of months. It is such a huge testament to their skill and expertise that they never panicked. They went straight into action mode: right, Greg is hurt, what do we do?

The following day I could hardly even walk, but Dan told me to turn up at the track. Was he mad? I wanted nothing more than to bury my head in a pillow and wallow in my misery, but Dan wasn't having it. He got me holding on to a rail and doing some drills. I remember it hurt quite a lot, but he kept telling me, 'Just work within your pain barrier.' This approach was so unlike the traditional British model. If it had been under a different regime, I would not have seen Dan again until I was fully fit. Instead, he had me performing functional rehabilitation from day one.

Meanwhile, Gerry was constantly in and out of my room working on my hamstring and giving me acupuncture to settle everything down. From the first couple of days, I was also connected to an FSMT (frequency specific microcurrent therapy) machine, which sends mild electrical currents through your soft tissue to help speed up the healing process.

I wasn't, I admit, always the ideal patient. Part of me worried that it was such a bad tear that my Olympic chances really were over, even though it was only January. I actually went out drinking with my room-mate, the pole vaulter Steve Lewis, to drown my sorrows. So much for that New Year's Eve promise to myself!

We ended up roaming – or in my case hobbling – around the streets of Stellenbosch and partying quite hard. In a funny kind of way, it might not have been the worst thing to do, because when I got drunk I was able to move around smoothly and without pain, the booze having dulled my senses. It also gave me the chance to switch off again, to distract myself from the spectre of London 2012 and stop stressing so much about the Olympics. For every British athlete, the London Games were a true once-in-a-lifetime opportunity, and the pressure of that could consume you if you let it. An escape was quite welcome.

When we got home, we carried on with the intensive therapy and, by the time we went out to America two months later, on

21 March, for our second training camp of the year, I was already back in shape. My mindset for the upcoming Olympics had also crystallised. I'd become convinced I would get on that podium. People would ask me when I'd be on, and I'd reply, 'Well, qualification is on the third of August, the final is on the fourth, and the medal ceremony is on the fifth.' They'd laugh when I mentioned the medal ceremony, but I kept telling myself I could do it. I think it's something many people don't appreciate, or train, enough. The mind is such a powerful tool when it is used right.

From the end of 2011, every single day when I walked my dogs or went training in the woods, I would mentally rehearse winning the London Olympics. I would assume the role of the stadium commentator, talking about my competitors' jumps, and then my efforts. And if no one else was around, I'd raise my voice and talk through the competition running through my head. Sometimes, I would add twists and turns to make it more interesting – like one of my rivals jumping further than me, or it lashing down with rain. But each visualisation would always end with: 'And Greg Rutherford has won the Olympic title!'

I often get asked about the secret of my success, given that I don't necessarily jump miles further than my rivals yet consistently win or get a medal at major events. Obviously, it comes down to a lot of things, including my belligerent refusal ever to accept that someone is better than me, and my excellent coaching team. But one aspect people don't appreciate is how much I work on the mental side. Even if nobody else in the world thinks I have a chance of winning, I will always back myself if I am fit. These mind games have helped me massively. It's no good your coach telling you that you can do it, if you don't genuinely believe it yourself. I mentally rehearsed winning the London 2012 gold medal thousands of times – so when it became a reality, I wasn't as shocked as everyone else, because it had happened so many times already, in my head at least.

Unlike many sportspeople, I have never had a sports psychologist to confide in. I am entirely self-taught, and I believe mental preparation has to be extremely personal. What works for me will not necessarily work for another, so it's hard, but not impossible, to teach. There was one occasion in 2007, while recovering from my second round of surgery at the Olympic Medical Institute, when I saw a nice lady, but I really didn't enjoy it. I vaguely remember that at one point she talked about sucking a lemon, and that she rambled on for about half an hour. But when I walked out I said to myself, 'I am never doing that again.' I have no idea what relevance sucking a lemon has to long jump. I just didn't need somebody to tell me how to believe in myself, because I already did, and I had to learn how to believe on my own terms.

Unfortunately, when you are injured, no amount of mental resilience is going to make you jump the distances you need to win an Olympic gold medal. But throughout my treatment, Gerry was great at telling me, 'I will get you back, don't you worry.' He had been brilliant at helping me recover from other injuries before that, so I had faith in him. And then amazingly, by the time I got to America, I could again picture myself winning the home Olympic Games.

Just before I flew back to the States, I saw that British Airways had a sale on, with upgrades from business class to first for only £400 more, return. I was sorely tempted. I'd never flown first class, and, after spending so much time trying to rehabilitate and stay as mobile as possible at all times, the idea of all that extra space was awfully attractive. As usual, I phoned Andrew for his take. 'Do it!' he said – so I did. Part of me also saw the extra cost as a sort of investment in my own career, something that not enough athletes probably do. If I can afford it, even if it's a stretch, and it might help, then it's worth it.

I stepped on to the plane and turned, for the first time in my life, left at the door. I had no idea what to expect. I was wearing jeans, a T-shirt and – my token attempt at smartness – a blazer. I had no clue what people wore in first class – maybe I was horribly underdressed? The cabin crew seemed to be addressing everyone by their first names: did they know all of these international jetsetters already? I felt such a fish out of water. At one point, everyone seemed to be standing by their seat, as though it was some sort of protocol. If you tried that in economy, you'd be virtually pushed back down by a stewardess.

Fortunately, although I felt as if everyone was probably wondering who on earth had let me in first, most people's attention was taken up by the fact that the US pop singer Katy Perry was on board, being loud – and I found her manner obnoxious. Most of the other passengers seemed to be businessmen who all knew each other, so there was some classic British head-shaking and eye-rolling between them. During the flight, I actually walked past her when she was asleep, and was tempted to take a photo of her, mouth open, not looking very Hollywood, but I managed to restrain myself.

Despite being a complete novice at the whole thing, and not knowing how to get my bed flat, or why it was that we were allowed metal cutlery when economy were only trusted with plastic, I absolutely loved it. When I was a kid, the idea of travelling first class had always seemed like some ultimate, unattainable luxury – the true sign that you'd really made it. And there I was, doing it.

When I got to Los Angeles, Andrew broke the news to me that he was considering retiring. He had suffered a lot of injuries since running brilliantly in the 400m and the 4x400m relay team at the Beijing Olympics. I told him that if I won London 2012, he wasn't allowed to quit – I would take care of all his bills and training costs for a year if he stayed on.

Having watched me train, Andrew reckoned I was in such phenomenal shape that he'd better start thinking about his plans for 2013. Pretty soon I backed up those impressions with the biggest jump of my career. I'd already jumped in Chula Vista the week before, posting a respectable 8.20m, but I knew there was more in the bag. In fact, I was so confident that, even though I was due to fly back home, I extended my trip for three days to jump in San Diego again the following week – and Steve Lewis and I paid for Dan to stay longer too.

Yet the day beforehand I checked the weather forecast, which predicted rain. I said to Dan, 'I'm not sure about this – my leg doesn't feel right either.' But he said, 'Well, we've committed now. We'll go down, we'll warm up, we'll see how it goes. If you're still good, we'll jump; if not, we will just pull out, it doesn't matter.'

I warmed up and felt pretty good. So good, in fact, that I jumped 8.35m, equalling Chris Tomlinson's British record. I was thrilled to bits and so was Dan, but he came over to me and simply said, 'No more today, let's just leave it there. If you keep jumping, you'll jump far, and then that might cause us problems.' Two years later he was proved right when I jumped 8.51m and some queried it because the board didn't have plasticene on it. Part of me wanted more, but equally I was happy, and celebrated with a four-pack of Coors Light lime while sitting in the hot tub, listening to my favourite song at the time, 'Wildfire', by SBTRKT.

That performance was also vindication of something Dan and I had been working on during the previous few months. After what had happened in Seoul the year before, we had talked about how my long stride before take-off was putting greater pressure on my hamstrings. Dan changed my approach so that I used a lateral movement on my second to last stride. This is another facet of the genius that is Dan. He has such an array of technical weapons in his arsenal to try to improve you. If one adjustment doesn't work, he'll try something else. We used to spend time on video analysis and biomechanics, which Frank didn't much believe in, and it paid off.

Dan was also a big believer in learning from the greats of bygone eras: 'Watch what they do, and see what you can learn,' was his philosophy. One of the first things Dan said to me was, 'By the time you finish working with me, I want you to have the equivalent of a PhD in the long jump. I want you to know the ins and outs of the human body. You will learn about your event, not just do it.'

I hate giving Carl Lewis any props because he was subsequently found to have tested positive three times at the 1988 Olympics trials (though he claimed his usage of the banned substances was accidental), but there's a video of him jumping in Mt SAC in, I think, 1985. And, every round, he jumped over 28 feet – or 8.53m, which is the distance I am desperate to achieve. What I noticed when they showed the head-on view of the jump is that he went to the side slightly before he took off. I spoke to Dan about it. And he said, 'Oh, that's the right old step, which is a fantastic way for speed-based long jumpers to control their speed.' So I said, 'OK, let's give it a go.'

We started working on it, and I got it almost instantly. It was a complete joint effort: I watched it being done, but Dan showed me how to do it. And that tiny adjustment became a very important thing.

I had a few up and down performances after that, jumping only 7.98m in Doha and 8.12m in the UK trials in Birmingham, despite trying very hard. I think the problem was that I felt a bit flat because I had little competition. Still, I was happy. I remember Andrew and I went to a Pizza Express afterwards for a nice meal with a glass of wine, and he reminded me that I had qualified for my home Olympics, I was ranked number one in the world, and I had been jumping really well. I was ready.

I just needed to fine-tune a couple of things, which I fully expected to do in my last two competitions before London 2012, in Madrid and Crystal Palace. First was a small meeting in the Spanish capital. The Australian Mitch Watt was there, and in the first round he jumped 8.26m, which didn't bother me in the slightest. I charged down the runway, convinced I'd be able to beat it. But at the point of take-off, what felt like an electric shock shot up my hamstring into my glute as I jumped 7.81m. Dan asked if I was OK. I told him I wasn't sure. I prodded it a couple of times and there was a tiny amount of pain. Competitive Greg was whispering in my ear, 'Go back and jump again and win the competition.' But for once Sensible Greg won out by pointing out that 'today is not the day'.

It was a really close decision and, when I think about it, it gives me a bit of a chill. If I'd kept jumping, I would have torn that hamstring properly and I would then have had no chance of competing in London. I wouldn't be sitting here now, able to write a book about my career, and I certainly wouldn't be sitting here having been an Olympic champion. In fact, I might have had to quit at that point – that's how fragile the line between success and failure can be.

Instead, I was sensible and pulled out, went home, and had a scan. I was right to be cautious, as I had fluid pooling round one of my ligaments high up in my hamstring. In layman's terms, I had a small tear to my hamstring. I really felt it the next day; and, even though it was an ache rather than that horrible nerve sensation I normally have when I hurt my hamstring, I was thinking I would be out for a month.

I had jumped in Madrid on 7 July. The qualification round of London 2012 was 3 August. I didn't have a month to give. I had 27 days to recover and get into peak condition again, for the most important competition of my life. The stakes were precariously high.

I was determined to do everything possible to get back, so I ended up sitting in a hyperbaric chamber at St John's Wood hospital twice a day for nearly two weeks. The principle behind it is to deliver higher levels of oxygen to the body at double the normal atmospheric pressure, enabling injuries to heal faster. But the practicalities were a bit grim: I had to sit for hours in a big metal tube, about 6ft wide and 5ft tall, breathing oxygen through a face mask. It bored the hell out of me and it made me feel sick initially. Bizarrely, Chad Smith, the drummer with the Red Hot Chili Peppers, was often there too, as he'd picked up some form of drumming injury, so at least I had some interesting company.

Sometimes, I would be able to stay in a hotel in central London, but on other occasions I had to leave my home in Woburn Sands at 5am to get down there for treatment, which wasn't ideal Olympic preparation. On top of that, Gerry would also be treating me every day, which of course was always extremely helpful. I must admit that he did look a bit worried at times, but I'd tell him, 'Don't worry, mate, it's all right. I'm still going to win the Olympics.'

Perhaps there was an element of bravado there, but I was trying to stay as relaxed and positive as possible. I needed to be with Dad, who is always melodramatic whenever I pick up an injury. Even if I got the smallest strain, he'd say, 'Right, that's it – your season's finished!' So you can imagine what he was like before London 2012. I'd keep telling him, 'Don't worry, I'll make it.' And, after two weeks of intensive treatment, I believed it too. My fitness was back – and so was my confidence in winning gold.

CHAPTER 20

Gold

Just before the Olympics, I flew out with most of the British athletics squad to our holding camp in Portugal to put the finishing touches to my preparations. UK Athletics had booked somewhere that was particularly popular with Germans, and rather bizarrely appeared to be full of German swingers. There were a lot of boobs on show, and rumours that rather a lot of free loving was also taking place. Of course, my sole focus was on the upcoming Games.

In Portugal, I felt completely separated from what was going on in London. The athletics programme was scheduled to start a week after the opening ceremony, so I watched the first few days of the Games in between training sessions. It all seemed so distant, unreal, at that point – just something that was happening to other people.

The last big jumping session I did was on the Saturday, six days before I'd be competing in London in the qualifying rounds. Dan had planned a session of six jumps, but at the second one I put in a really fantastic jump. 'Right,' he said, 'that's it. You're done. We're ready.' Perhaps after all the stress I'd been through with my various injuries, he wanted me to go into competition with a great last jump in my head, knowing I was in good shape. As ever, he was cunning with his use of both training load and language, giving you what you needed, and nothing more.

It was time to enter the fray, to fly into Olympic London, a version of the city that seemed completely removed from its everyday cynical self – instead, a place of excitement and smiles. I was competing in the first two days of the athletics programme, along with Jessica Ennis and a few others, so we flew in together and then jumped on the bus taking us to the athletes' village.

I sat right across from Jess on the bus and, as we were approaching the village, we drove past a large high-rise with this massive banner of her down the side of the building. Everyone seemed to see it at the same time, and instinctively we all turned to look at her. We all knew Jess was the poster girl of London 2012 – but here she was, literally on a poster. She had a small smile on her face; if she was nervous, it didn't show. She was so professional, nothing seemed to faze her.

But, bloody hell, the pressure she must have been feeling! Everyone had already hung that medal around her neck, and she hadn't even started competing yet. I knew full well the fragility of athletics, how things can go wrong and how the smallest thing – a tiny injury or a minor illness, say – can see that medal slip out of your reach. Yet she completely took it in her stride. I felt part admiration, part worry, on her behalf. I found it hard to believe someone could have that level of stress and still cope, though, of course, Jess being Jess, that's exactly what she did.

When we reached the village, I was first into my shared apartment, where I nabbed the bedroom that had an en-suite bathroom for myself and my room-mate, Steve Lewis, who would be arriving a few days later. Our balcony overlooked the Westfield shopping centre, and you could watch people excitedly milling around, before they headed into the Olympic Park.

It was my first realisation of how massive the Olympics in London were becoming. As the squad had left for Portugal before the real buzz started, we'd been a bit disconnected from it all. And still, there was some doom and gloom around, especially for the first couple of days. The weather was up and down, British gold medal chances came and went, and the few critics who believed that staging the Olympics was a waste of money began to shout louder. But then came the Team GB successes, and everything changed. Sport dominated the news and everywhere people were smiling. It was as if the government was pumping serotonin into the water supply.

I was in a great frame of mind too, helped by the fact that the food in the village was the best I've ever had at a major event. There was a big food hall with loads of choice, and I particularly loved the Caribbean selection, with amazing plantain, chicken and salad – I think I ate that every day. It was where everyone went and you'd find yourself surrounded by all these incredible athletes and sports stars. At any one point, up to six thousand athletes might be there, eating their dinner. It was a lot of fun – a really sociable, well-designed place to hang out and chat to people and soak up the experience.

The recent experience of my third Olympics in Rio really puts in perspective how superior London was. I'm afraid to say that the food and the organisation at the 2016 Games were pretty dire in comparison. In London they created the perfect environment to succeed. There was even a coffee kiosk around the corner from my apartment, where I could go and grab a half-decent brew – which naturally made me very happy.

A surprising thing about the Olympic village – and this is true of all of them – is that there was also some pretty unhealthy food on offer and all of it was free. It's pretty hard for people to resist a free McDonald's or unlimited cake. I was at that point the leanest I'd ever been, and was thankfully strong-willed enough to resist the burgers and cakes. But there were athletes who'd gorge themselves on multiple Big Macs, nuggets, fries and milkshakes galore, especially after they had finished competing. Perhaps that's why I stuck to my plantain and chicken every day – turning it into a routine made it a little easier to ignore temptation. If you are not extremely disciplined, the Olympic village is ironically the perfect place to ruin four years of hard work.

I was due to compete in the qualifying round on the Friday, and I wanted to look good, so the day before I called my friend

George Martin for a trim. I'd met him originally at a hairdresser's in London – he actually used to be a really good 800m runner in his time.

He was happy to come over to Stratford, but we had a problem: there was nowhere obvious for him to cut my hair. So rather than get his scissors out in the street, he suggested seeing if one of the salons in Westfield would let me use one of their chairs. We went into a salon called The Ginger Group, which seemed appropriate for me. George told them that I was competing in the Olympics the next day, and asked if it would be OK to borrow a space. The guys there were really nice, and said, 'Yes, sure, no problem.' No one else spotted me or wished me luck, because no one knew who I was. My next visit to Westfield a few days later would be entirely different.

Ahead of big events, I had got into the habit of calling my best mate Andrew and talking through my preparation, almost as a pep talk to help settle my nerves. Even though I'd done it a million times before, and since, I needed that reassurance; in fact, I still do it to this day. Of course, I knew exactly how things would go; it's pretty simple – I run in a straight line and jump into a sandpit. Nevertheless, I always rang Andrew to talk it through.

But in actual fact, the main subject we were discussing this time around was that I had gone £3 into an overdraft that I hadn't actually arranged, and I feared that my credit report was going to be affected. Yes, really! Here I was, just before the biggest opportunity of my life, the possibility of winning an Olympic title, and I was worried about my credit rating. It's probably not what you'd expect potential medallists to be thinking about, but it just shows you, normal life does go on. Andrew said, 'Look, don't worry, we'll sort it out – it really isn't an issue now. Let's focus on you actually preparing to jump in the qualification of the Olympic Games.'

I took his advice and by the time I got to the warm-up track – along with Dan – I was actually quite relaxed. Strangely, though, I did something I'd never done before, and still don't do now: I listened to some music. I've got a fairly eclectic taste and had a playlist with everything from 1960s' pop tunes to drum and bass, but the song I really remember from that moment was Nero's remix of 'Blinded by the Lights'.

I suppose I was trying to get focused, but actually it was a really odd decision, as the last thing you should do before a competition is suddenly change a routine that doesn't need changing. But this event felt so huge, so different, that instead of being my usual chatty self, I thought I had to be super-focused.

Standing in the tunnel waiting to emerge was an amazing moment. I could hear the crowd going wild at almost everything that was going on, really getting behind everybody in a British vest, and I just wanted to get out there and be part of it.

Walking out into that noise, I knew I was ready. All I needed to do was qualify for the final. I had three jumps to do that. Anyone who jumped over 8.10m or was in the top 12 places would go forward. So, ideally, what I needed to do is jump 8.11m in my first jump, and my work would be done. I could go back to the village and relax for Saturday's final with my feet up.

My first jump was 8.08m – close, and a good distance, but not quite enough to have it all done and dusted. I took the second-round jump, and cleared 8.06m. By this point I was in a good position – fourth overall – so I had nothing to worry about; I'd qualified. And although my distances weren't huge, I felt pretty good. Perhaps most importantly, I'd really enjoyed the experience of competing in a home Olympics, which boded well for the final.

What's more, not leaping a huge distance probably helped, as no one was putting a huge weight of expectation on my shoulders. That night, I spoke to Andrew again. We talked about how Dan hadn't been hugely impressed by the qualifying, and then went through everything as usual. I was confident it would click when it really mattered. I hung up and then went to see Gerry Ramogida, who had been instrumental in ensuring that I made the Olympics in one piece, for a final tune-up. He was checking me over, prodding and pressing as chiropractors do, and making an adjustment to my back, when suddenly my groin went into a severe spasm. It was strong enough for him to feel it under his hands. The pain was so sudden and sharp that I actually screamed.

Who knows what happened: perhaps I was a little dehydrated and my body responded badly. But Gerry stood there with a look of utter panic and horror on his face that I have never seen before or since. The poor guy! At that moment I think he genuinely thought he'd ruined my chances of winning an Olympic title, and after he'd worked so hard and brilliantly to get me there. I found out later that he didn't sleep a wink that night, he was so anxious.

Gerry used acupuncture needles all through the groin and adductor muscles, to settle it down. The head of UK Athletics, Charles van Commenee, actually walked in at one point, not realising the pain I was in, laughing and asking, 'Do we need to wrap him in cotton wool tonight so he doesn't get hurt?'

I went to bed that night hooked up to my FSMT. And, thankfully, the next morning I woke up and the groin didn't feel too bad. So my internal self-belief just powered on: 'It'll be fine,' I thought, and so it was. The same inner voice that had been there since I was a kid, telling me that I was going to be a professional athlete, that I was going to win a gold medal one day, was so crucial.

And when I thought about who I would be up against in that final, who my rivals were, I didn't believe that any of them was much better than me. I convinced myself that if I had a good day, I would win.

There were athletes in the British team who struggled with the weight of expectation. They worried about the pressure of the home Games and the reaction of the press and the public, and it all got too much for them. But I thought it was incredible – this once-in-a-lifetime opportunity, not long after I had jumped the greatest distance of my career. Why not bloody win the Olympics? That was how I saw it. Nobody else has been on great form; you might as well go and grab it.

By the time of my warm-up, I'd forgotten all about the groin pain. I warmed up with Mitch Watt, chattering away to him – and didn't use music again. I had a chat with the Swedish jumper Michel Tornéus as well. We were all just getting ready; probably all thinking we had a good chance. Mitch, Sebastian Bayer, Chris Tomlinson too – each of the finalists no doubt saw a good opportunity.

But I was also looking around and thinking that everybody – Michel, Will Claye, all good friends of mine – looked so serious. I remember thinking to myself, 'Guys! You need to relax a little bit more and enjoy it! This is wonderful, it's a brilliant Olympics, we are having a fantastic time, the stadium is amazing, the crowd is out of this world!'

I felt, even then, that they were overstressing about what was going to happen. But then I had an awakening myself. Just as we were being held in the tunnel, a huge picture of Jess Ennis appeared on the big screen and the crowd went absolutely wild. It was insane – all they'd seen was a picture and gone completely nuts. And then we were walking out and the ripple effect as the crowd caught sight of us was just incredible. It was like a Mexican wave of noise that reverberated around the stadium. At that moment, I had a tear in my eye.

I had to check myself. Because, while it was an unbelievable experience, I couldn't get too emotionally involved. Knowing that every person in that stadium was willing me to succeed, because I was competing for Britain, was truly mind-blowing. At that moment, it really, properly hit me for the first time: I was competing in an Olympic final in my home country.

Yet strangely, as I stood on the runway, listening to the crowd clapping to spur me on before my first jump, I didn't feel any pressure. But then, all of a sudden, when I was halfway down the runway on my first jump the noise became so ear-piercingly loud that it actually distracted me. I was thinking, 'Bloody hell, this is noisy,' and I mistimed my jump and barely got over six metres. Being able to tune out the crowd has always been one of my strengths; but I had never competed in anything close to the noise that the 80,000 people in the Olympic Stadium were making that night.

I went over to Dan for feedback. He said I'd got too caught up in the moment, and told me to just get the second jump in properly. He also said that he didn't think anyone else looked great, and that I had to seize this opportunity. So I started walking back to prepare for the next one. And, as I did, it very briefly went quiet in the stadium, just for a moment. And from the crowd a voice yelled out, 'Come on, Greg, this is your time.'

I have no idea who it was, but those words rang in my ears. 'You're right,' I thought. 'It is, and I will.' So when I stood on the runway for my round two, I had that conviction fully in focus. I charged down the runway, this time ignoring the noise, and put in a decent jump of 8.21m. I was in the lead at the home Olympic Games.

Whenever I watch the footage of that jump, my body language suggests I didn't think it was that much of a deal. But trust me, inside I knew it was.

For one thing, it wasn't actually that good a night for big jumps. There was a chill in the air, and with a slight headwind too. That is often overlooked when people criticise my winning distance in 2012, but the upshot was that my jump had not only put me in the lead, but piled the pressure on everyone else. One of the things I'd worked on, over and over again, with Dan was how to jump in any conditions. It was one of the real strengths I took into that final.

In round three, I fouled, much to Dan's dismay, but right then I watched Jess cross the line in the 800m, the final event of the heptathlon, to win her gold medal. I saw how the crowd responded to her victory and it made me want a gold medal of my own more than anything in the world.

So I jumped. And this one was better – much better: a leap of 8.31m, which stretched my lead by ten centimetres. After this one, I did celebrate, just a little. Because looking around at the seven other athletes still in the competition, I was convinced that none of them was going to jump further than that. Of course, I pushed that thought to one side, but I saw in their faces that they didn't believe they could do it – and I think they saw in my face that I very much thought I could.

There were still two rounds left, however, and anything could happen. My seven opponents still had a possible 14 jumps with which to beat me. It's no exaggeration to say that watching those last jumps was the most stressful experience of my life. Generally, there's a really good camaraderie between the long jumpers; we all know each other well, compete all the time, have a chat and a good time. But at that moment, it didn't matter if they were the nicest people on earth, I wanted to beat them.

At one point in the last round, I was literally praying for some kind of biblical intervention to end the competition right there, leaving me as the winner. My thoughts were pretty much reduced to: 'I don't care if there is an earthquake or a bolt of lightning hits the pit and they have to stop it – but please let this end now.'

My biggest fear of all came when Mitch Watt took off for his final jump. He had gone out to 8.54m in 2011, so I knew that even though it was cool and the wind was against us, he was capable of a monster leap. This time, his jump initially looked big as he left the board; but just as I was starting to panic, he came down like a stone and ended up with 8.16m. Enough for silver, but no more. Perhaps there had been some biblical intervention after all.

Then it was the turn of Will Claye, who was now in bronze medal position, to jump. I knew his personal best was shorter than the 8.32m he needed to beat me, so the pressure on him was immense. When I saw he'd fouled, the stress I'd been feeling as I watched turned to utter relief.

I still had to jump, one last time, but as I stood on the runway I was almost laughing. I simply didn't know what to do with all these emotions. I'd rehearsed how to jump under duress, up to the point of winning Olympic gold, but this was a whole new experience. I ran down – and ran through the pit. That was it; it was done.

I then saluted the crowd and they went every bit as wild as they had done for Jess and would do for Mo Farah later. It hadn't yet sunk in, but I was the Olympic champion. I took off my jumping spikes and looked up to the heavens. Then I walked to the long jump pit, and scooped up a little handful of sand. I thought, 'This is Olympic sand, this is the sand I won an Olympic gold medal on. I'm taking it home with me in my pocket.'

My lap of honour is a blur. Even at the time, I was aware of how brief this moment would be, and I wanted to savour every wave, smile, clap, cheer and breath, so I took as long doing that lap as I possibly could. It still finished too quickly. As I jogged around, someone threw me a Union Jack to wrap around myself – and then I saw my parents, who were wearing 'Go Greg' T-shirts. I leapt into the crowd to hug them. There were tears, more hugs, and a whole load more emotion. Then I was off again. I saw my long-term supporter Ian, with his wife, both crying with happiness. A man so strong was like the rest of my friends and family, crying with joy.

On that lap of honour I also had the best seat – well, stand – in the house for the end of Mo's 10,000m final and his first, of many, gold medals. I was standing just under the Olympic flame as he crossed the line. I could literally feel its heat on the back of my neck as I watched a moment of sporting history.

My initial reaction was, as a team-mate, to run over and celebrate with him, but I knew this was his moment. As an athletics fan, I loved seeing an amazing performance like that. Then he too did his lap of honour. I was still standing there, transfixed, as the stadium emptied around us. A photographer came over and snapped Mo and me together. I remember saying to him, 'You're Olympic champion!' and he said, 'Yeah – and *you* are Olympic champion!'

Then it was through to the anti-doping area. That's always an odd moment. You have this sense of sheer euphoria and then suddenly you are sitting in a kind of office, waiting to pee into a jar. Naturally, you want to get that over with as quickly as possible – but peeing quickly when you are dehydrated is not as easy as all that . . . I waited and waited and waited, and with all my press and media commitments, I didn't leave the stadium until 1am.

I headed off and was walking around in something of a daze, trying to find a way back to the village. At that moment, Mo, together with Galen Rupp, the American silver medallist in the men's 10,000m, and Alberto Salazar, the pair's coach, appeared, so I dived into their car with them. The whole thing felt totally unreal now – all of us in a car, all basking in Olympic success, as either medallists or the coach of medallists.

From the village, we went to the Team GB house where I saw my family. I was tired by that point, but we hugged and kissed and celebrated together. Then I walked back to my room, and, although I was exhausted, I was genuinely scared of falling asleep. I had the irrational fear that if I dropped off, it would all turn out to be a dream when I woke up. The medals had not yet been awarded, so I had nothing tangible to prove that I'd really won. I crept into the room and saw that Steve was asleep. I was trying not to make a sound because he was competing the next day, but I obviously did, because he kind of dozily rolled over and said, 'Hey, well done, mate!' before going straight back to sleep.

I lay in my bed and stared at the ceiling in a state of disbelief, trying and failing to take it all in. I stayed like that, with my heart still racing, my brain whirring madly, until about 4.30 in the morning. Eventually, I gave up, got dressed and went for a wander around the village. At that hour, there were plenty of drunken athletes and coaches, who had finished their own events, stumbling back to their rooms. I ended up in the food hall, just sitting there, poking at something to eat, trying to comprehend what the hell was going on. Some swimmers I knew came in, and congratulated me – they were completely smashed. I thanked them but was still really quiet. The biggest thing that had ever happened to me, and I simply couldn't comprehend it. People expect a great victory to produce unadulterated joy, but the feeling I had was very different, more like a profound sense of intense relief.

More drunken athletes stumbled in. I hadn't had a single drink that night. At about 6.30am I wandered back to the apartment to meet the British Olympic Association press woman and start the day. I hadn't slept a wink.

So began one of my busiest days ever. I think I spoke to every news outlet going. I'd done interviews before, of course, but now I was Olympic champion, on Super Saturday, the most successful night in British athletics history. Again, I hadn't taken that in at all. To me, it was just that Jess, Mo and I had won. But to everyone else, beyond the bubble of the village, it was a momentous occasion in our nation's sporting history. There were questions and more questions about the whole night. It was bizarre. Suddenly, I was being referred to in the same sentence as two of Britain's greatest ever athletes.

I think I was incredibly fortunate that it all happened in London and within that golden 46 minutes at the Olympic Stadium. No matter what my achievement, I don't think anyone would remember it as fondly without the fact that I was sandwiched between Jess and Mo. Being part of that particular moment changed my life far more dramatically than might have been the case had I won the previous day, say.

One of the hardest things in all those interviews was to put into words what it all meant to me. What I was mainly thinking involved rather a lot of swearing: 'Fucking hell, this is just unreal,' for a start. I loved it, though, that whole day. Everyone was so wonderfully positive, and the enthusiasm ensured that I soon forgot about my lack of sleep. I talked to the BBC, Sky, ITV, Al Jazeera – anyone who asked. I did every single television programme going. I truly wish I could do it all again, even though I started getting knackered and losing my voice because I was talking so much. Nothing will ever be that good in my career again; I know that now.

That evening I was back in the Olympic Stadium with a gold medal around my neck, watching the Union Jack being hoisted into the air. I was so emotional that I struggled to sing along with the anthem and the whole way through I was thinking, 'Don't cry! Don't cry!' and that sort of overtook everything. But of course I also thought of all the sacrifices my parents had made to get me here, as well as the skill and dedication of my coaching staff and the support of my friends. But mostly I was trying to savour the moment as I stood there on that particularly special podium, full of pride in myself and my country, thinking, 'This is the greatest feeling ever!'

The instant that gold medal was around my neck, my life went absolutely bonkers. The first inkling of how people were going to treat me differently came a couple of days after I'd won, when I went into Westfield shopping centre, the same place I had anonymously strolled around only a few days before. I wanted some new clothes and headed to All Saints, as I'd always liked their stuff. It turned out that this particular branch was their London hub, and, after walking in as a normal punter, I left with a load of free clothes. Stuff I'd normally spend a fortune on was simply handed to me. It was surreal. It was quite a change from a few days before the Olympics, when I'd had my hair cut in that same shopping centre and no one knew me from Adam.

In the feverish atmosphere of London 2012 everyone wanted to be associated with a British gold medal winner. And so too in restaurants. I would go to pay my bill, only to be told, 'You're a gold medal winner, this is on us.' No one wanted anything in return. The whole country had got so caught up in the Olympic spirit – and, remember, the Games were still going on at this point – that everyone wanted a little part of it. For a few days, I had to get into private cars every time I left the village because of all the attention.

I'll be honest: I absolutely loved it. Overnight I'd gone from a complete nobody in most people's eyes to somebody everyone wanted to give free stuff to, talk to and get to know, and it was brilliant. It was so totally different from the life I had led before, of an anonymous working-class lad from a famously boring part of the country. In some ways, it was a life I'd always secretly dreamed of living. Every single night, I was invited to event after event, parties and restaurants filled with celebrities, and I was being photographed everywhere I went.

One of my first experiences of the celebrity world was at the

GQ Men of the Year Awards. There were a few athletes there – Chris Hoy, Victoria Pendleton and others. I was given a Hugo Boss suit, for free, which was a heck of an upgrade from the tatty River Island one I had back home. I was even invited on stage to be presented with an award, and had yet more free stuff thrown at me. Afterwards, Matthew Freud, the PR guru, invited a few of us back to his house in Primrose Hill. That was an eye-opener for me – this massive house in an incredibly expensive part of London, a real glimpse into how the other half live.

It turned out he's a big table tennis fan, and had his own table in the basement, so we went downstairs to play a bit. And as we did so, Sacha Baron Cohen greeted us with: 'Hey, it's the Olympians! Let's give them a round of applause.' I was so star-struck. I couldn't believe these people even knew who I was, let alone felt moved to applaud me.

At that party, I remember seeing Bono chatting to Liam Gallagher, as well as Michael Fassbender and Damian Lewis having a good time. I couldn't help thinking, 'What the hell is going on – this is the most bizarre night of my life.' They were all standing around, chinwagging, probably doing what they do all the time. Totally normal for them. And there I was, wearing really uncomfortable new shoes that had given me huge blisters, feeling like I'd landed among them from the moon.

I was actually rather sensible that night, as I was due to compete soon afterwards, so I went home reasonably early. Part of me probably thought, 'Oh well, I'll have plenty more nights like that.' I now wish I'd stayed and truly enjoyed it. Apparently, I even missed a fight that broke out between two really big stars later on, after I'd left.

The *GQ* awards were one event among many I went to after London 2012 because I was determined to capitalise on my gold medal. Some people lambasted me for this – the following year the BBC TV pundit Denise Lewis was a particularly vocal critic – but the way I saw it, I wanted to experience a different life as well as earn a few quid by doing TV programmes and appearing at events. I was not a big name in the run-up to the Olympics, and didn't have the luxury of any large endorsement contracts to make the most of the home Games, so I couldn't turn down these well-paid work opportunities. Don't forget, I entered London 2012 with literally minus three pounds to my name! When you think back now to 2012, I bet you can't name all 29 of Britain's gold medallists. And I noticed this very quickly; I knew I'd be forgotten, and I had to seize the moment.

I also saw the exposure and all the media work as hugely important for my future. Making contacts in the TV world, turning my hand to new things, setting up possibilities for when I was retired – no athlete can go on competing forever, after all.

I was working hard, as well as drinking hard, really burning the candle at both ends. I'd be up at 5am to do a radio slot or TV show, then perhaps more interviews, then another show, then in the evening a dinner or an event, late into the night. Then I'd get up the next morning and do a whole different series of shows, or interviews, all over again. I could easily do five or six things a day, five or six days a week. Sometimes, I wondered how there could always be so many companies and businesses holding these events, night after night. They never seemed to stop. One evening I would be at a party with Niall from One Direction, the next it was someone from MTV, or a TV presenter. I was out every night, and spending so much time in London that I was hardly ever home.

This had one major impact, pretty soon. My relationship with my girlfriend Liz had, if we're both honest, not been going brilliantly for the last couple of years. We'd been together for eight years but even before the Olympics, with all the travelling I was doing, we'd been growing apart. It was a huge shame, as she'd always been incredibly supportive and sacrificed a lot for me, but we'd really drifted more into being friends than anything else, so I felt it was time for it to end. I'd been quite unhappy for a while, and had put it down to the stress of preparing for London. I used to say to myself, 'Once London is out of the way, we'll be fine,' but I realised quickly this was very much not the case.

Given how long we'd been together, ending the relationship was always going to be painful, even if it was the right thing to do. When you've been with someone for that many years, people don't question it; they just assume everything is perfect. Even your family and friends fail to understand; they also think all is fine and dandy. So, we split up, and it was tough.

It was way easier for me, of course, because there were plenty of distractions. I was hanging out in London, and staying most of the time at the Mayfair Hotel. That, in itself, was another eye-opener. I was being put in suites where some of the rooms were bigger than my entire house and paying very little in return. Previously, if I ever had to stay in a London hotel, it would invariably be at the cheaper end of the spectrum. Now, I was practically living in one of the capital's most luxurious rooms.

And, of course, as a young man who'd been a bit of a lad back in the day, I loved this lifestyle. You'd even be given free credit at the bar, to the tune of £250 a night – just because the hotel wanted you to be seen hanging out there. One night Joe Calzaghe was there; the next night, the whole cast of *Strictly Come Dancing.*

Alcohol came with everything I was doing. Whether it was at the hotel, or having wine with dinner, your glass was constantly being refilled before you even noticed it was empty. And it was all free. It goes without saying that I ate some fantastic food too, but, really, I found myself drinking an awful lot. It wasn't that it became a true problem – I wasn't suddenly a borderline alcoholic – but it was a huge part of that lifestyle, and it did end up having a bit of an impact on me.

Another insight into the mad celebrity world came when I found myself on the front page of the *Daily Star.* I'd been on Alan Carr's *Chatty Man* show along with loads of other athletes. It was a big special, I think, and also appearing were Jonathan Ross, Leigh Francis and Tulisa from N-Dubz, who was an *X Factor* judge that year. There was a big audience, and to get everyone relaxed, they had drinks including some punch they'd had made. 'Help yourself,' they told everyone, but all the athletes were kind of sitting around quite meekly, not sure what to do.

So I thought, 'Well, I'll just get some then.' But I was really nervous, and was shaking so much that it was difficult to pour the stuff into glasses for everyone. I was really struggling to control my nerves in this world I didn't know. Later, some of the other athletes left, but Louis Smith and I were still there; we had the same management company, so I guess we were waiting to be picked up, having a chat outside the studios.

Then the car arrived, so I started saying goodbye to everyone I'd met. In that world, everyone seems to hug and kiss everybody else, even if they hardly know each other, so I was merrily going along with that. Then, just as I said goodbye to Tulisa – whom I'd never met before – some paparazzo managed to stick a camera through the fence and take a picture of it. A couple of days later, I was on the front page of the *Daily Star* – 'Tulisa finds a new Olympic hunk', or something similar.

I was taken aback by that. And, in fact, during this period I actually became somewhat obsessed by the idea that someone I knew might sell a story about me to the tabloids. At the Teen Awards, when I had just broken up with my girlfriend, I made some vague comment about how it had been a stressful week, and one of the showbiz editor types then immediately wrote a story about 'Trouble in the love life of Greg Rutherford'. Yet I hadn't said a thing about it to anyone; it was a completely private matter, and I hated the thought of it becoming public reading material. It was a wake-up call that brought home to me how careful you have to be with certain ruthless media outlets about absolutely everything you say, and how they can then twist anything you do say.

Social media was another aspect of the new world I found myself in that shocked me. Overnight, my Twitter following grew hugely, from something like 6,000 to over 100,000, and suddenly I was getting sexual offers – quite open ones, no messing around! Alongside the more explicit overtures were marriage proposals, people telling me they loved me, mad people wanting pictures of my feet or for me to send them socks. It was a revelation, to say the least.

There was also, of course, a flipside to that – the nasty trolling, which was again quite new to me. Before, everyone I'd interacted with had always been very positive, because I probably only had followers who were really into athletics. Now, I had a whole load of people who just wanted to hurl abuse.

That was very difficult, because the fiery side of me wanted to react, and respond in kind. I genuinely wanted everybody to like me, and I couldn't understand why I was suddenly the target of some people's hate. That's still the case. I have always struggled to comprehend why some people decide they don't like me, having never met me and without knowing anything about me. I have not changed either: speak to those who knew me before London 2012, like Andrew, and they'll tell you I'm still the same person I was back then. I have never got too big for my boots, and I am sorry that, by virtue of my success on the track, or maybe just because of the way my face looks, I seem to have riled some people.

However, the sexual offers were at least interesting and made me laugh. And it wasn't only young women: I seemed to have quickly developed quite a big gay following as well, which was really flattering. Who doesn't want to be told by people that they find you attractive? I never acted on any of these offers, but later in the year I did get tweeting to one fantastically witty, smart and attractive person who ended up being the mother of my child. So, despite the abuse, Twitter can be a wonderful thing.

Amid all the craziness engulfing my life, I was still competing. I jumped in Birmingham at the Grand Prix and, perhaps unsurprisingly, didn't do too brilliantly. I had some soreness anyway after the Olympic Games, but the lifestyle I'd suddenly been plunged into can't have helped.

After that, I went to Newcastle for the CityGames. I had been due to get the five o'clock train up on the Thursday night before the games, but I was out drinking, so when it got to four I said, 'OK, I'll get the six o'clock.' That came and went and soon it turned into a heavy night out. I had to jump straight on a train early the next morning, to do the media before the event. I staggered into the press conference, where Mo Farah and others were waiting, all fresh and professional and ready to chat. There I was, basically wearing the same clothes I'd had on the night before, still half-cut, walking up and down a track for photographs.

By now, the groin injury I'd been carrying was actually quite bad, and I think perhaps that's one of the reasons I didn't take the post-Olympics competitions too seriously. Neil Black, who had just been named as the performance director for British Athletics but up to then had been chief physiotherapist, was treating me at the time and he was up in Newcastle. I vividly remember – who wouldn't? – that he carried out the old-school hernia test where you, er, insert a finger up a certain private area then ask the patient to cough. He said he could feel bulging, which basically meant the start of a hernia. So he advised me not to jump. But I'd travelled all the way up, and really didn't

Suited and booted in Hugo Boss at the *GQ* Men of the Year Awards in September 2012 – and to think that before the Olympics I'd been worrying about going £3 overdrawn. *(PA)*

he Olympic victory parade through London was a wonderful occasion, and I have to say that I enjoyed myself to the full in the aftermath of winning gold. *(Getty Images)*

Dad, Mum and Natalie join me as I receive my MBE in February 2013. *(Getty Images)*

It seemed like a good idea at the time: Sara, Andrew and David join me in the Hyde bar to see i the New Year in 2013.

Hill-sprint training with Robbie Crowther in Australia in 2013.

Too far to jump! Enjoying the scenery at the Grand Canyon in 2013.

Getting ready for the skeleton run was the easy part. The 34 seconds it took me to get to the bottom were so thrilling.

Double joy. (Left) Celebrating th Commonwealth gold medal at Hampden Park in 2014, which ensured I wouldn't be condemne as a one-hit wonder. Seventeen days later (below), I added the European title on a cold evening in Zurich. *(Getty Images)*

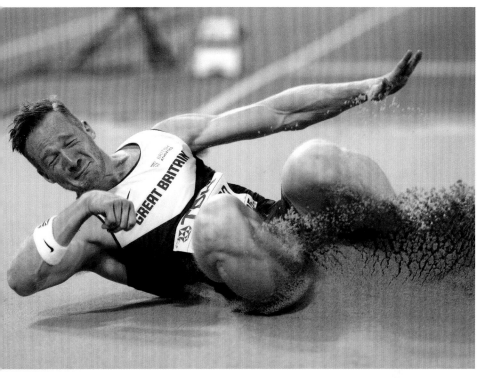

I am so proud to have completed the career grand slam. I won gold in Beijing in the 2015 World Championships, which meant I held all the major gold medals simultaneously. *(Getty Images)*

I still wonder if I should have gone to the BBC Sports Personality of the Year event in 2015 after I'd made it clear that I objected to the presence of Tyson Fury on the list of contenders. *(PA)*

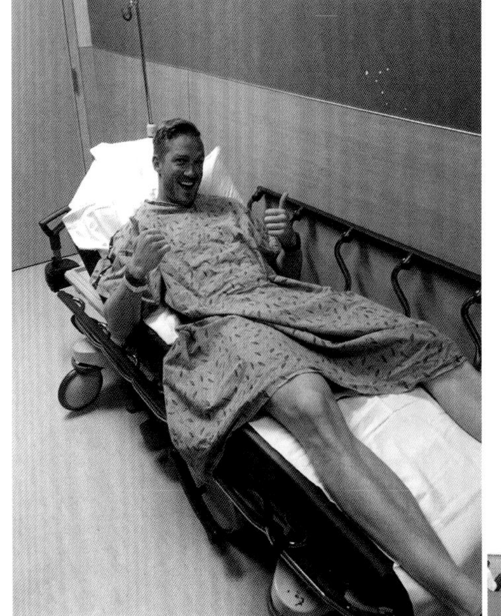

If ever there was a moment that made me value the NHS even more, it was when I had to go to hospital in the States with an appendix problem.

It's not all glamour – getting running repairs in the Rome Diamond League event in 2016.

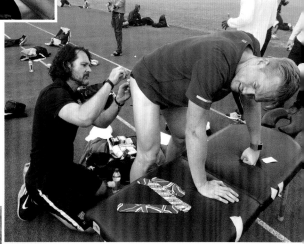

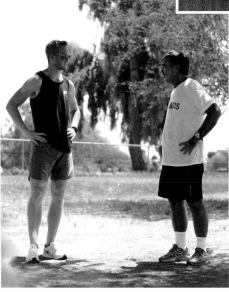

Dan Pfaff has been a brilliant coach and mentor to me over many years. His approach has always helped get the best out of me.

Contrasting emotions: gold in the 2016 European Championships in Amsterdam, and bronze at Rio. *(PA)*

My photocall for *Strictly Come Dancing* – it was a great opportunity to try something new. *(PA)*

At home with my dogs in the sand pit I built in the back garden so I could do as much training as possible there. *(Getty Images)*

With Susie and Milo. Having a son has been a huge spur to do my very best all the time.

It started with a tweet. Me and Susie proving that sometimes good things do come from Twitter.

want to let people down. However much partying I'd been doing, I always felt that if I'd made a commitment, I should stick to it.

So I ended up jumping, and it wasn't too bad. I didn't win; in fact, I think Chris Tomlinson did, and typically he made some kind of snide comment about beating me. But I was happy that I'd managed to get through the competition, and then afterwards had yet another big night out. By that point my season was effectively over – though there was a moment when Andrew and I decided to go for a jog around Green Park and loads of people started to follow us. It was like the opening sequence of *Austin Powers* . . .

By mid-October, I knew I would be slowing down anyway, as I needed surgery on the foot issue that I'd been dealing with for a few years, since before working with Dan. My hernia had to be fixed too. Before then, however, the party lifestyle I'd been enjoying since London 2012 also came to a head.

One day I woke up for another 5am start, ready to be rushed off to spend the day talking to everyone, telling my story a thousand times, jumping in and out of cars, going to photo shoots and then to more events. Usually, I wasn't complaining, and I was still loving all the new experiences – it's just that my body was so exhausted it gave out on me. I felt incredibly ill.

I remember once having a conversation with Andrew about what real flu is like, as opposed to the bad cold that people sometimes claim is flu. He said that his dad, Dr Chris Steele, always put it this way: you know you've got real flu if you feel so ill that, if there was a huge pile of money on the floor outside your door, you would be willing to let someone else take it. Well, that was how I felt that morning. My body completely and utterly crashed. I'd been living this crazy life for eight weeks, trying to compete a little between times, and not really treating my body right. I felt so awful that I ended up spending three days, alone, in my hotel room trying to recover.

The management company I was with at the time was certainly keen to flog me around. They turned up at the hotel just when I couldn't have felt any worse, and demanded I come to an event. But I was so clearly unwell that no one would have wanted me anyway. I looked like death.

Shortly afterwards, I had surgery on my hernia, which went fine, but the odd thing was that my parents chose that moment to blow up at me. They had taken my split with Liz badly and had also seen a couple of stories about me in the tabloids, which, as usual, had been given a hefty amount of topspin. I was at home and couldn't even sit up in bed. So I was lying there when my dad appeared, and a huge row broke out. He was shouting at me, 'You are having a nervous breakdown!' I was saying, 'No, I'm not. I've just been enjoying my success a bit!'

I actually felt that some of the decisions I'd taken, like splitting up with Liz, should have been made long before, and the catalyst just happened to be the fact that I'd won the Olympic title. But I suppose my parents didn't see that; they thought I was all over the place, this young man riding a wave of something insane that he wasn't ready for, perhaps ditching a relationship so that he could misbehave, rather than because it wasn't working.

The row had probably been brewing for a while. I'd already had a little falling-out with them because of my appearance on *Celebrity Juice*. In the episode, Keith Lemon did this skit, 'jump face, or cum face', and my mug was superimposed on some X-rated image of a girl being shagged by a porn star. Obviously, it was pretty rude, and I told my parents not to watch it, but they were intrigued to see me so they tuned in.

And so, to no one's surprise given how religious they are, they were hugely embarrassed that they and everyone else in my family had seen it. My dad said to me, 'You'd never see Jess or Mo on a programme like that. I can't believe you've degraded yourself in that way!' Then, funnily enough, the very next week Mo appeared on it, and the week after that it was Jess. But my family didn't know how to deal with stuff like that. It was so far out of their experience – even more than mine, perhaps.

Appearing in the papers, as with that *Daily Star* cover, didn't help. They would see stories about me and come up with their own conclusions about what I was up to – none of which they liked. The fact was that, while I might have been drinking too much, I was hardly playing the field. I was too wary of anyone selling a kiss-and-tell to the tabloids.

Unfortunately, it felt like I was really badly managed at this time, and was doing far too much – often for tiny amounts of cash. I also noticed there was something of a backlash from other athletes, particularly on social media, where people I knew were writing cryptic tweets or backhanded compliments that upset me. It was as if now that I was standing out, and no longer one of the bunch, people felt it was OK to have a pop at me.

Even after my surgery, and my falling-out with my parents, I kept partying. One night out in particular sticks in my head, because it began with what seemed at the time like a totally trivial chat, the kind of conversation you have all the time. But it was to end up becoming probably the most important one I'd ever had – because that was the very beginning of me and Susie.

My friend Leo, a former decathlete, had come over with one of his best mates, David. This was about ten days after my operation, and I was bored out of my mind. I was at home, falling out with my family, all my friends seemed to be away or somewhere else. I was fed up and a bit lonely. But Leo was around with David, so I said, 'Hey, let's go out!'

It was daft, because I was still in my bandages. They both told me not to be silly and that we should hang out at home. It was around Halloween time, and the *Strictly* special was on TV, so we watched that, joking around and talking about it on Twitter with other people, the way you do. And Leo said to me, 'Oh, you should follow this girl Susie – she's funny, you'll like her tweets.'

So I flicked to her profile and saw that she was really attractive, but at the same time slightly intimidating because she was clearly very intelligent and wrote really well – and some of her tweets were quite brutal. But I thought, 'Well, I'll definitely follow her' – and pressed that button. That really was all I thought of it at the time, because I was still determined we were going out that night.

Dave in particular tried to talk some sense into me, but I went upstairs, jumped in the shower and looked down at my foot. The stitches were still in, and it was all swollen and puffy. But I crammed it into a rather tight leather brogue anyway, and said, 'Come on, guys, I've booked a taxi, we're off out!' So that's what we did. We ended up in Oceana again, just like we had on my birthday in 2009; this time, thank God, there was no mass brawl outside KFC.

In late November, I had another big night out for my birthday, and that was when I had the realisation that I was drinking too much. I can see now how people, especially in that kind of environment, can become dependent on alcohol, because if you are even vaguely in showbiz or part of that weird, intense, celebrity world, booze is always in front of you.

For my birthday, I brought loads of friends down from home, and had a big party at the Rose Club in London. I even went to Selfridges and spent an absolute fortune on a designer outfit. I had money in the bank, real money, for the first time in my life. When I'd gone shopping in London for the first time years ago, I'd been in a store and seen a scarf, and just idly looked at the price tag thinking it was quite nice – and it was £120! I couldn't believe it. I had to walk out of the store, embarrassed that anyone might think this lad had the temerity to presume he could afford something like that. And now I was going to a posh department store and spending huge sums without batting an eyelid.

Although the party was great, it was a bit of a turning point. I had a brilliant night, but a couple of days later, I realised something was going very wrong when I found myself really wanting a vodka in the morning – almost to the point of thinking that I 'needed' it. It was a horrible moment. Drinking every day had become so normal to me that my body wondered where the booze had gone. That was the time I realised that things had gone too far.

Actually, looking back now, I desperately wish I could live those four months again. If I were able to do that, with the head I now have on my shoulders, they would be a billion times better. But by the end of 2012 I was burnt out, because I had just done too much stuff. One of my last TV appearances was a panel show, and I remember the management company had brought in someone to help me prepare. She was much better and more sympathetic than the other people I'd been working with. I turned to her and said, 'That's it, I'm done. I'm going on holiday, and getting out of here.'

I'd just been given a car on a year's lease. Up to that point I'd been driving a Ford Mondeo, so imagine my astonishment when I woke up one morning to find that a set of keys had been dropped through my letterbox, and a free Range Rover was parked outside my door. I'd hardly had a chance to drive it before now, but I'd had enough and needed to get away. I rang Andrew and said, 'Right, we are going skiing. Come and meet me; we'll take the car and just go.' So the next morning, in mid-December, we drove to Heathrow, dropped off the car, and the next thing I knew, we were in Val Thorens.

Even though I'd not been on the snow for years, my legs instantly got back into it. We had such a fantastic time. We did crazy things like seeing how fast we could go using high-tech goggles that actually measured your speed on a mini screen, and on one of the runs we managed to clock 97km/h. We skied really hard for about five days, then came back home for Christmas.

As my family don't celebrate Christmas I was on my own that day as usual. I rang my friends David and Darrell and asked them if they fancied popping over for a bit as I was going to cook. Perhaps because I never had it as a kid, I really love cooking Christmas dinner. I bought a turkey crown, a leg of lamb and a beef rib joint and cooked all three of them. And we ate it all – just me, David and Darrell. The whole lot. Pretty tragic Christmas, really. I tweeted a picture of it, and when I look back at it now I just think how tired I look.

I knew it was time to stop all this craziness, and return to training. I might have been living a hedonistic life but deep down I was still an athlete.

Nevertheless, the year did end with one last wild adventure. On 30 December, I hatched a mad plan. I texted David and Andrew – who had just got engaged to his now wife, Sara – and said, 'Fancy coming to Vegas in the morning for New Year's Eve?' They texted back, kind of laughing and saying, 'Don't be silly, come up to Manchester, we can hang out there.' 'Get back to you in a minute,' I replied.

At 11 that night, I rang Andrew, David and Sara individually to tell them I'd booked them all tickets to Vegas, and that they needed to be at Heathrow by 9am the following day. I gave them no time at all, and that was that, we were jetting off. I paid for the flights, the hotel and everything – but, of course, they spent the entire time complaining, only partially in jest. Well, who doesn't when their mate whisks them off to Vegas for a free holiday?

We arrived at about 4pm on New Year's Eve and were all absolutely knackered; we hadn't slept, and were totally jet-lagged. I had thought it would be epic, but what actually happened was that no one really wanted to do anything. I'd flown everyone out to have a wild party, and we ended up sitting on the hotel bed watching the fireworks from the window, then going to sleep. I think Andrew even snoozed through the whole display.

The next day, though, we had more of a party. Compared to what usually goes on in Vegas, it was probably a quiet night in, but we went to the Hyde bar in the Bellagio. The waitress serving us was stunning, and obviously she was charming because her job was to get us to spend lots of money. I was ordering bottles of vodka and spending an absolute fortune, mainly because I really fancied this girl, who clearly had no interest in me. At the end of the night, the bill arrived and it was an astronomical $4,500 – and I was trying to act like this was normal for me. I was completely drunk, of course, but not so blotto that I didn't think, 'Bloody hell, that's a lot of money.' But I guess I was trying to look like more of a high-roller than I've ever been, and to save face, so I ended up giving an extra $500 tip to this girl. The rapper Lil Jon was at the next table along, so I felt under pressure to look big time. Just because the waitress was attractive. Looking back, all I can think is, 'You complete prat – what on earth were you thinking?'

While I didn't gamble a single cent in Vegas, I did something else that was a little crazy to remind me of just how epic 2012 had been. I had the words 'Citius, Altius, Fortius' – the Olympic motto and Latin for 'Faster, Higher, Stronger' – tattooed just below my navel. And that was that, really. The end of the greatest year of my life. From Vegas, I travelled straight back to Phoenix and to Dan. It was time to begin training for the 2013 season, to actually live like an athlete again.

CHAPTER 21

Susie

I'd been following Susie Verrill on Twitter since that Halloween night in October 2012, and gradually and naturally, it progressed from exchanging public messages, to exchanging direct messages, and then texts, after we'd swapped numbers around January 2013. All of it was very tame – I distinctly remember us talking about David Attenborough and *Antiques Roadshow* – barely flirting. The chat via messages went on for about six weeks or so. And then, when I was back in the UK for a bit, I thought, 'Well, she's good fun, she's clever, incredibly attractive – why not meet up with her, if she's up for the idea?'

Fortunately, she was. I think it was a Wednesday when I suggested it, and on the Thursday I jumped in my car and drove into central London to pick her up from work – she was working on *Look* magazine at that point – and we went bowling. I'd obviously never met her before in my life, and there I was, turning up in a Range Rover outside her office to take us bowling. Probably not a bog-standard move for a first date. But when you talk to someone for a while, via Twitter and text and so on, you feel like you know them, before you really do.

What I loved about Susie straight away was that she was direct, funny and not afraid to take the piss. I also liked the fact that, as it turned out, she hadn't watched any of Super Saturday. She'd been at a wedding, and when she got home her mum said, 'Oh this lovely ginger smiley lad won a medal in the long jump.' And Susie – probably still half-drunk from the do – wasn't particularly fussed. She didn't care at all about track and field, which I found really refreshing. None of it fazed her in the slightest. Talking to her was so easy and natural; it was easy to forget that we'd only just met.

After bowling, I dropped her at a friend's house. Then the next day we met up again at her house, and I didn't get home until about 4am – not because we were partying but because we lost track of time, talking and talking for hours. The next day, I just wanted to see her again.

So, we started hanging out together a lot. So much so that when I was getting ready to go and receive my MBE – an honour that I was immensely proud to receive – she was actually staying with me at the hotel. We had just clicked, instantly, and time spent not hanging out with her seemed a waste.

One funny moment early on in our relationship came when I was invited with four friends to appear on the TV programme *The Cube*, which was recorded in the spring of 2013 but not actually shown until Christmas. My brother Rob, Andrew and Darrell agreed to come along. Then I asked Susie if she'd like to come too, and she said yes. At the beginning of the show, you have to tell everyone who you've brought with you. So I duly said, 'On the left we have Andrew Steele, who is a very good close friend of mine and a training partner, and we have the beautiful Susie "Ver-ille" here as well, who has been a good friend for a long time now.' I actually pronounced her name wrong. She gave me a look that said, 'OK then.' I couldn't call her my girlfriend because we hadn't had that conversation yet. But getting her name and the length of our relationship right would have been a good start.

But while this new relationship was going brilliantly, I was only at home in the UK for a couple of weeks before I had to head off again, and get back into serious training and competition mode.

Normally, I would have headed back into training with Dan. But something unexpected had happened when I'd returned to him at the beginning of the year. To start with, everything went great. While it was instantly clear that I was somewhat out of shape because of all the drinking and partying of the past four months, as soon as I got back into hard training I felt fantastic. I think I was running faster on the flat than I had ever done before. Perhaps it was confidence, or perhaps the result of taking that real break and having the operation to resolve the foot problem that had bugged me for years.

Either way, I went back into it, putting all the recent craziness behind me. In my head I'd never stopped being an athlete, and now my head was right back in the sport.

While I was in the US I got to know the American football quarterback Tim Tebow, who was quite a big name in the NFL at the time. He had come to train with us in Arizona to work on his speed. One day, he threw a Hail Mary to test me and I outran his arm – basically, I ran faster than he could throw it, which is very rare. It seemed to impress one of the offensive coaches at the University of California Los Angeles, who was there with Tim at the time.

One night, we were at dinner with Tim, his brother, the coach and a few others in an amazing Mexican restaurant, where Tim and his guests ate for free, of course. During the meal, Tim turned to me and posed a question: 'Greg, what if I told you you could train for one or two years and then join the NFL as a wide receiver?' I laughed it off, but he stuck with it. 'No, really, I spoke with the coach – he thinks you could do it.' He was seriously imploring me to try to become a wide receiver in the NFL, by virtue of my speed and, perhaps unusually for a track and field athlete, my ability to catch. It must have been my football and rugby experience when I was younger. I'm also quite big and heavy for a long jumper; at six-foot-three and over 90 kilos, my body type is surprisingly suited to a wide receiver.

So, all of a sudden, I was thinking maybe I should go for it. I bought myself a proper American football and I started doing catching practice with Andrew, and sometimes with Tim himself, every day. At one point, it became quite a real opportunity; the offensive coordinator from UCLA invited me to try out for their college team, which was even more tempting because I might have been able to take a history degree too. For several weeks, it genuinely seemed as though the idea could become a reality, but it was a chance I didn't feel ready to take. I still believed I had a point to prove in track and field, especially given that so many people had thought my victory at London

2012 had been a fluke, so, rightly or wrongly, I politely declined. It seemed so far-fetched that I could have a chance of making it, having had no experience in the sport at all, but I guess my speed blinded these guys to my other weaknesses. As it happens, over the years since, I've often practised a timed 40-yard dash, one of the key performance tests in the NFL, and regularly run faster than the all-time record.

It was during this training camp in Arizona that, out of nowhere, the owner of the venue presented me with an invoice, claiming I owed $13,000 for around six weeks of training there. I'd just sat through a whole presentation about their ambitious plans for the future, and I'd been really enthused. Then at the end of it, they hit me with this huge bill for only five or six weeks' training, and not even including any medical or accommodation fees.

It threw me right back to the time my old coach, Tom, had cornered me in his car to ask for a big pay rise from me when I was just a kid. To me, it felt as though these people were trying to rob me – the sum was so vast and disproportionate given that I'd only been there a few weeks and, as far as I'd been told, UK Athletics were supposed to be paying Dan until April 2013. I just muttered something like, 'Oh, OK, well, I need to figure this out,' and left the room. Andrew, who was also there, was similarly astonished.

I avoided the track for a few days, but ventured down when the main guy went away on business. There was a really frosty atmosphere. It felt to me as if the few staff members had turned against me, leaving poor Dan stuck in the middle, not knowing what to do. After five weeks, I had to go home anyway – the reason being a nice one: I was getting an MBE – and I was glad.

I was hurt and worried by the whole experience. I felt taken advantage of, as though everyone around me had decided I must be a millionaire or something because of my gold medal, an assumption which was about ten times over the odds. So when it came to planning what to do next, I spoke to my agent and he said, 'Well, Australian Athletics have invited you to compete on their circuit for a month.' Andrew had spent a lot of time out there, so we talked about it and decided to go for it.

I knew there were some great coaches in Australia – Gary Bourne, for one, who had done so well with Mitch Watt – and other good long jumpers coming through. I hadn't been there since the Commonwealth Games in 2006, and I thought it would be worth investigating a new set-up – because I feared that with the whole situation in Arizona, I had lost Dan forever.

One of the promises I'd made to Andrew was that if I won the Olympics, I would fund his training for a year. So this seemed like my opportunity to come through on that pledge – and have some fun. I booked him on the same flight as me. Through all this, I was chatting constantly with Susie, but as it was still such a new relationship and this was such a good opportunity, I felt I had to take it. I also decided I would bring my parents over to watch me and see Australia too, which was a trip of a lifetime for them.

Our first stop en route was at a nice hotel in Singapore, where I went to pay for something and my bank card was declined. 'God, that's strange,' I thought. 'I know I've got plenty of funds in my account.' I rang my bank, explained what had happened and asked them to check. They came back and said, 'Yes, Mr

Rutherford, sorry about that, you have a very healthy balance at the moment of a £120,000 credit, so I'll just lift that block and you can carry on.' Well, Andrew and I just sat there looking at each other in awe. It seemed incredible – £120,000 in my account! And only a few months before I'd been fretting about my unauthorised overdraft. The phrase 'very healthy balance' stuck with us . . .

Then we arrived in Australia and got back to work. We were based at first in Perth and I was supposed to be getting a nice car supplied for my use. Well, there was a car but it was the most beat-up old wreck you can imagine – it had a huge dent in the side, and was barely holding together. But it held up, and we had a great time, rolling around the amazing beaches in our banger. Perth was also the track where Fabrice Lapierre had put in an absolutely massive jump in 2010 – 8.78m, which would have been the longest since 1995, but it was with an illegal tail-wind. I was pretty excited about jumping at that track, but I discovered very quickly that I was out of practice. Australian Athletics had billed this meet as me versus Mitch, but we were both in a bit of trouble. He had a few injuries too, and I jumped awfully. I still won, and I was chuffed about that – it even made the front page of the local paper – but it wasn't a great performance, all things considered.

Although I was training and competing properly, I wasn't in as good shape as I could be, and I wasn't always being strict on myself. Part of me still wanted to enjoy myself, go out for dinner and have a glass of wine, because it was a great experience travelling the world again, having fun with my best friend.

And also, I was a bit lost at that point. I didn't know what was going on with Dan. I knew I had to try to figure things out, but I thought perhaps it was a good time not to take it so very seriously.

Next, we flew from Perth to Canberra and I started falling apart a little bit. I wasn't training the same as before, wasn't lifting weights, or doing all of the right sessions. The knee on my take-off leg began to hurt a lot, every time I tried to sprint or jump. From Canberra, it was over to Melbourne, via Sydney, because I had never been there and it gave me an opportunity to catch up with my parents.

In Melbourne, I was once more jumping against Mitch, and again the press had been building it up. Although I hadn't been able to train much, I jumped quite well, and even broke the stadium record with 8.10m – though it's been surpassed since. Mitch is a mate of mine, and I like him a lot, but I was pretty pleased to beat him twice in his own backyard. I'd also thought of that trip as a kind of recce, to look into coaches. But I hadn't found anyone I desperately wanted to train with, and certainly nobody who would be a patch on Dan.

So we flew back, via LA, and a random night out in a diner where we bumped into Andi Peters and Chris Moyles, to Arizona. I just had to hope that nothing else had happened at the training venue and that I wasn't presented with more huge bills.

After a week, I noticed that even with Dan things had become very awkward. He was stuck between a rock and a hard place, really. It was now beyond the time that British Athletics had agreed to pay him, so officially he wasn't my coach any more. Instead, his paymasters were a company called Altis, who I was now having this dispute with.

A couple of years later they did admit they were in the wrong, and apologised. But at the time I felt extremely frustrated because I had become the Olympic champion and now couldn't even see my coach properly without somebody chasing me for money. It was such a tricky situation that I decided to go back home. But I was a worried man. After winning gold in London, I'd had visions of finally being able to create my perfect training set-up; instead, I effectively found myself without a coach or a place to train. On top of that, I no longer had a kit sponsor, as negotiations with Nike had taken a negative turn.

At the end of May, I was due to compete again at the Prefontaine Classic in Eugene, the scene of a few happy memories. But I was feeling down, partly because I didn't know if I had a coach or not and partly because I was going to be away from Susie for a bit. On the day I left, we were sitting in my car at Milton Keynes train station at 7am and it was lashing it down. She had already taken an extra couple of days off work to hang out and she just said, 'I wish I didn't have to go to work today.' So I asked her if she'd be willing to come with me to Oregon that night. Luckily, she said yes and British Airways had a spare seat, so we were on our way, with almost no notice.

It was all a bit of a mad start to a relationship. For the first few weeks in London, we were seeing each other constantly. Then suddenly I'd disappeared off to Australia. Now we were flying out to America together. I saw that my lifestyle, with me jetting off all over the place, was not conducive to getting to know someone properly, so I thought I'd take the plunge and ask her to go with me.

It turned out to be a good week, both professionally and personally. I jumped 8.22m to finish third in Eugene behind the Russian Aleksandr Menkov, who jumped an insane distance despite being well behind the board. Then Susie and I travelled around to take in the sights, including a visit to Vancouver.

There were just two flies in the ointment: my relationships with my sponsors and my coach. While I was in Oregon, I had a conversation with Nike, who were annoyed that I had spoken out about what I felt was a derisory offer to renew my sponsorship deal with them. But I held my ground. I knew they were offering me a lot less than some mediocre athletes in other events who were never going to win anything, and they kept low-balling me in our negotiations. I guess they might also have seen my London victory as a fluke, so I did something they didn't expect: I walked away.

Meanwhile, the situation at the training camp in Arizona was coming to a head. In retrospect, I think I approached the whole matter the wrong way: I should have said, 'Look, I don't think the fee you want is fair. Let's discuss it and come to an agreement so that I can keep working with Dan.' Instead, as I had done in the past, I buried my head in the sand and hoped the problem would go away. Soon after that, I went back home and that was the last time I saw Dan all year – by that point, the whole scenario had become unworkable.

Professionally, it was a really difficult time. Often, I felt lost trying to work everything out, with so many decisions to make. A few short months before, I had a great coach, great chiropractor and an amazing training environment; and now I was faced with having to figure out a whole new working pattern and support system without help from anyone, not even UK Athletics.

But I comforted myself with the fact that I had Susie – and that was a massive, massive plus.

CHAPTER 22

Frustration and Loathing in Moscow

After that America trip with Susie in late May and early June, my season began to slide desperately downhill. I competed in the Birmingham Diamond League and the European Team Championships, finishing second and third without jumping particularly far, so I knew I really needed to step it up at the big Paris meeting in early July.

Bizarrely, the night before I was due to jump, I had the horribly vivid sensation that something was about to go wrong. I don't believe in signs or omens and all that baloney, nor am I superstitious, but there have been a couple of occasions in my career when I've had the premonition that I was about to pick up an injury and a day or two later it has happened. So I made sure I got my hamstring rigorously checked beforehand. It all looked OK, and I appeared to be moving fine when it came to the warm-up, so I thought to myself, 'This is just nerves: you are in shape, you'll be all right.' Yet I also had nagging doubts about the knee issue that had developed while I was in Australia, which was affecting my approach to the board. That certainly played a part in what was to happen next.

The meeting hadn't started well. The organisers in Paris had decided to stage a parade for all the Olympic champions who were competing there, but for some reason I was the only one who didn't get invited. I remember the great American jumper Dwight Phillips was disgusted on my behalf, saying, 'This is typical for field event athletes – we are always treated worse!' I appreciated his comments but it soon turned out that the parade snub was the least of my problems.

My opener was 7.99m, which was not fantastic but not too shabby either. On the second approach, I hurtled down the runway and, as I planted my leg to take off, I heard an almighty bang. I couldn't believe it: my old nemesis, my hamstring, had gone again. As I was lying in the pit, one crushing thought kept coming into my head: your career has just finished. That's it. Kaput. It was that bad.

Having suffered a couple of dozen hamstring tears in my life, I could probably write a thesis on the subject, and I knew this one was different. It wasn't that it was more painful, but it felt like something had gone very seriously wrong in the back of my leg.

When I flew back home and looked at the scan, I could see a straight line of tendon and then a gap. I turned to Noel, the doctor from UK Athletics, and said to him, 'I've ruptured my hamstring, haven't I?' He confirmed I had, and pointed out the two-centimetre gap in my tendon. Noel told me I had to hope that the tendon would reattach itself to the broken part; but he also warned that the injury was so serious I might not be able to jump as well as before. All of which left me thinking, 'Shit, my career possibly really is finished.'

For the next few days, I was pretty low. I threw a big barbecue at my house for my close friends in track and field and my family, which I traditionally do at the end of each season, and it felt like I was saying farewell to my athletics year in mid-July. To cheer myself up, I also went out and got a new dog. Some people eat ice cream and watch television when they are upset; I buy dogs.

Something really strange and inexplicable happened, however. Despite this being without doubt the worst hamstring injury I'd ever suffered, from the point of view of both pain and clinical diagnosis, within a week I could walk without it hurting and suddenly I began to wonder: should I start training again? The gap between the Paris Diamond League and the World Championships long jump qualifiers in Moscow was 39 days. It seemed impossible to get back in time. People around me were chastising me for even thinking of training so soon after such a bad injury, but I couldn't shake off the idea.

This has usually been the pattern with injuries throughout my career: my body gets hurt very easily, but it heals quickly and I'm then able to do things again far sooner than other people. The standard prognosis is almost invariably wrong in my case. I don't know why, it just happens; it's my very specific and vague superpower.

I continued to improve, so nine days after my injury I went to the track in Milton Keynes to see whether I could do a few strides. My approach with every hamstring injury has always been the same: I will sort of walk until there is no pain, then I will jog until there is no pain, then I will run until there is no pain, and then I will move on to sprinting and finally I will jump. And as I jogged around the outside of the track it was clear that, while there was a slight tugging in the hamstring area, there was no pain.

I was thinking, 'This is not normal – nine days ago I ruptured my hamstring and now I am almost running.' Over the next week, I continued to improve and so I spoke to Neil Black, the boss at UK Athletics, and told him: 'Something weird is going on here . . . If I can get fit, will you still take me to the World Championships?'

In a very rational, calm way, Neil pointed out that what I was describing was unlikely, because his doctors had taken multiple scans that showed I had a fully ruptured hamstring. I think he maybe thought I was so desperate to make the team that I was deluding him – and perhaps myself. But he kindly said, 'Look, we will leave the spot open when we pick the team, and we will then do a fitness test as close as we possibly can to Moscow. If you pass the fitness test, then we will let you go.'

After those words, I snapped right back into athlete mode. I started running up hills and even doing boxing training to give myself every possible chance of making it to Moscow.

A few days later, Neil turned up at Milton Keynes for the fitness test and he genuinely couldn't believe what he was seeing. I did my full warm-up, all my drills, and then some sprints in spikes and take six jumps off a short approach. Three weeks after my hamstring injury I felt fine. It was incredible: I had somehow defied the laws of science, and all of a sudden I was going to be on the plane to Moscow after all.

I even started to believe that I might still be able to get a podium spot. After all, I knew I could rise to the big occasion; and, as I pointed out to reporters, I'd had similar problems before the 2009 World Championships, yet been able to produce a jump of 8.30m.

As the event drew closer, the doubts grew. I did another set of sprints and realised I hadn't got my speed back to where it needed to be. I spoke to Andrew on the phone and asked him, 'Should I just pull out?' He argued persuasively, telling me that I had defied expectations so many times before that it was worth giving it a shot; that I was lucky to have the opportunity to be there at all so I should see it through, for better or worse.

I agreed. I knew the deck was stacked against me but I felt that I had to give it a go. You can say what you like about me, but I have never been a quitter, and I have never been too proud to put myself at the mercy of the competition, no matter what shape I'm in.

When we arrived in Moscow, I noticed that some in the British team were acting strangely in my presence. I'd always been one of the lads, so it was an unusual experience when fellow athletes avoided eye contact or sort of nodded and then looked away. I felt further ostracised when one team member put out a cryptic tweet about an Olympic gold medallist in the squad who had become a complete arsehole – they were clearly referring to me. And what really hurt was that other athletes retweeted it or replied with similar veiled comments. I thought, 'Hang on a second, most of you were my friends before London 2012, what has changed?' I certainly hadn't, only my athletics CV had. Yet, here they were, sticking the boot in. Recently, I talked to that athlete and we're good again, but it made for a very strange atmosphere in the team.

My room-mate, Steve Lewis, seemed to be getting the cold shoulder too, as a result of his link to me, which was odd and incredibly unfair on him because he is a great human being. As we walked around, we'd be wondering, 'Bloody hell, nobody wants to talk to us! What did we do?'

I should stress that it wasn't the entire team who were behaving that way. Most of the girls were fine. Yet despite still being ordinary Greg, happy to chat to all and sundry, willing to wish everybody good luck and support them, there were those who wouldn't give me the time of day. I wanted to scream, 'I haven't changed!' – but some people clearly thought I had.

Even to this day, many athletes in the British team treat me differently from the way they did before London 2012. I find that really weird, because as people who have been my friends for a long time, such as Andrew Steele and Steve Lewis, and my family will tell you, I am exactly the same person I always was. The only real difference is that in the past four years I have made a bit more money, so I have been able to enjoy a better lifestyle. I had that aspiration before 2012, I just couldn't afford it so much. Andrew used to joke that I *had* to win gold in London, simply to meet my lifestyle expectations.

In Moscow, I had to develop a thick skin very quickly. Soon it got to the point where it thought, 'Well, if you don't like me, I'm not going to waste my time trying to change your mind.' I'm a lot more brutal nowadays. If people don't like me, whether it be on social media or elsewhere, I am not going to spend my time worrying about it.

Something else frustrated me while I was in Moscow. Given that I had no coach after falling out with Altis and being separated from Dan, I started referring to Paul Brice, who is an incredible biomechanist and was actually helping me train at the time, as my coach. Most people's response would have been, 'OK, so what?' But – incredibly – my comments so offended the other British coaches in Moscow that they complained to Neil Black, who then approached me in the dinner hall to talk about it.

He explained that the other coaches had decided that because Paul was not an accredited coach, I shouldn't be allowed to refer to him as such. I laughed, and thought, 'Are you serious? We are on the eve of a World Championships – surely these people should be more focused on their own athletes and not on whoever is coaching me or what label we give him?' Unfortunately, too many British coaches are not only mediocre, but can be negative and spiteful people to boot, and that incident highlighted how petty they can be.

Steve and I had a laugh about it later, both of us saying, 'Well, nobody on this bloody team seems to like us!' I ended up referring to Paul as my Technical Watching Assistant Teacher – I'll leave it to you to work out the acronym – which was a dig aimed squarely at other coaches not him, because he is one of the best in the world at what he does.

Paul was ruthlessly honest too. Four days before I was due to jump in Moscow, he put the speed gun on me because I was concerned that I wasn't running fast enough, and he found that I was a metre per second slower than I had been before London 2012. That was crushing, because I still clung to the hope that I could go out there and somehow conjure up a performance out of thin air. After all, my hamstring had magically mended itself, so why not?

When Paul told me the result, I was so taken aback that I said to him, 'Are you sure you did everything right?' I was desperately trying to hold on to something, even I recognised that. He is an exceptional biomechanist and wouldn't have made a mistake. 'Sorry, mate,' he replied. 'That is what it is.'

It made me think of Muhammad Ali's famous quote before fighting Joe Frazier the first time. 'Frazier's got two chances. Slim, and none. And Slim just left town.'

I knew then that I couldn't win the world title, and that my chances of getting a medal were also very slim. I was just too slow. As I lay in my bed I thought, 'Should I just leave now?' In hindsight, I should have cut my losses and walked away. But I didn't want to let anybody down, and I'd put so much effort into making it to Moscow that I felt I had to give it a shot, however forlorn my chances.

And I did. I gave it my absolute best. But I finished with my worst performance of the season – 7.87m. I was 14th overall, five centimetres off making the top 12 places that would have got me into the final. Even though I had been expecting it, I was still gutted.

No sooner had I taken my third qualifying jump than Chris Tomlinson, who had missed out on a place in the World Championship team, put the boot in hard. 'Words can't describe my anger. Season ruined on media profile and not current athletic form, thanks for the support from the athletics community,' he wrote in a tweet that he later deleted.

I felt really hurt by that. And it simply wasn't true either. Not only had I jumped further than Chris on multiple occasions that year, but I had beaten him in every head-to-head competition except for when I was injured. What's more, I was Olympic champion, so it was a no-brainer that I should get the nod.

His tweet led to me getting a torrent of abuse on Twitter. Scroll back a year, and my feed was exploding with well-wishers telling me how much they loved me. Now, I was getting a ton of hate dumped on me every day. Of course, all those who had decided they didn't like me because I was appearing on lots of TV shows came out in force again to tell me how pathetic I was, how shit I was, and how lucky I had been in London 2012.

Perhaps it is the British way, to cheer people on the way up and smash them brutally on the way down. But it seemed excessive, so unnecessary: almost playground in its simplicity and nastiness. I wanted to say to each of them, 'Look, I ruptured my hamstring just 39 days ago and have thrown everything at trying to recover when I probably should have spent the rest of July and August putting my feet up and hanging out with Susie. I have tried my utmost to do my best for my country. Yes, I have failed this time – but it is not for want of trying.' And while I hadn't made the final, it was not like I'd jumped six metres – I'd missed out by less than the length of most people's little finger. But I wondered if it would actually have changed anyone's opinion of me. I doubt it. Logic and reasoned argument don't come into it in the realm of social media. There are always some, who have no idea about athletics, that come out of the woodwork to tell me how bad I am.

I have always bitten my tongue when Chris has criticised me, as I have felt he has on numerous occasions. But I think the fact that he hasn't had results as good as mine kills him, and if he was honest he'd admit that. I don't think I was alone in believing that he had been jumping abysmally that season, and hadn't demonstrated that he had the ability to succeed at major world events, so I doubt he would have made the final in Moscow. But, of course, I doubt he would accept that.

Given that the Russian Aleksandr Menkov produced a jump of 8.56m to win gold in Moscow – a distance he has never come close to since – I would have struggled to overtake him even if I had been at my best. However, I'm sure I would have made the podium if only I hadn't gone to Paris. Jumping there got me a tiny appearance fee, and ended up ruining my year entirely. Not a good trade-off.

The Moscow championships had ended up being not just

uncomfortable, but a failure. One thing about my competition record is that I am never scared of failure, I am always willing to put myself out there, but this one led to more people questioning whether my success at London 2012 had been an accident. And it made me even more determined to prove the doubters and critics wrong.

CHAPTER 23

17 Days of Glory

After Moscow, I did what I always do at the end of the season: I stacked the fridge and booze cabinet with every unhealthy treat I'd been resisting and ate and drank myself into a larger human. But by late September, earlier than I'd ever started winter training before, I was back at the track itching to prove I was no one-season wonder.

By then, I had gone for another scan, which showed that, remarkably, my hamstring had done exactly what the doctors had hoped and reconnected itself to the tendon, rather than the tendon to muscle. It meant I could crack on with running up hills with my dogs and lifting heavy weights, each day fuelled by an angry fire and desire to prove the doubters wrong.

There was one major problem: I didn't have a coach. I couldn't go back to Dan Pfaff, and I hadn't found anyone to replace him. In my mind, there were no decent long jump coaches in Britain, but I knew that Steve Fudge, who trains Adam Gemili and James Dasaolu, was a highly regarded sprint coach so I spoke to him. Unfortunately, he turned me down.

Nor was there any chance of me working with the other main sprint coach in Britain at that time, Rana Reider. After London 2012, the chief executive of UK Athletics, Niels de Vos, came up to me at the parade and said, 'We've got your new coach! He's this American, Rana Reider,' which I found really odd given I was with Dan at the time, and, as far as I knew, didn't need a new coach. But when I eventually met up with him he seemed hugely frosty.

First of all, he warned me that the Olympic triple jump champion Christian Taylor was the main guy in the group, and then he said I would have to be voted in by the other athletes. To top it off, he said, 'I've never seen you jump and I've been coaching Chris Tomlinson to beat you all year, so I'm not sure how this is going to work.'

It wasn't hard to read between the lines: I wasn't wanted. But, for my part, I had no desire to be in an environment where people are giving you orders and there's a hierarchy within the group. Dan has never operated like that. He works with lots of athletes, including long jumpers who are rivals of mine, but no one athlete is more important or more of a favourite than any other. He makes sure he gives his time equally.

Then, slowly, another option dawned on me. Jonas Tawiah-Dodoo was a young but very bright sprint coach who had been working under Dan before 2012, and was familiar with his methods. I met up with him and we very quickly agreed that I could train with him; we'd carry on Dan's programme to a certain extent, and he would add bits here and there.

I did some of the sessions at home; for others I travelled to Lee Valley to train with Jonas' group. I was working out with the guys quite a lot, and getting to know them. The amount of talent in those young kids was phenomenal, but a couple of them were leading lifestyles that were definitely not conducive to being successful in sport. I think perhaps Jonas hoped that having me around as a slightly older and more experienced athlete might provide some guidance for the more wayward ones. But, actually, I suspect most of them looked on me as some posh kid who'd had it easy; none of them had any idea, of course, what my upbringing was really like.

There was one lad who had to move because some guys broke into his house wielding a gun. Now, it never got that serious for me, but I remembered that, back when I was his age, I'd moved myself out of certain social groups because I knew they were going to steer me down the wrong path. But often these young lads weren't prepared to listen. They just said, 'Oh, Greg, you don't know,' and joked around, but they evidently thought I couldn't possibly understand.

The best sprinter in the group was CJ Ujah, who was lightning fast and clearly a massive talent. It was no surprise to me at all when he became one of those rare British sprinters to run the 100m in under ten seconds. Like many young sprinters, he needs to focus his mindset and know when to knuckle down, but he is an incredibly exciting prospect for British sprinting. I hope he comes to realise that he is as good as anyone in the world, and that he makes the most of his amazing talent. I also gained a fantastic training partner, and an even better friend, in Jermaine Olasan, who has now moved on from athletics to rugby sevens. He was a breath of fresh air, a calming influence and would join me on future US trips.

From the outset, I really enjoyed working with Jonas. I suppose it was a different dynamic; he's the same age as me, so it wasn't a kind of master/disciple relationship. He was always receptive to me having a level of control over how things went, which is really important, particularly when you are working with older athletes who already know what works for them.

I was training well, but of course it was almost entirely sprint work. Going into the start of the indoor season, I hadn't done a single jump session. So when I took part in my first competition indoors, in Birmingham in mid-February, I was pretty pleased to jump eight metres exactly. Just as importantly, jumping far again had produced no negative effect on my body, which was a huge relief. After that, I felt I could truly get back to my best once more, something which before that season I had seriously doubted.

I thought we would probably all benefit from some warm-weather training at that point, so I talked to Jonas about flying out to San Diego. He had to figure it all out, and I had to do a fair bit of convincing, because he had a lot of youngsters in his group who couldn't afford much. But San Diego, as I knew well, was a great place to be and to train. It was relatively cheap too – $18 a day to use the track and the gym.

Soon after we got out there, with my training picking up and getting better, we decided to do another jump session.

And, immediately, I felt almost a shock in the back of my knee and I had to stop straight away. It wasn't that I couldn't walk, or anything dramatic like that, but it was sore, and clearly a problem. I spoke to the British doctors at home, and they set me up with a doctor in LA, where I had something called prolotherapy. They inject a kind of sugary substance just under the skin, and it's supposed to help calm down the nerves and take the edge off.

It was extremely frustrating because I was training really well, at least as far as sprinting went. I was even sometimes beating some of the very fast sprinters in the group over 40m, so I knew I was in pretty good shape. I've often wondered just how fast I could run a 100m with the right training; maybe one day I'll have the opportunity to find out, though I'm getting on a bit now.

After the prolotherapy, I did two weeks of adapted training. There was a competition in San Diego coming up, and I thought I'd give it a go. I'd been watching Will Claye and his group train and I knew they were looking good. I'd also, incidentally, spoken to Will's coach Jeremy Fischer about joining in, but because he was tied to USA Track and Field he wasn't allowed to coach any foreigners. I thought, 'Well, I've got to test myself,' and if you are going to test yourself it might as well be against the best. I also knew San Diego was a great place to jump, because the setting is perfect, and conditions are usually excellent – warm, and conducive to big jumps. What's more, it's exclusively a jumps competition, so the small crowd can gather right next to the runway and there's a great atmosphere.

It was a bit of a leap in the dark: although I felt I'd pretty much healed, and I knew I was really fast, I had almost no jump practice under my belt. And there were some great athletes in that competition.

It didn't start particularly well. I fouled the first two rounds. I felt oddly under huge pressure, which was weird because, despite all the big names, in many ways it was essentially just a training environment. But in round three, I jumped 8.18m, which put me into third. At that point, Will had jumped 8.27m and Tyrone Stewart a personal best of 8.39m, but I still thought I could beat them.

It was a good day to jump. A very good day. The winds were ideal, the hot sun was starting to drop – and there were no killer bees or coyotes. It was just perfect, really. A perfect day for the best jump of my life.

In that fourth round I went for it hard, taking full advantage of my new-found sprint speed, and, after hitting the board spot-on, it seemed as if I was floating for an age before my skin finally hit the sand. It was enormous, I knew that straight away.

I always believed I could jump big. After the 2012 Olympics, plenty of armchair heroes chuntered on about how it was the 'shortest' winning jump since 1972. But conditions have to be right for big jumps, and, in any given competition, you can only beat whoever is in front of you on the day. It is such a strange criticism: what would people have preferred, that I didn't win?

People also forget that most of the major titles I've won have been in adverse conditions for big jumps. Jumping is very much affected by the weather, and if it's cold, rainy, or you have a headwind, no one is going to be putting in stellar distances. And, actually, when a gold medal is on the line, distances be damned. Major championships are about one thing, and one thing only: winning.

However, I always felt – and still do, in fact – that I could have jumped further in my career. And when they called out a huge personal best distance of 8.51m, it felt like finally I had some confirmation of that. Little did I realise that it was going to cause such a ridiculous amount of controversy. You really can't win sometimes.

At that event, there was a French Paralympian guy recording all the action. He's a bit of a movie maker in his spare time, so he put the jumps together in a cool compilation video, with some nice editing and effects and posted it online. Incredibly, it triggered a snowball effect of allegations and dispute, all stemming from comments made by Chris Tomlinson to the effect that my 8.51m jump was a massive foul – which, of course, was in absolutely no way related to the coincidence that I'd just smashed the British record he had previously shared with me. I'm not so sure Chris would have been quite as ready to criticise anybody else's jump, but, since it was me, denigrating this performance seemed to become his mission, though he denied it was a case of sour grapes on his part.

This was incredibly frustrating. I'd jumped far enough to win the Olympics, I'd jumped huge in San Diego, and then a guy who I thought was clearly dealing with some fairly major jealousy issues just had to get stuck in. I thought, 'Give me a break and give me my dues.' Instead, Tomlinson and his dad seemed to embark on what struck me as a bizarre personal vendetta to try to have the distance removed from the record books, despite the US track and field authorities firmly stating it was completely legitimate. They lobbied the media, UK Athletics and the IAAF to get them to change their minds. I felt it was unbelievable. Perhaps he was struggling to deal with the fact that his career was coming to an end, and that now he wouldn't even appear in the record books. I found it ironic thinking back to Paris in 2011 when he'd broken the British record – which was mine prior to that – and remembering how I'd congratulated him. My first thought had been, 'OK, fine, now you have to jump further' – not to embark on some pointless campaign.

Of course, for all his protestation, the authorities dismissed his claims outright. All that came out of this ridiculous episode was more attention on the fact that I'd jumped a British record, and I don't think he emerged with any credit from his response.

I shrugged it off; I had slightly more important things to think about at this point – because Susie was pregnant. I'd missed Nugget's first scan – the name we gave the baby growing inside her back then – as I had been in San Diego, and was really upset about that. But the drive I had to succeed for my future child was enormous. I was disappointed when I was narrowly beaten in my next meeting, in Hengelo, after jumping 8.26m, but I was happy with my competition overall. All of my jumps were over eight metres, which hasn't happened often.

When I finished, I noticed that because an athlete had withdrawn through injury, there was a lane free in the 100m. I was knackered, of course, but I thought, 'I'll have a go at that.' I went and got myself into the race, but then realised I only had jump spikes, not running ones. So I borrowed a pair from a nice German hurdler. A series of eight-metre jumps does take a lot out of your body, so in the warm-up I was definitely feeling a bit tired. I did a couple of practice sprints, then it suddenly dawned on me, when talking to Jonas, that I hadn't run out of blocks in years. I had no idea what my settings should be, so we had to quickly figure that out before I raced.

Soon afterwards I got a stark reminder of the difference between the call rooms for sprints and long jumps. The call room is where you wait to be brought out into the stadium. Jumpers tend to get on: we have a chat, a laugh, and calm our nerves together. With sprinters, it's as if everyone wants to kill everyone else. So I walked into the call room, giving it the usual long jump chat, 'How are we, guys? Ready for a good day?' And everyone just looked daggers at me.

The race itself was fine. I got off to a great start and was even, up until about the 30m mark, leading, I think, but then the tiredness kicked in and I just died a death. I pretty much jogged across the line – well, I ran 10.44, so not really jogging but I knew I was a lot quicker than that. There's a reason, though, why you don't generally run a 100m race after six rounds of the long jump.

All my focus that year was on completing the Commonwealth Games and European Championships double, and so far everything had been going to plan. But then my fragile body started misbehaving again.

I was preparing to compete in the Diamond League at Hampden Park in Glasgow when I noticed a pain in my knee. After what had happened in Paris the previous year, I wasn't about to take any chances. The doctors found I had a nerve problem, where fluid was accumulating on my take-off leg, and ten days before I was scheduled to compete, they gave me an epidural – the same procedure is administered to pregnant women to temporarily reduce pain, and it's often used in sports medicine to settle nerve issues. Fortunately, the knee responded fairly quickly to this intervention, and within a few days I was able to run and jump again. The double, it seemed, was back on.

I knew I had a task on my hands attempting to win two majors in the space of 17 days, with the Europeans following so hot on the heels of the Commonwealths, but despite feeling like I was being held together by tape, I was up for it.

My old adversary Chris Tomlinson was there in Glasgow for the Commonwealth Games, but he was on the decline so I wasn't worried about him. Instead, the main threat came from the South African Zarck Visser, although I definitely felt that I was the man to beat.

Qualification went fine. I jumped in long tights, which is unusual, but it was absolutely bloody freezing. And, of course, I didn't care about huge distances, just getting through to the final safely. I jumped 8.05m, qualified easily in first place and thought, 'Fine, I'll open up properly in the final tomorrow.'

After that, there was a mad 45 minutes of signing autographs and taking photographs with the brilliant crowd. Eventually, one of the officials tried to lead me away, but there were loads of kids there, patiently waiting, so I ducked under his arm and made a break for it to go back and do some more. The official got a load of abuse; he was just trying to do his job and ended up being shouted at by his boss down the radio, ordering him to pull me back. I didn't set out deliberately to annoy the organisers, but a lot of the spectators – many of them children – had paid a fair bit of money to watch and it seemed far more important to me to sign a piece of paper for them than to worry about holding up a press conference by 20 minutes. Funnily enough, my great escape from that guy even made the news bulletins.

The night before the final wasn't all that restful. The prefab houses they'd used for the athletes' village had paper-thin walls and ceilings, and every time anyone moved around it sounded like an elephant stampede. I jammed in earplugs just to try to get some kip.

The next day, conditions again weren't great. But I felt totally relaxed and thought to myself, 'Right, time to put in some effort. You've got a great opportunity of winning here.' Although I'd done so little jumping in training that whole year, my speed was good and I knew I could do it.

And so I did. I jumped 8.20m and won by eight centimetres from Visser – a margin that felt more comfortable at the time than it seems on paper. As I stood on the podium, my overriding emotion was, 'Wow, I've done it – I'm not just a one-hit wonder.'

The post-games partying was quite something, too. I spent a couple of days in the village afterwards, before I had to leave to get ready for the Europeans, and all sorts of stuff was going on. For a lot of the athletes it was the end of the season again, and they were out on the lash. One of our weightlifters had a big fight with an Aussie guy and laid him out in the middle of the street next to where I was staying, and then got removed from the village. A couple of Aussie boxers also got into trouble for fighting as well. There was a very weird end-of-season vibe. But for the track and field athletes, the season wasn't yet over.

After a major championships, it's usual for the body to switch off. All the adrenaline disappears and it's as if the system just wants to collapse. I was so keen to do the double that I had to fight this urge – there was still another big competition to go, and keeping my chances alive was as much a mental battle as a physical one. I went out for one night, to have a meal with my agent, and that was that. Back home, and back into training.

I wasn't exactly up for partying; all I wanted was to see Susie, who was very pregnant by now. She had come up to watch the Commonwealths with my family, but she'd been really tired and headed home straight afterwards, so I really wanted to be back with her.

All too soon, though, it was time to head to Zurich, where once again I felt that I was the one to beat. I hadn't competed in the Europeans since 2006, when I'd won a silver medal as a youngster. Now I was coming in as a favourite, trying to claim my second title in 17 days.

As with the Commonwealths, qualifying went smoothly. I jumped 8.03m and it felt easy. I knew I didn't need to push myself, and that I should save it all for the final. It was an odd, but brilliant, position to find myself in: the luxury of not needing to take all my jumps to qualify, and being able to put the pressure firmly on everyone else.

The weather had been rubbish all summer across Europe, and

it was no exception in Zurich. There was a bit of a headwind, it had been raining, and it was pretty cold. Not an afternoon for anyone to put in big distances. My confidence was high, but as I went through my warm-ups ahead of the final, there was a problem: Jonas, my coach, was nowhere to be seen. I started to get annoyed because there was no one to watch my runway, and spot the little things I was doing wrong. So when he finally appeared, I had a right go at him, bang in front of the packed stand, before charging off.

What I didn't realise was that Jonas had been suffering with dreadful stomach problems and been stuck in the toilet. So not only was he feeling grim, but his athlete was yelling at him in front of everyone. And he was hardly going to turn around and announce that he'd got severe diarrhoea, was he?

Of course, I apologised profusely, and Jonas' initial absence didn't affect my performance. In the second round, I jumped 8.27m to go into the lead, and when I went two centimetres further in the fourth I knew I had it in the bag. I performed a mild celebration – a small fist pump, if I remember – then walked back and looked into the faces of my main rivals, Louis Tsatoumas, who was second, and Kafétien Gomis, who came third, and I knew they had nothing left in the tank.

Such was my dominance on the day that I had the three longest leaps of the competition. It was a strange feeling, though, as the crowd didn't seem to be interested in the long jump at all. I celebrated, but there was nothing coming back, so I felt a bit deflated. It really couldn't have been less like London 2012. No one threw me a flag – which, as you will know from the TV, is pretty much the first thing that normally happens – so I just headed back to my seat and started packing my bag to leave, thinking, 'Well, that was a bit of an underwhelming finish to a major competition – and my second major title in a couple of weeks.'

At that point, Britain's victorious women's 4x100m relay team were coming around on their own lap of honour. I've always got on really well with those girls, especially Asha Philip, who is great and a real laugh. She very kindly said, 'Come with us! Join us!' So I sheepishly tagged along for part of their victory lap.

I had just won my third major championship, and somehow I was only a guest on someone else's lap of honour.

CHAPTER 24

Milo

Before that eventful athletics season of 2014, Susie and I had moved into our new house. It was February and we were surrounded by boxes, the usual chaos of moving day. I was in the kitchen, with a clear sense of priorities – trying to reassemble the coffee machine, first things first – when Susie burst in from the bathroom: 'I'm pregnant!' I had absolutely no idea what to say. It just stunned me.

I was so, so excited but I was unable to take it in at first. A minute before, I'd been thinking, 'Wow, there's a lot going on at the moment' and then suddenly this. Then the pure elation hit: 'I'm going to be a dad!'

A couple of months earlier over Christmas, Susie and I had been talking about the future. We knew we wanted to have children together, and we'd talked about how, if it happened now, it wouldn't be a bad thing. But I don't think either of us expected it to happen that quickly – it was virtually instant.

But one thing we immediately worried about was how to tell my family. This baby would be my parents' first grandchild, which you'd hope would be a cause for celebration; but, then again, their religion made things less straightforward, and my parents' reactions to big events are never predictable. After all, Susie and I weren't married – we still aren't, in fact – and, for my parents, that mattered.

They came over to the new house; it was still very much a work in progress and my dad had just been sanding down a wooden floor. There was dust everywhere, and Susie was actually feeling nauseous. We had a short break from the DIY work – though, true to form, my dad couldn't just chill out and was sandpapering a corner where the machine wouldn't reach.

My mum, I think, sensed that something was going on, and stood there, looking at us. And Susie gave me a look that said, 'Just do it, just say it now.' And I was panicking. I had a silly grin on my face – I couldn't get rid of it – but I was also scared about how they were going to react. What if it was really bad, or awkward? I was concerned for Susie too. So, I just froze.

Thankfully, Susie took control. 'Right, Andrew and Tracy ,' she said, 'we've got something to tell you. Could you come here, please?' My dad looked up at us from the corner where he was working and said, 'Yes?' Susie got them to sit down at the table, while I sat there with this silly expression on my face giggling. 'We're having a baby,' she announced.

My dad's reaction was fantastic; straight away he looked thrilled to bits. My mum, however, broke down crying. I was slightly alarmed, thinking, 'Oh God, she's so upset.' But she soon realised and said, 'No, no, I'm not crying because I'm disappointed! I'm crying because I thought I'd be waiting ages to be a grandparent.' We all hugged, and it was brilliant, exactly the response I'd been hoping for.

As well as having three children of her own, my mum has been a maternity nurse for the last 25 years, so she quickly slipped into that mode, asking about dates and scans and so on. It brought us all closer.

We had to tell my grandmothers, too – Grandma Carol, my mum's mum, and Grandma Gina, my dad's mum. My grandma Gina looks years younger than her real age and is one of the most stylish 85-year-olds I've ever seen in my life. Because she lived in Harpenden when I was young, I didn't see her that much, but now she's moved to Bletchley I've been delighted to get to know her better. I'd actually spent much more time with my grandma Carol and always got on well with her. When my granddad was still alive, I used to stay with them for weekends and had a great time. So her reaction particularly mattered to me.

We sat at the same table in my new house and I gave them the news. Grandma Carol looked instantly furious. She's one of those people who is terrible at hiding their emotions and will say whatever she feels, regardless of who she might offend. Her immediate words were: 'Well, I presume you are going to get married now, then?'

Susie replied: 'At some point, when we find the time.' And my dad added: 'Good luck with that.'

She'd had opinions on other family members having children out of wedlock, and her view hadn't changed. So she didn't take the news well, but at least she's a woman who stands by her morals.

Grandma Gina, meanwhile, had been sitting there in total silence. Eventually she said, 'Lovely, well done, dear,' and then walked into the back room to play with the dogs for a while. She stayed with us for a few hours, still not really saying anything, then eventually asked my mum – who had driven her over – to take her home as it was time for her to leave.

Grandma Carol's reaction was upsetting, of course, but I couldn't bring myself to be too down about it because Susie and I were so thrilled. Later on, she did congratulate us, and even attended a baby show with us where she bought our son's first rattle.

Soon after that, I had to fly to San Diego. As I've mentioned, the worst part of that trip was missing my baby's first scan. I was devastated not to be there with Susie, but her mum went with her, so she wasn't on her own. I couldn't help feeling I'd missed out on something very important: those little pictures you get – the first time you lay eyes on your future child – all of that was happening thousands of miles away. With the time difference in the States, it was night for me when the scan took place, so I got up ridiculously early and rang Susie. She immediately FaceTimed me so that I could see the photos. It was such a special moment, even over the phone.

When I got back home, we decided to make it public. We put a picture on Twitter of me and Susie standing on a balcony, holding a blown-up scan of our tiny baby – who would eventually be called Milo.

The story of how Milo came to have that name is quite a funny one. After the European Championships in August, Susie and I decided to take a little break together, and enjoy some time alone before we were a family of three. We went to Bath and stayed in a lovely hotel on the Royal Crescent. We had a beautiful big suite with a bedroom and lounge, and I was flicking through a posh magazine when I came across an article about a World War II pilot called Milo something. As a kid, I'd thought about joining the RAF and becoming a pilot – even now I still dream of obtaining my pilot's licence.

For some reason, this article resonated with me, and I thought how much I liked the name Milo. I mentioned it to Susie, who really liked it too. Coincidentally, she had just seen the name in a newspaper article and liked it too, but hadn't yet mentioned it to me. We didn't tell anyone else but, for us, Milo just felt right. We even researched it a bit on Google: nothing much came up apart from an ancient Greek wrestler called Milo of Croton, who was famed for his amazing feats of strength and won six medals in the ancient Olympics.

So that was it for me. I thought, 'We've got that flying connection, the Olympic connection – it's perfect.' From the first scan, we'd been referring to the bump as Nugget, but from that point I started calling him – as we knew it was a boy – Milo. Susie kept telling me not to, just in case when he was born we both decided he didn't look like a Milo, but in my head he already was.

Milo's arrival was anything but smooth. Susie had always wanted a water birth, and that's what we'd prepared for, along with hypnobirthing. But when she went into labour, it seemed as though everything was happening so fast and when we got to the hospital, there were no pools available, or any proper rooms, so we were put in a small side room. That threw us a bit. From there on, everything seemed to go wrong. Susie was in labour for hour after hour after hour, and nothing was happening – Milo was totally lodged in position.

Thankfully, he wasn't in any distress – his heart rate wasn't dropping or anything – but the doctors were saying that they had to get him out.

After eight hours of this, still nothing. Milo had somehow managed to flip around so that he was 'back to back' – which made labour both slower and much more painful for poor Susie. They tried to give Susie an epidural – a pretty painful process in itself – but it failed. They tried again – failed again. Third time – still no luck. At this point, I was getting quite distressed and emotional for her – she looked so incredibly tired and the anaesthetists weren't helping, just putting needles in her spine that didn't seem to do anything.

Finally, they said, 'Look, just let us use forceps and we can have him out in three pushes.' But the one thing Susie had said to me before we went to the hospital was, 'Whatever happens, no matter what, don't let them use forceps on me. I'll be in a dark place, in pain and everything – but just don't let them.'

I'll never forget it. Susie seemed to be drifting in and out of consciousness by that stage. Sometimes she was there; sometimes somewhere else entirely. The doctors asked her about the forceps too and she said, 'Yes, yes, do it.' Now I didn't know how to respond. She'd been so categorical before, saying that even if she was out of it, even if she said OK, not to let them use those forceps. I was torn between wanting desperately to protect her from this pain and for it to be over, and respecting what she had demanded of me.

I had to ask everybody to leave the room so that I could talk to her alone. I was quite tearful at that point, and felt so powerless. I had asked what the risks of using forceps were, and they'd explained the dangers, including permanent injury or disfigurement or even death. Of course, I knew, somewhere in the logical part of my brain, that these were remote possibilities, but still. They were terrifying words to hear.

Susie was hardly present, but I managed to hold her hand and get her to focus on me. I said, 'Look, are you sure this is what you want? Because it's the one thing you've told me not to allow, and I'm scared of getting it wrong.' She wasn't fully there, even though she was looking straight at me. Her body was just shutting out the pain, I guess, putting her somewhere else. But she said, 'Yes, do it – let them do it.'

So the doctors came back in, got everything ready, and cut Susie while wielding what looked for all the world like bloody salad tongs. They got hold of Milo's head and then, as they'd said, three pushes later he was out.

Susie was amazing. I remember her saying hello to him, all calm and relieved, I suppose, that he was out. And I was just a total blubbering mess. It had been such a stressful moment – far worse for Susie, of course, than for me but I was so scared I'd screw up. She actually said afterwards that she didn't think she had enough energy left in her body to cry; she just wanted to lie there with Milo, our brand-new little boy, on her chest.

That was the proudest, greatest moment of my life. Nothing in athletics or anything else comes close. All that mattered in that instant was my perfect little boy and the fact that Susie and he were both OK. He had a bit of bruising down his face caused by the forceps, but the doctors checked him thoroughly and reassured us there was no permanent damage and that the marks wouldn't last.

It wouldn't have mattered if they did. Nothing could take away from the fact that I was the happiest, proudest person in the world. An Olympic gold medal might have been the greatest thing to happen to my career, but nothing could match the joy I felt when I saw Milo's little face.

Or, to give him his full name, Milo Andrew William James Nugget Rutherford. William and James after our granddads, and Nugget to preserve the nickname he'd had when just a bump.

There's no doubt that having a child changes you. No parent would deny that for a second. And no amount of prenatal classes or lectures from your midwife, mum or friends with kids can prepare you for the initial lack of sleep or the crazy new routine you are suddenly plunged into: changing nappies, winding, feeding, winding again. Over and over, 24 hours a day.

It certainly wasn't easy, but from the beginning it was fun. I loved every minute of it. Even the distinctly unglamorous ones: I vividly recall being on a packed tube train, coming home from London with Milo. I was holding him and he puked all over my top and trousers. I was wearing head-to-toe black, covered in baby sick. I swear everyone was looking at me with a mixture of pity and horror. But I bet there isn't any new parent who doesn't have a similar story.

It's one hell of a steep learning curve, too. Susie was amazing from the start. She was breastfeeding, and I was in charge of winding. She would feed, I would wind, and then we'd do it all again what seemed like five minutes later. Of course, we were hideously sleep-deprived – what new parent isn't? – but we co-slept together and that really worked for us. In fact, after the first five or six weeks, things seemed relatively calm. We were prepared for the chaos to last, and for it to be extremely hard, but actually he slotted easily into our lives, and we made sure he could come everywhere with us, with minimal fuss. It helped, of course, that I wasn't really training or competing at that point, after a successful season. The absolute last thing I would have wanted to do was be away from Susie and Milo, even for a minute, in those early days.

Even when I went back into training properly, it all seemed to work fine. A lot of athletes talk about how having a child can have a positive effect. Sure, you are a bit sleep-deprived at first, but it does give you a whole new perspective on life. Things that might have stressed you out before – minor irritations – suddenly seem insignificant. But, at the same time, I had by no means lost my drive. In fact, I now felt I had more reason to do well. I had a family to provide for, a house to pay for, and a son for whom I desperately wanted to win every time I stepped on to the track.

CHAPTER 25

Bob Skeleton and Bake Off

I have never wanted to be defined solely as an athlete. Sure, it is an important part of my life, but when I hang up my spikes I don't want to be living off London 2012 anecdotes on the after-dinner circuit. So, in 2014, just as I had the previous two years, I juggled my track career with opening myself up to as many interesting new experiences as possible. However, I don't think many people expected that would include setting up my own clothing label.

After I fell out with Nike over their reluctance to offer me a decent contract, I thought, 'Why not give it a blast?' My idea was to create a range of quality but affordable sports gear, which would be at least as good as the big brands but at cheaper prices. And so, in May 2014, I created a small batch of clothing, under my own label, GRavity.

Would it surprise you if I said the whole process proved a little trickier than I expected? To start with, I signed a deal with a company in China, who made stuff that was so bad it burned a £10,000 hole in my pocket before I'd even got going. Then I had to find another manufacturer and pay them £25,000 to design everything and give me what I thought was enough stock. The problem was, I bought way too much, particularly because within a year, I ended up signing a new deal with Nike.

I enjoyed it on one level, even though it cost me a huge amount of money, because I learned a lot about business. Some days I'd send out a promotional tweet and we'd get 40-plus orders. Susie and I would then bag them up, write on the addresses and send them on – yes, it was a real cottage industry. Unfortunately, it became a bit tricky to run a business while also trying to win medals, and it also coincided with Susie becoming pregnant with Milo. Despite its brief, yet sweet existence, the GRavity brand provided me with a great learning experience and one that I hope to be able to build upon one day in the future.

As you will have gathered from the antics I got up to as a young man, I have always been a risk-taker. At the start of 2014, I admitted that I would love to represent Britain in the bobsleigh or bob skeleton at the Winter Olympics. It might have sounded crazy but I was completely serious: one of the attributes you need in both sports is speed over a short distance and I knew I had that in abundance.

Shortly after Milo was born, I left him and Susie for a few days to give it a go. My ideal world would be one in which I travelled all the time, but always with my family accompanying me. Susie, though, hates flying, and travelling with a child is a particularly testing challenge. I've always loved flying, and have never been remotely scared of it – but, funnily enough, on that trip, for the first time ever, I experienced a moment of fear. It wasn't that I was nervous about the flying itself, but it occurred to me that I was now responsible for another human being, that I should be thinking twice before doing anything that might put me in harm's way – for him, not for me.

At any rate, I flew out to Oslo with Andrew, and we then drove a few hours north to the great Olympic city of Lillehammer. We joined up with the British skeleton development squad. They were identifying young athletes with talent and had around ten in the programme, who were spending quite a lot of time on the ice.

I was being followed the entire time by a film crew, and was riveted by the whole process. Then it suddenly dawned on me that I was actually being put in a tray for the first time. The head of the British skeleton team took me to the shed, sized me up, and said, 'Right, OK, let's go and slide.' The fascinating thing about a sport in which your speed is controlled by gravity, not by your own volition, is that there's really no halfway between doing it, and not doing it. Once you are on the course, you're going down, whether you like it or not, whether it's your first or thousandth time.

High in the Norwegian mountains, I walked the course with the performance director, talking about the different turns and how to handle them. He mentioned that I should be particularly careful at turn 13 because a lot of people came a cropper there. Even with this advice, I had no reference point regarding the speed, and I was rather blasé about the whole thing. When you are walking around, in non-slip shoes with spikes on, at about half a mile an hour, it all looks perfectly sane. The gradient didn't look too bad, I thought – and nowhere near as terrifying as I'd expected it to be.

Then suddenly I was on a sled, and a coach was holding on to my legs, with a rather fragile-feeling grip. 'Oh God,' I thought. 'This is a really bad idea!' Then he let go.

For the first few seconds, I thought, 'Well, this isn't too bad.' Then I went into the first turn travelling much too fast and the acceleration was just outrageous. Of course, you have a helmet on, and you are lying prone, in a streamlined position. But adrenaline was coursing through my veins as I got quicker and quicker and quicker. I was desperately trying to work out where the hell I was on the course, whether I was anywhere near turn 13, but the corners were coming up every half-second, and everything I'd been told about technique had completely gone out the window.

Precisely 34 seconds later, it was over. The run had finished; I was still on the sled and I was half-whooping and cheering because it was such fun. My instant reaction was, 'Let's do that again!' So we jumped into the car, drove to the top, and I was off again.

It was a crazy, amazing experience. I ended up doing a third run as well. Afterwards, I chatted to the British skeleton people and they said they would happily teach me more if I was serious about taking it up full time because I had reached speeds of 100km/h and clearly had potential, despite being raw and new to the sport. While the idea of potentially competing in a Winter Olympics as well as the Summer Games was incredibly tempting, I was back on track having won Commonwealth and European gold. If it had been 2013, I would most likely have taken them up on their offer. But now that I had three of the four major titles in the bag, I desperately wanted the World Championship title in Beijing in 2015 to complete the set.

One of the other things I thoroughly enjoyed taking part in that year was *The Great Sport Relief Bake Off*. I've genuinely always loved cooking and, when I was younger, I even thought I might end up owning my own restaurant. My mum has always made amazing cakes, as has her mum, and when I was a kid I would love to get involved in helping her out. There was nothing my dad liked more than coming home from work to homemade baking. My mum's speciality is chequerboard cake, with pretty squares when you cut it, but she's also a dab hand at rock cakes and sponges. The masterpiece she made for Milo's first birthday was incredible.

Working as a waiter killed any ambition I'd had of going into the restaurant business, but I still loved cooking at home and when the celebrity version of *Bake Off* came along I thought, 'Fantastic! I'd love to be a part of that.' What's more, I definitely thought I could win it.

I'd baked for years, and, because of my diet, had even been experimenting with gluten-free recipes, so I thought I would be able to impress Paul Hollywood and Mary Berry. When I met them I felt nervous, although I thought that was a good thing – it only happens when you really care about something. I put a lot of pressure on myself going into the opening bake.

Our first challenge was to make ginger biscuits – the irony was not lost on anyone. I made them with a homemade lemon curd, so that they looked like eggy soldiers. The biscuits were the bread fingers, which were then dipped into the lemon curd/egg. They looked, I think, very good – and tasted great. But Paul walked over and gave his verdict: 'There's not enough ginger in your ginger biscuits.' I was instantly deflated. Great. There I was, a ginger, and I'd not put enough in my biscuits!

To be honest, I bristled a bit. Everyone who watches *Bake Off* knows how Paul can be, and it did get my back up. In the second challenge we had to make a banoffee pie, including our own shortcrust pastry. I didn't get it right, even though shortcrust pastry is really easy to make. Mine was terrible. There were cracks in it; I didn't leave enough time for the banoffee filling to set, and, when the moment came time to present the pies, mine looked like its innards had spilled all over the table, having escaped through the pastry.

Still, it was fun. I'd met British sprinter Jason Gardiner, who was also on the show, before and we had a laugh together, mainly about how terrible my pie looked. Ridiculous as it sounds, though, I was a bit annoyed with myself. Whatever makes me an athlete also makes me very competitive, and I couldn't turn that off, particularly when it concerned something I'd thought I was quite good at. It was a bit of a shock to discover that Paul didn't think I was nearly as accomplished as I'd thought.

The next day, we were asked to make a cake – whatever one we wanted. I decided to play to my strengths, and make something really epic. The idea was that it should say something about you as a person, so I created one with caramel peanut brittle on top, which was meant to look like sand in the long jump pit. Inside was a lovely chocolate cake, which I was really proud of because it was one of the best I'd ever made. I also thought it looked pretty impressive.

Again, Paul crushed me. Everyone else was complimenting me, 'Wow, your cake looks great!' But Paul came over, looked at it, took a bite and said, 'It's under-baked.' I was totally deflated.

When I got home, I rang my mum and kind of complained to her: 'You always said you liked my cakes!' 'Well, I always liked to encourage you,' she said. It turns out that I make quite a heavy cake compared to some people – including my mum, with her beautiful light sponges. So, perhaps it's partly my mum and my grandma's fault for being too nice about my cooking. Yes, I may be scratching around for excuses here.

CHAPTER 26

Glory in Beijing

The start of 2015 was magical: I was on a massive high, spending time at home with my beautiful baby boy, watching him change and grow with every passing day. But I also felt the responsibility of needing to provide for Susie and Milo, to make sure they never lacked for anything – and an overwhelming desire to make Milo proud.

Looming on the horizon was the biggest test I'd faced since London 2012, a second go at success in the Bird's Nest stadium in Beijing, at the 2015 World Championships. A major motivating factor was that I wanted Milo to be in a position where he would never have to worry about anything; he'd go to a good school, do all the activities he wanted, and lead a great life. My parents worked so bloody hard when I was a kid; I wanted everything for Milo that they hadn't been able to give me. I also knew that most professional athletes are past their best by their early thirties. I was now 28, so time was of the essence.

My new level of determination to win and bring home the bacon for my family seemed to be working. I jumped 8.17m early in the season, indoors, and I was delighted with that. But the thing that preoccupied me most was that I desperately wanted to go back to train with Dan Pfaff. Despite all of Jonas' excellent work and exceptional talent, I believed Dan could make the vital difference in me winning the World Championships in Beijing that August.

Steffen Kiel, my competition agent, spoke to the guys at Altis and finally we managed to iron everything out. We agreed that I would pay a fee to go there – I think it was $500 a week – and train with Dan. I couldn't have been happier.

When I arrived back in Arizona for the first day of training, I was really nervous, having left the last time under a cloud of negativity. But now the training centre was so different. When I'd first trained there in 2013 there were about six or seven of us; now there were 70-odd people – athletes, coaches, dedicated support staff. It felt like a totally different place. Everyone seemed quite happy to have me there, including Dan. He's not one to show his emotions, but I like to think he had missed me as much as I had him.

It was great to be back, and we just cracked straight on. We'd kept in touch with emails and the odd WhatsApp message in the intervening period, even though he wasn't officially my coach. Jonas knew about this, of course, and he too would ask Dan's opinion about things, so he'd always been there, in the background. Now I was properly back with him, so the moment I got there I said to him, 'Look, I want you to be fully my official coach again and come to competitions.' Thankfully, he was happy to do so, which was a huge relief and a fantastic result for me.

I trained in Arizona for a month and felt in good form. Apart from a minor tweak to my hamstring in my first week there, there were no major concerns. For most of the camp – as now seems common with me – I ended up focusing not on jumping but on the rest of the training. That tweak may well have happened because I was trying to impress Dan and the other jumpers there, and probably pushed a bit too hard early on.

However, I managed the injury so I was able to run quickly again, and when Dan had to leave in the last week of the camp, I did a load of really intensive sprinting with the others. Then, from the 40°C heat in Arizona I headed back to the UK to jump in Manchester, where it was about ten degrees. It felt more like December, such was the nasty headwind. Considering the grim conditions, a winning jump of just over eight metres was a satisfying result.

From Manchester, I travelled to Shanghai for the Golden Grand Prix. I was certainly moving between some extremes of temperature in those few weeks. There, I had one of my best jumping days, though the results didn't reflect it. I felt so fast, and was putting in huge leaps, but kept ever-so-slightly fouling, with a toe just nudging over the line. Small fouls, and big, big jumps – in the 8.40m region, pretty much every round. But the only one I managed to land legitimately was 8.08m, which was only good enough for seventh place.

It was an odd competition. I absolutely hammered my body, and, in fact, on the fifth round I tore my adductor muscle. I was pushing my body into a position that it had never been in before, thanks to the incredible speed I'd achieved. While the jumps weren't coming together yet, I could see from the reaction of the other coaches that they knew I was in good shape.

I returned to the UK and underwent some intensive work with my physio, Andy Burke, who did a great job of fixing me. However, when he came to watch my sessions in the lead-up to the next competition in Birmingham, I complained to him that I felt awful. He said, 'Hey, don't worry, you are moving fine!' But I felt as if I was very slow and that it was the worst week of training ever.

Of course, as soon as I got in front of the British crowd again, it was better. I jumped 8.35m – the joint second-furthest in my career – which was brilliant considering I'd had a tear four weeks earlier and had felt dreadful in the build-up. This constantly inflating and bursting bubble that was my body was showing signs of delivering something really special.

From that point on, I was just rolling; it was a near-perfect selection of competitions. After Birmingham, it was off to Oslo for the Diamond League. Again, it was cold, and again, I won. This prompted someone to comment that I was the best bad-weather jumper in the world, and the idea seemed to catch on. It was shaping up to be a fantastic season.

But there was one blip in this rosy picture and, unfortunately, it happened at the Anniversary Games – unfortunate because I was jumping in front of Milo for the first time and was desperate to do well. Also, naturally, I always want to perform well in front of a home crowd, and it was the first time I'd been back in that amazing stadium since 2012, so I had many reasons to feel quite emotional. Looking back, perhaps I tried too hard. I couldn't get it together. I gave it everything I had but I simply couldn't land one.

I finished third in the end, with 8.18m, behind the American Marquis Dendy and the South African Zarck Visser. I won't deny I was totally gutted. Afterwards, many of the crowd came surfing down to the barriers in front of the track, wanting selfies and autographs, and while I was hurting inside I made sure I took the time to smile or sign for every one of them. It's so important to engage with the fans, especially the young ones, because for the health of the sport athletics needs them to keep returning, year after year. If British athletes want to keep British audiences and continue to enjoy the profile they currently hold, they must never take the fans for granted.

Then, to my surprise, the next morning I woke up to one of the most ridiculous newspaper articles ever written about me, by a journalist from the *Independent*, who clearly knew little about me, or track and field. For a start, in order to flex his athletics credentials, this guy had a pop about the fact that I'd been lying on a towel. But at every competition since 2011, I have taken a towel to lie on, or something waterproof if it's wet, between my jumps. My former chiropractor, Gerry, had been obsessed by me lying down rather than slouching on a bench because it was better for my back. Plenty of other athletes do it too. But for this journalist, it was clearly beyond the pale.

He also wrote about how I looked like an 'Olympic tourist', and then had a pop at me for hanging around with spectators rather than rushing over to speak to the journalists in the mixed zone. Of course, just as we do with the fans, we have a duty to engage with the media if we want our sport to survive.

What was bizarre to me then – and still is – is the notion that spending time chatting to people, signing autographs for kids who want them, could possibly be seen as a negative. It wasn't as if I was there on a jolly. I was gutted to finish third, and desperately wanted to have jumped further and won. But after that was done and dusted, people were still being kind enough to want to talk to me, and I would certainly never dream of being so rude as to ignore them. I've seen some other big athletes disregard their fans, only sign a few autographs or take one or two pictures and then skulk off – that doesn't help anyone, not the athlete, and certainly not the sport that gave them their living.

At that point Dan had come to the UK to stay with me, and rightly urged me to forget about what had happened in London and move on to the next meeting in Stockholm, a few days later. I was keen to avenge my defeat on home soil by Marquis Dendy, and also in the back of my mind was the knowledge that Mitch Watt had jumped 8.54m in Stockholm, on a beautiful day in perfect conditions, in 2011. But, of course, when we got there, and it was wet and cold again. I swear most of the competitions I've been in have taken place in terrible conditions! I certainly don't have much luck with the weather.

I did have the fire in my belly that day. Underlying everything was a desire not only to prove a point, but to make this year the one in which I won the overall Diamond League long jump title – which meant doing as well in as many individual competitions as possible. For each win, I got $10,000 and there was also a bonus of $40,000 for whoever came top at the end of the year. Compared to some other sports, this is a tiny sum; plus, of course, you have to deduct your agent's fee and taxes and so on. But when I think back to what things were like when I was growing up, it was obviously a substantial amount of money.

In Stockholm, I only took four jumps, and it was the first time I'd ever had two 8.30m-plus jumps in the same competition. It was a great series: 7.98m, 8.14m, 8.32m and 8.34m. I was delighted with this, *and* I beat Dendy. That meant I still had a chance of clinching the overall Diamond League, and had won my final big competition going into the World Championships in Beijing. I was excited, thrilled and nervous about what they might hold.

Every time I went away for a competition, regardless of the success or otherwise, I missed Milo and Susie dreadfully. Having Milo was a huge spur for me to succeed, but it was hard to be away from him and to miss out on big events in his life. Luckily, Susie is amazing, and has always been incredibly supportive. She understands that the life of an athlete can be intense – and brutally selfish at times – but that I've always tried to include my family as much as I can.

The desire to be close to my family was one of the reasons why I asked my dad to help me build a competition-standard long jump pit in the garden of our house, so that I could train there without having to waste time travelling. Of course, Milo was delighted by this; as he got bigger, he started playing with plastic buckets and spades in the sand. He probably has the biggest sandpit of any child. We also had a gym installed in the house so that I could do my strength work too. It means that when I'm in the UK, all my training takes place either in my gym, garden or in the woods that back on to our house. Everything is within about a 200-metre radius. If you are resourceful, you don't have to trot off to the gym every time you want to work out.

I arrived in Beijing ten days before the World Championships, in great shape but arguing with UK Athletics – or British Athletics as they now were – on several fronts. For a start, I found their decision to replace the Union flag on our tops with their own logo to be a case of staggeringly bad judgement. I had tweeted a picture of the kit and said it was a stupid move. I even made a joke about stitching my own little flag on my kit. I am proud to compete for Britain, and I wanted to make it clear that I was jumping for my country not for the brand of British Athletics.

Every athlete I spoke to agreed with me – we all wanted the flag. A lot of people then blamed Nike, who had manufactured the kit, but I think that's nonsense. British Athletics buy it from Nike, so they are the ones putting in the order and giving directions on what to make. Besides, the previous year's Great Britain kit was manufactured by Nike and still had the flag.

I was also pretty annoyed that British Athletics had refused to release my lead therapist, Andy Burke, to come to Beijing in time for my arrival, instead keeping him at the team's holding camp in Japan to work with athletes who weren't really medal hopes. It seemed a bit vindictive. It's not as if you can simply swap therapists; in fact, the others who turned up then said they couldn't work with me because Andy was my guy. So I had no one to help keep my body in one piece, until Andy was finally allowed to fly in the night before I was due to compete.

This is such bad practice for an elite sporting organisation. People like Andy never get any credit, but seeing and being in constant touch with your therapist is an important part of preparation for a major competition. They are the people who keep your body, and indirectly your mind, in the right place to compete. And yet I only got to see mine on the warm-up track before the start. I was genuinely outraged.

It seemed that the unwritten hierarchy within British Athletics was at work. There were well-known inconsistencies – Mo had his full set-up of coaching and medical staff, while Jess had two therapists, but here I was going into the championships as a clear medal hope and I had nothing. Dan also got extremely angry and had a massive row with one of the team doctors. That lack of support had been symptomatic of their approach since London 2012.

I spoke to the *Guardian* on the eve of the World Championships, and in the interview I revealed that I had been paying for my own medical treatment for the last 18 months, and that I had asked British Athletics to help and they had said no – or rather they had told me that in order to receive any treatment I would have to make the three-hour round trip to Loughborough, an entirely counter-productive stance to take. The really frustrating part of this was that I knew there were athletes who had access to home treatment, funded by them. Of course I don't begrudge them having this, but I felt it should be more widely available. As I put it at the time, it's 'as if your national governing body is more of a hindrance than a help'. I cannot see why an athlete should ever have the perception that they have to fight British Athletics; but the decisions of the powers-that-be often made me feel that they didn't believe in me.

In fairness to British Athletics, after I won gold in Beijing they asked me how much I had spent over the past two to three years and, by going through all my records, I was able to show them it was something like £130,000. This was my own money that went directly on training and expensive medical support. They then agreed to help me in 2016, but as the interview with the *Guardian* demonstrated, it took a lot of public prodding to get them to change their ways.

One of the problems has always been that most athletes don't speak up – but I do. Some might say too much. Yet I truly believe we should be more vocal, because talking about it once you are retired doesn't help anyone. Some fellow athletes suggested I shouldn't be causing this controversy.

I guess if you aren't experiencing the inadequacies directly, you won't necessarily be aware that it's not the same for everyone else. In my opinion athletics in Britain requires its own formal union, to which all those who wear a GB vest must sign up. Its aim would be to protect the athletes, and to set clear and transparent rules governing what the federation is obligated to do for those who perform in their name. This is something I am extremely passionate about, and hope to get off the ground in the near future.

It wasn't just my contemporaries telling me to shut up. Before Beijing, the former Olympic 200m and 400m champion Michael Johnson also claimed I should do 'more jumping, and less talking'. For some people these aggravations would be distractions. But I used them – and my army of armchair critics – as further fuel to fire my desire to succeed. Only recently, a journalist wrote that I sometimes seem to thrive off some 'grit in the machine', and perhaps this is true, but I'd rather not have the grit at all.

I don't want to be a retired athlete in years to come still talking about what I did 20 years ago. I want to have helped the sport succeed; it's my life. In any other profession, if you're high up you can express an opinion and it will be treated with respect. Athletes aren't just robots within a machine, we make it. Why can't we voice our concerns and address problems as we see them? I always try to make sure my comments are well worded and thought through. I pick my battles, and don't rant on social media or postulate post-competition when I'm caught up in the adrenaline rush of the event.

In Beijing, I very much had a point to prove, and I couldn't wait to silence my detractors. I breezed through qualifying with a leap of 8.25m, while Dendy, who was considered my main rival, didn't even make it through after a huge jump of his was unlucky enough to be ruled as a marginal foul. Everything was going perfectly. Yet, just as always seems to happen, something went wrong in the 24 hours before the final.

I woke up with a nasty headache, feeling rough as old boots, and took a whole load of paracetamol to try to kill the pain. But it didn't have much effect, and by 2pm that day I was certain I wouldn't be able to jump. I felt that bad. I couldn't believe it – it was like a replay of the 2008 Olympic final when I'd ended up with a kidney infection and tonsillitis. It seemed barely credible that something similar was happening again in Beijing.

I don't know why it keeps happening, perhaps it's due to nerves and the stress of competition, but the body seems to be more susceptible to illness and injury right at the crucial moment. Adrenaline, though, is an incredible thing. I got to the warm-up still feeling a bit groggy and heavy-headed. But as soon as I stepped out into that stadium, the adrenaline kicked in. Almost instantly, I was pumped up and couldn't wait to get going. Just like that, a switch flipped, and I was ready.

The other jumpers, it seemed, were having more problems coping with the pressure. It was a fascinating competition. The runway was incredibly quick and some of the others were really struggling to nail any jumps at all. Jeff Henderson, a serious threat, crashed out halfway through, having failed even to reach eight metres, while another American, Mike Hartfield, fouled all three of his jumps.

I took only four rounds to win the World Championships – and two of them were fouls. It wasn't until a long time afterwards that I saw that one of those foul jumps was massive, the biggest jump of my life by a long, long way – easily over 8.60m, though obviously it didn't count. It was the one that got away. It was actually after that jump that Dan gave me a bit of a talking to. 'What on earth are you playing at? Why are you failing such massive jumps?' he said. 'Just get on in and close the night.'

The next round I managed to catch a big one, 8.41m, putting me firmly in the lead. And with that jump victory was sealed. Part of me wanted to keep going and land an even bigger one. But I was in the gold medal position, and in the end won by nearly 20 centimetres from the Australian Fabrice Lapierre who took silver. I now had the full set of major medals: Olympic, World, European and Commonwealth, the grand slam, placing me on a very short and prestigious list of British athletes alongside Daley Thompson, Sally Gunnell, Jonathan Edwards and Linford Christie.

Once again, I had managed to prove my critics wrong. As I flippantly put it to the BBC and Michael Johnson afterwards: 'Well, Michael, how do you like me now I am world champion?'

It was an emotional victory. I struggled not to cry but all I could think about was that it was Milo who'd won it for me. All of that day, in the lead-up, I'd been missing him and watching videos of him on my phone. He'd started saying 'Dad' and I had some lovely clips of us playing together. While I was away in Beijing, he'd taken his first couple of steps – and I'd missed them. It made me sad, but also utterly determined to win for him. If I'm not going to be there for these key moments, I knew I had better do my absolute best while I was away. When I was on the phone to Susie that day, I'd heard him chatting to himself in the background, and that had just pumped me up even more.

One of the reasons I didn't take all my jumps at the World Championships was that the final event of the Diamond League was scheduled for the following week in Zurich, and I still had a job to do – for me, for Susie, and for Milo. Those two events were stupidly close together, and I needed to place at least in the top three in Zurich to win the $40,000 bonus. And, to do that, I had to get there in one piece.

Going into that meeting, there was some fairly hostile talk from the American jumpers. They were piping up all of a sudden, saying that I was lucky to win in Beijing and, in that very American way, that they were going to 'take me down' in Zurich. Perhaps they thought if they got under my skin, I'd screw up; but they obviously didn't know me well enough, because I always find such gamesmanship funny. They didn't realise they were just providing that 'grit in the machine' that I seem to thrive upon.

During our first night in Zurich, Andrew, Steffen and I were in the dining room in the hotel. The Americans were there too and either pretended they hadn't seen me or looked at me with a smirk on their faces. I just gave them a big grin and was deliberately overly friendly in return, because I enjoy this kind of psychological stuff. No athlete has ever managed to get inside my head. I love it when they think they can, only to realise it has no effect.

So we went into competition. It was one of those nights when the lead switches back and forth; and I had a bit of fun messing around with the Americans. Dendy had jumped into the lead, and I was just lying there on my towel. I hopped up and said, 'OK, no problem.' I got on the runway and jumped

8.32m to equal him exactly – winning the night on a countback as well as that $40,000 bonus.

It was the perfect end to a perfect year. I'd said I wanted to win the Diamond League *and* the World Championships and I'd done it. At one of the first meetings of the outdoor season when I'd announced that was my target, some of my rivals were chuckling away. They weren't laughing now.

CHAPTER 27

A Rumble With Fury

Being nominated for the Sports Personality of the Year award at the end of 2015 was a huge honour. This award ceremony holds a special place in the minds of all aspiring young sportspeople, so it was almost a dream come true when I was shortlisted. I say 'almost' for a reason. Now, the 'personality' part of that title has always been tricky to define; we could argue until the cows come home about what exactly it should mean. There are plenty of deserving sportspeople who've been nominated in the past who probably don't fit the classic definition of being a 'personality', but I am fairly sure the award shouldn't go to the person in sport who can be the biggest arsehole.

This is why I found it difficult to swallow that the name of the world heavyweight champion Tyson Fury was on the shortlist alongside mine. I was horrified, and I wanted no part of it.

A few weeks earlier he had given an interview in which he said: 'There are only three things that need to be accomplished before the

Devil comes home. One of them is homosexuality being legal in countries, one of them is abortion and the other is paedophilia.'

To come out and equate homosexuality with paedophilia was disgusting. He is evidently a very troubled, and possibly unwell, man. And to use religion, in particular, to condemn other people was just wrong too. Perhaps having a gay young sister made me particularly sensitive to the distress and dangers caused by Fury's comments, but I have a pretty strong moral compass and would have spoken out against him regardless. This calls into question the very notion of whether, as sportspeople, we have a duty to be role models. I believe we do. Why else do we celebrate our sportspeople if it's not to excite and inspire ourselves and others to work hard to achieve our own goals? Some feel otherwise, of course, but it is my belief that if you are in a position of influence thanks to your sporting ability, then the moment you choose to speak publicly about something other than your sport, as Tyson did, you by default become responsible as a role model.

I called Andrew, and told him I was thinking of pulling out. Initially, he was shocked, but when I explained that I really wanted to make a stand, he was behind me. We sat down with Susie and decided to write a letter to the BBC. I thanked them for the opportunity, and politely asked to be removed, stating my reasons as logically as I could – the crux being that, though it was their choice who they nominated, I would feel uncomfortable being part of a ceremony celebrating a group of sportspeople that included a man with views which clash so much with my own.

The management team that then represented my commercial and media commitments were very much against this, and tried to persuade me not to pull out. The phrase they used was stark, and in my eyes inexcusable: 'principles have a price'. That was when I knew I would be leaving their agency.

I was actually quite proud of the letter I wrote to the BBC. I felt it was very measured, not some big showy statement. The BBC immediately got back to me, asking if we could please leave it with them for 24 hours, which seemed fair. What we hoped might happen was that they would decide not to nominate Fury after all, as they were coming under a huge amount of scrutiny for it. Naively, I thought perhaps they could de-nominate him.

The BBC took a while to get back to me. In the meantime, people in the agency started muttering that I'd been a fool, and ruined my relationship with the BBC, the major broadcasters of athletics events in Britain. They were advising me that, if I wanted to be any kind of pundit or presenter in the future, I had to get on with them and not rock the boat. As you may have gleaned by now, I am somewhat impulsive and cared not a jot about this.

A couple of days passed, and I still hadn't heard from the BBC. As far as I was concerned, I was no longer going to be attending the ceremony and my name would not be on the list at all. However, while waiting for their response, the story somehow became public, first reported by a BBC news source. But, and to my astonishment, it had been spun, claiming that I was 'considering' pulling out, which wasn't the case at all – there was no consideration about it, I'd written to them and clearly asked to be removed already.

I am not sure what was going on behind the scenes – although

I have my suspicions – but the Beeb's statement unfortunately made it look as if I was fishing for sympathy or future votes. I started getting phone calls from presenters and friends, saying that it was a really bad idea to withdraw. People warned me against it, and then someone even said the Olympic pentathlon champion Mary Peters, who had won gold at the 1972 Games, wanted my number to talk to me. It started to feel faintly ridiculous.

In the meantime, I attended the Sports Journalism Awards. Along with Jess Ennis, I won the main award, which was fantastic. I was also encouraged to come forward with my opinion because a lot of people there agreed with me about Fury and wanted my thoughts first hand. They'd actually invited him initially but then withdrawn the request after he made threatening comments to the *Mail on Sunday* journalist Oliver Holt, in the wake of the interview that started the whole furore.

I got the impression that the BBC were actually almost stirring it up, like it was some kind of weird pantomime. The running order of the show was meant to be secret, but I was told by another athlete on the nomination list that if I attended I was supposed to be first up, which would put me in the incredibly awkward position of having to respond to possible questions about the situation, with Fury having the last word. I actually rang up and quizzed them about this and their rationale was – in all seriousness – that boxing was a violent sport so it had to be on later. This, in a show entirely about sport. Insane. If the sport, in their eyes, is too brutal to show at 7pm, then perhaps best not nominate its main protagonist anyway?

Things had escalated way beyond what I'd originally intended, which was to protest quietly and just withdraw from the whole shebang. I wasn't trying to make some big public statement about how morally correct I am. I simply wanted it to be known by the BBC that it was my strong belief that Fury should not be involved and that I felt uncomfortable being put in that situation.

Meanwhile, my mum and dad then got in on the act. They were particularly annoyed by the fact that I had pulled out because it was something of a dream of theirs to see me nominated for that award. I really, really fell out with them over it; this was a rupture of serious proportions, even by our standards. I didn't speak to my mum for about six weeks afterwards because, the way she saw it, Fury's views didn't affect me directly, so I should have stayed out of it.

In the end, I felt compelled to go. I didn't enjoy it one bit; I turned up late and left as soon as I possibly could. Looking back, though, I should have stuck to my original decision because, by the end of it, it got me nowhere and I looked like I'd done it for show.

Another shame in all this is that, at some point in the chain, someone leaked news of my withdrawal for their own gain. I no longer think the BBC was at fault, though of course at the time I couldn't help but draw that conclusion. My suspicion is now leaning towards the idea that someone on my side perhaps threw me under the bus to protect their relationship with the BBC. I sincerely hope, though, that I am wrong and that it was purely a case of a genuine, unintended leak.

What followed was the worst period of abuse I have ever suffered on social media; the trolling was disgusting, with Susie and even Milo also threatened, it was truly horrendous. I guess that pathetic phrase 'principles have a price' was correct.

CHAPTER 28

A Far From Ideal Preparation

I was thrilled to join the elite list of British athletes who have completed the full set of major titles. Yet heading into 2016 I was chasing an even more alluring prize: becoming one of the very few people to retain an Olympic long jump title. The plan for the year was simple: go to the World Indoor Championships in Oregon in March, then the European Championships in Amsterdam in July, and, of course – the big one – Rio in August. And, of course, win them all.

I hit the ground running at the start of the year with an indoor competition in Albuquerque, New Mexico, where I jumped, in my very first outing of 2016, 8.26m – a new British indoor record. To say it wasn't the greatest jump technically would be an understatement. When I saw it on YouTube I thought I was as rusty as hell. But it felt pretty easy. Given that there were still six months to go before the Olympics, it was an early indication of the form I was in.

However, the next day I woke up in a lot of pain. In the lead-up to the event, I'd been running through my standard drills, the ones we do every session, six days a week. I did one – a very basic foot drill – a bit too fast and hard and felt a small pop. I had some treatment, and everything seemed more or less OK; so, because I was really keen to go to Albuquerque and jump against Mitch Watt again, I went ahead.

That night, I was hobbling a bit, and it was starting to get a bit sore, but by the following morning it was obvious that I had torn – yet again – an adductor on the left side of my groin. I remember thinking, 'Oh, for God's sake, I can't possibly have pulled an adductor doing a simple ankle dribble – that's just nigh-on impossible.' But I had. Already, after my very first competition, my plans for the year had gone completely awry. I'd have to miss the World Indoors in Oregon.

It was disappointing, of course, but there was a silver lining, as it meant I had to return to the UK early for a scan, so I got to see Susie and Milo sooner, and also pick them up and bring them back to the States with me. Susie, understandably, wasn't keen on flying on her own with Milo. What sane parent wants to fly long haul with a baby, on their own?

The scan showed that there was a 2cm hole in my adductor, so I had a few weeks of treatment at home to let the injury heal. Then we all set off for America, where we would be staying in the same place together as a family for three months. It was a bit like we were decamping and moving the family to Arizona.

It was extremely frustrating to have to follow the World Indoors on Twitter, knowing I should have been there. Missing out on an opportunity to win that major title – one of the few not on my CV – was a big blow.

I always hate pulling out of a major event. Not only is it disappointing to see a medal chance slip by, but it also gives a sign to your competitors that your body must be fragile and that perhaps things aren't going so well. But far more worrying news was to follow. Dan hadn't been feeling well, and now it turned out that he had a stomach illness. It wasn't cancer but it was serious enough to mean that he would have to receive chemotherapy as part of his treatment. When I got back to America, he was in hospital in Austin, Texas. Dan is not just my coach but a good friend, so his condition played on my mind a lot, particularly as I feared he was underplaying the gravity of it to me.

On a more selfish level, it also meant he was not going to be around for most of that year. So I was training solo, worrying about Dan and building up my rehab. But it helped hugely that I had ended up living in some sort of multi-family home in Arizona. There was Susie and Milo, and also my best mate Andrew – who, in the light of my struggles with agents, had now formally taken on the role of being my manager – and his wife Sara, plus one of Andrew's training partners, Richard. At various points in the trip, my mate David, his girlfriend and even my mum, Susie's mum and her stepdad also came to visit. It became like some sort of commune.

I was starting to train very well when my body clearly decided that having a torn adductor muscle wasn't enough in an Olympic year, so why not throw in appendicitis as well? We had gone to a park to play with Milo. I was feeling a bit rough, like something I'd eaten hadn't quite agreed with me – nothing major, at that point, just a bit sore. But it started getting a lot worse. Andrew laughed at me; he thought I had a case of really bad trapped wind. So picture the scene: the idyllic American family dream, with parents throwing balls to their kids, picnic blankets spread out, happy, smiling people. American as apple pie. And there's me, on a blanket in the middle, with my bum up in the air trying to dislodge what I thought was gas. I looked like a complete idiot, and we were all laughing about it.

Then the others decided they were hungry, so we headed off to get a burger. As we were leaving, the pain was becoming increasingly troublesome and I thought, 'If this is wind, it's a bit bloody intense.' I got into the car and Susie said, 'Look, let's go home and get you into bed.' But I insisted, 'No, no, I'll be fine, it's just wind.' I didn't want her to miss out on the burger, because Andrew and Sara had been talking it up and saying how good this place was and, thanks to my diet, we very rarely eat out.

It was about a 20-minute journey to the restaurant and, by the time we got there, I was in so much pain I really shouldn't have been driving. I was sort of semi-curled up on the seat, just about able to hit the accelerator or brake, but twisting into different positions to try to fend off the searing pain in what turned out to be my appendix. I parked up, and said to the others, grimacing, 'I can't move. I'm just going to have to stay here.'

I was trying to downplay it as much as I could, so Susie asked, 'Want me to grab you some food?' I replied, 'No, do you know what, I don't want anything. I don't actually feel that well.' Anyone who knows me will tell you that me turning down food – particularly a famous burger – is unheard-of. So something was clearly very wrong but I insisted they go and eat. By the time they returned – it felt like forever to me but was probably about an hour – I was lying there, sweating heavily. The pain was becoming truly excruciating. Susie said, 'I've got you a burger and a shake' – nothing seemed less attractive than food at that moment. Then I drove back, but I was kind of in a ball, peering over the steering wheel, driving really slowly to keep her and Milo safe.

When we arrived home, I pretty much crawled through the door and into bed. I don't remember much after that except for being in a lot of pain, sort of drifting in and out of sleep and people coming and going. According to the others, it was clear I was in a bad way. They chose to keep a close eye on me and let me sleep. I didn't realise it, but they were all very worried and checked on me every hour.

Andrew rang his dad, Dr Chris Steele, who's been the resident doctor on ITV's *This Morning* for 30 years and in my eyes is a total legend. He'd been really helpful to us as a family when my granddad was ill, too. He advised Andrew on what to do and what to look out for.

When I woke the next day, the pain had eased a little. But when Andrew spoke to him again, he advised us to go straight to the hospital. He'd obviously been wondering about the possibility of appendicitis, and one of the signs, apparently, is that the pain can get better before it then gets a whole lot worse again, so he thought I should go and get it checked out. At that point, the pain had lessened from the levels of the previous night, but it was still radiating horrendously down my side.

We drove to the hospital – and into the strange, Kafkaesque world of private healthcare in America. The utterly bizarre experience started even before we got there, when we had to do some research online to check out which hospital had good ratings, in itself a strange concept for someone used to the NHS. But that turned out to be the more straightforward part of the day.

When I arrived, I quickly found myself on the receiving end of a slick sales pitch to relieve me of my appendix. Andrew and I walked through the doors, and I said, 'Hi, I'm not sure if this is the right place to come? I've got this pain . . .' The lady's response was immediately: 'Oh no, you must absolutely stay and have it checked out.'

I waited, and eventually got seen by the triage nurse. She asked me if I wanted some pain relief. I thought I was probably OK, but she was being quite pushy. Of course, in a British hospital you wouldn't think twice about this, so I agreed, only to find her coming back with morphine. I said that I wasn't in that much pain – I'd been thinking she'd give me some ibuprofen tablets or similar, and, besides, as an athlete, I couldn't take any morphine without a therapeutic use exemption from the doctor. Afterwards, we realised it was a sales tactic, as morphine was the most expensive drug. Luckily, I had the presence of mind to hold off . . .

Then they brought in a doctor, who walked in and asked, 'Hello, do you still have your appendix?' When I said yes, he replied: 'Well, do you want to keep it?' He hadn't even examined me at that point, literally hadn't touched me.

'Um, well, that depends,' I said, thinking the most important factor in all this was whether it actually needed to come out or not. How naive I was.

'We may as well whip it out,' he announced. 'Someone will

be in shortly to sort out the next step!' And he was gone. That was the only contact I had with a doctor during this whole process.

A good hour passed, maybe two, which was odd as it was a private hospital and appeared to be empty. Outside my door, no one seemed to be doing anything. My nurse was just sitting there, twiddling her thumbs.

Later, I realised that you got billed by each hour you were in that room, so of course no one was in any rush to get me out of there.

Then a woman arrived to take a deposit. I asked how much they needed, and she said, 'Whatever you want, as much as you like.' She just plucked figures out of the air: 'Well, some people do $500, some $5,000.' It didn't help that they had no price list for anything. We told her that private hospitals in the UK usually have some kind of price structure. Surely there must be a ballpark figure? 'Well,' she said, 'for some people it costs as little as $15,000, for others it's $100,000.'

How do you respond to that? It was only afterwards that I realised I had made two big mistakes: first, I didn't have travel insurance, and because of this I had told them when I arrived that I was going to be self-paying. That was error number two, and an invitation to them to mess me around. What I didn't know at the time was that if you don't have insurance, and don't commit to be able to pay yourself, they are legally obliged to treat you, at their own expense.

The ordeal wasn't over there, because the hospital then suggested I should get a scan, to be sure. 'How much will that cost?' Andrew and I asked.

'Oh, there's no way of telling,' came the reply.

'Of course there is – this is outrageous!' we said.

Eventually, they said that a CT scan could cost up to $3,500, which is unbelievable for something so relatively simple; it wasn't even an MRI.

At this point, we were still unsure whether my appendix was going to rupture, so we didn't really know what to do. Trying to think on our feet, Andrew frantically searched online for specialist travel insurance that you could buy when you were already abroad.

In the end I had the scan, and it showed that my appendix was inflamed. Unsurprisingly, this led to the doctor insisting I should have it out. But God, I really didn't want to pay $15,000, let alone a possible $100,000.

At this juncture, they suggested I stay overnight and make the decision in the morning. Again, Andrew and I asked how much this would cost and once more they refused to give a definitive answer: 'It's impossible to tell – all depends on what the doctors choose to give you.'

It began to feel as if we were dealing with a dodgy second-hand car business rather than a hospital. I think we'd all had enough at that point, so that was it, we decided to leave. Andrew called his dad again, who said it could be something called a grumbling appendix, where it can flare up, but then settle down again once you take antibiotics. We decided to risk it, and headed home.

I remember Andrew was really quite worried that night. He insisted that Susie left our bedroom door open and kept the phone on at all times so that we could mobilise the hospital and get there quickly if the pain started again, because if the appendix ruptures, you have to act quickly. Luckily it didn't, and eventually we managed to see a specialist who was much more sensible and just gave me the antibiotics to settle it down.

That whole episode ended up costing about $6,500 and made me profoundly, hugely, grateful for the wonder that is Britain's National Health Service. Sometimes, you don't realise how much of a good thing you have until you experience the alternatives.

The pain was much better but took about ten days to go away completely, and I was still feeling a bit rubbish. However, despite this – and despite it being so soon after such a serious medical complaint – I decided to jump at my first outdoor competition of the year, in Long Beach, just south of LA, so we all headed off to California. I knew it could potentially be a good competition, as I'd heard Jeff Henderson was going to be there too, more or less in his own backyard. The conditions, too, were perfect. Lovely and hot, great winds, a beautiful newly laid track – just wonderful for jumping. So, in round one I managed to jump a really impressive 8.30m.

Doing that is a great feeling. It's like putting down a marker, saying to your rivals: 'Go on then, do better than that.' I then jumped 8.18m and 8.19m after that, and I think Jeff jumped 8.19m, so I beat him quite convincingly, and that filled me with renewed confidence. Only a matter of ten days after appendicitis, preceded by a troublesome adductor injury, I was still capable of turning up and beating the best in the world. How could I not feel emboldened by that?

The night before that competition, something else happened

that really helped, too. Carl Lewis came out with a bizarre and massive rant about the state of long jumping, accusing us all of being lazy, of not wanting to jump big, and saying that if he'd jumped my winning distance in London, he'd have said, 'Don't measure that, make it a foul.' He implied that I was, in his words, pathetic. It was quite laughable really, coming from a guy who tested positive for drugs three times during the US Olympic trials in 1988 but was still allowed to compete in the Seoul Games.

Guys like him forget that most of the current crop don't cheat. I thought his remarks were pretty disgraceful, and I ended up returning fire by pointing out that I really didn't need validation from him. It seemed to me that he was just desperate to get back in the spotlight, and it was great to see that he actually got a lot of flak for his rubbish, whereas my tongue-in-cheek retort received the opposite. I think he expected people to agree with him; he certainly wouldn't have anticipated such a scathing reply from me. His comments completely backfired, particularly as people on social media were only too keen to remind him about the drugs tests he had failed. Comments such as those only diminish any performance legacy he has. In particular, his foolish and flippant points about Usain Bolt in 2008 have really fallen flat in the years since – why not just act with some dignity and class, and celebrate great performances, even if they're not your own?

My early season consisted of a few more competitions in California. They went pretty well, some better than others, but all too soon my spell in the States was at an end: it was time to return to Europe, where the real business would begin, with Rio edging ever closer.

I started back at the Manchester CityGames, in front of

thousands of spectators in Albert Square, with a leap of 8.20m. I was happy to take that given the conditions – cold and wet, of course – and the fact that on my first attempt the board broke, collapsing underneath my foot, which was very scary.

Next up was a trip to Rome for my first Diamond League of the season. I went in knowing that the IAAF had given the rules an unwelcome shake-up in the field events. In the long jump, instead of the top eight getting three extra jumps after the first three rounds, now it would be only the top four. Why they chose to do this, without consulting the athletes at all, I do not know. But that rule tweak had a flaw that was blindingly obvious to everyone except the Diamond League organisers: there would be hardly any time to rest between jumps in rounds four, five and six for the four remaining competitors. I didn't like that at all – nor did anyone else. Everyone I spoke to about it thought it was ridiculous, and also that it showed just how little the organisers seemed to value jumpers.

I wasn't that keen on going to Rome initially. But it's a great place to jump, and I'd done really well there in 2012 – also in an Olympic year. And while I won with a leap of 8.31m in those rushed final rounds, I also ended up jarring my neck. The last round was farcical: first, the whole thing was going too quickly anyway, but then, just as I was about to launch myself down the runway, a cameraman came and stood right in front of me to record the steeplechase.

I should have taken a rest after coming home but three days later I was signed up to compete in the Birmingham Diamond League. I was very tempted to withdraw, but when you reach a certain level in the sport, there are a few more things to consider before you think of pulling out of a competition. Of course, there is the financial consideration: you receive a quite generous appearance fee to compete, especially at home events, and to miss out on this would sting. Secondly, and most importantly, if you have a decent profile in British sport, you become a draw and one of the reasons fans will by tickets and come along to an event, and this adds a level of responsibility that should be shouldered. I felt it would be unfair on the supporters who had come to watch me, among others, compete and I didn't want to let them down; I wanted to do well on home soil.

If the sport is to continue to prosper, it needs its domestic stars to compete in front of domestic audiences. However, in this case I desperately wish that discretion had proved the better part of valour, and that I'd listened to my instinct to pull out. After a first-round jump of 8.17m, I thought I had shaken off the neck niggle. But on my second effort, something went wrong as I was in the air, and I ended up hitting the sand in a sort of split-leg position, which in turn caused me to whip my neck around at speed. I remember at the point of impact thinking, 'That was *not* a good position to land in.' I was frustrated, too, because it would have been a big jump had I landed it properly. But I got back up, climbed out of the pit, and waited for my turn to jump in round three. While I did so, the whole of my left side began lifting up; the result of my shoulder trying to protect the neck. But I tried to battle through, telling myself, 'I'll be fine; it'll be fine.'

It might sound a bit nuts, but in a competition I sometimes talk to my body as if it's a completely separate entity to me or my consciousness. I probably started doing it because my body has broken down so many times that it feels as though it needs a little coaxing along. I don't do it every time, but if I know there's a problem, I have a word with myself. I move around a bit and – this really is a bit odd – I apologise to my body for what I've put it through. And I ask it to give me one more jump, just one more, then I promise we won't jump again today, 'I'll take you home and give you a good rest.' It's as if I'm talking to a skittish horse, or how I imagine a rider talks to a horse: reassuring it – or settling it down like I do with my dogs.

So, at the end of the runway I was doing that, asking my body for one more half-decent jump. I charged down and jumped just over eight metres, which I knew wasn't good enough to give me three more jumps. Not that I would have taken them. Because even that third attempt was a bad idea and now I couldn't even move my neck.

I saw Andy Burke, my physio, who said that everything was exceptionally tight through and around my neck. He gave me some treatment to try to relax the muscles, and I got in the car with Susie and went home. I did what I often do after Birmingham, and stopped in Corley services on the way home for a KFC. I actually wait in the car and ask Susie to go and get it, because every time I stand in the queue for any kind of remotely unhealthy food anywhere in the UK, I get heckled by people telling me I shouldn't be eating that and I should be concentrating on jumping! But I needed my comfort food that day.

The following day, I went to London to have a scan to determine the extent of the problem. I had a quick assessment with Noel Pollock, a sports medicine doctor for British Athletics, who said that while the neck was very tight the scan didn't show any damage to the spine or the neck itself, which was reassuring.

Oddly enough, that morning I'd woken up with a bit of a blocked-up ear. My hearing seemed a little skewed and I'd found myself turning my head to listen to Susie out of my other ear. I'd said to her, 'I think I might be getting an ear infection,' because I really couldn't hear well at all.

So while Noel was telling me not to worry, it was nothing too bad, just a kind of whiplash injury, and I'd be fine, I asked him if he could have a quick look in my ear. I explained about my hearing and he had a look down the canal. There was nothing there, though. Even so, my hearing was noticeably deteriorating, from being a bit muffled to almost complete deafness. Noel thought this was odd too, and referred me to an inner ear specialist on Harley Street .

I headed straight to see the specialist, who did lots of tests. I had to go into a silent booth and put headphones on and try to listen to certain sounds. He then had to push an electrode through my eardrum to be able to reach the inner ear part he wanted to test, so there was a horrible build-up of pressure as they pushed what felt like a drawing pin through. Just thinking about it now makes me feel nauseous. Then they ran some more tests and said, 'OK, we won't know any results until tomorrow, so go away and come back in the morning.' The last thing the doctor said to me was, 'This is pretty bad.' He was an odd one – not exactly the most tactful bedside manner . . .

So the next day, I went back. The hearing hadn't improved at all; if anything it had got worse, but I wasn't sure if that was because of the stuff they'd shoved in my ear. The doctor sat me down and said, 'Right, I've got the test results back, and this is pretty severe.' I was a bit stunned. 'What does severe mean?' I asked. 'Well, you have a significant loss in hearing, and it's something quite unexpected with the trauma that you've told me about.'

I was thinking, 'God, this isn't good. This expert, a real specialist in ears, is telling me it's bad – it must be really bad.' Noel was there with me, too, and he asked lots of questions because we were all trying to figure out what was going on. It transpired that the trauma I'd experienced – the whiplash – had been severe enough to force fluid into a compartment of my inner ear. That overloaded the amount of fluid that was meant to be in there, which in turn blocked the hair cells that received information. In simple terms, I had lost the ability to hear properly in that ear – at least for the time being.

They used a scale from one to 15 to measure hearing response and, if I remember correctly, for quite a few of the tests I scored zero. So, clearly it was not great.

Naturally, there was a big question I needed answering. 'So,' I asked, 'what's the likelihood of me getting my hearing back?'

'You've got a one-in-four chance of being permanently deaf in one ear,' came the reply.

This was all really scary. Dealing with the possibility of permanent deafness was bad enough, but what I didn't realise was that my balance was also being affected. It was horrible and incredibly frustrating: I couldn't have a proper conversation with anyone because if there was noise in the background, my brain couldn't work out what was happening where, or the difference between the sounds. One ear was struggling to do the job of two.

I rang Andrew in a panic. Perhaps over time it would be fine, but I really didn't want to be deaf in one ear at the age of 29. I wasn't even thinking of the impact it might have on performance, just about my life as a whole. I know now that Andrew had done some research and found out that this could affect my balance and coordination, and therefore my ability to jump, but he didn't mention it to me so as not to scare me further. A couple of days later, however, I woke up, got out of bed and everything was moving around me. I was completely still, but it felt like I was waist deep in the sea, with the tide pulling me back and forth. My balance was all over the place. So now, on top of worrying about my hearing, I couldn't even stand up properly. It was shocking to realise how something as innocuous as jumping into a sandpit, which I'd been doing all my life, could be so potentially damaging to my health.

I genuinely feared that not only were my Olympic chances ruined, but perhaps even my long jump career as a whole. Andrew and I discussed the possibility of me having to pull out, and how we would deal with that eventuality – how I was going to pay the mortgage, what contracts would be void and so on.

The whole experience really shook me. I'm not sure I've got over it even now, as I write this, several months on. There are medications available to help combat the side effects, but the reality is I'll probably have this problem lurking, if not actively harming me, for the rest of my life. The condition is called cochlear hydrops, and, according to what I've been told, when you damage the inner ear a certain level of trauma never goes away. The specialist also said that I'd probably damaged it before without realising, because they could tell from the tests that there was evidence of previous trauma, the recent one just adding to it.

Though the balance issues improved, this setback unnerved me like no other injury had before. With the European Championships only a month after Birmingham, and the Olympics on the horizon, it was a very stressful time. The initial treatment even prescribed five to ten days of prednisolone, a medication that needs a therapeutic use exemption from the IAAF under World Anti-Doping Agency rules, but simultaneously dampens your immune system. Thankfully this was outside of competition, but as well as the ear condition harming my ability to train and compete, the medication was also putting me at risk of illness, so I couldn't train. I felt so horrible on it, I actually stopped taking it early.

TUEs in sport are a contentious issue, and it has become clear that they can be misused, especially in endurance sport. I guess it's like anything, if it's open to abuse, some people are going to take that opportunity. In my career I've been unfortunate enough to need other TUEs to treat various injuries, but every time I've had one I've felt so awful. I couldn't train properly and I had no idea what sort of form I'd be in when I got to Amsterdam for the Europeans.

With Dan being unable to travel to Europe, I went out to meet him in Arizona for an extremely short training camp. Although a logistical challenge in terms of all the travel, it was worth it in order to be able to work with Dan to get me back in shape.

I arrived in Amsterdam with Steffen and Andrew as my coaching staff. Things didn't get off to a great start. When I found my room at the team hotel, it was really hot and ridiculously humid. Andrew and I had been sitting chatting for about five minutes, and we were already covered in sweat. We went to reception and were told that the air conditioning in my room was broken. I asked if there were any rooms that might be cooler, but no, they were fully booked.

I'd only returned from America two nights before and was still really jet-lagged and desperately needing to sleep, so I packed my bag again, checked out and went to find another hotel. I knew I wouldn't have slept a wink in that sauna of a room. As I left, I saw a member of the team staff looking at me, shaking her head as if I was being a real prima donna and considered myself better than anyone else.

All I did was go and find a room that wasn't actually hot enough to cook in – I wasn't asking them to pay for it. That got my back up a little bit. I have always taken ownership of and responsibility for my performance, whether I am travelling with the team or not; if I can do something better to help me perform, I'll do it. This was a simple matter of changing hotels, on my own bill, but for some reason certain team staff chose to see it as some sort of act of rebellion. I was a grown man fixing a problem.

When it came to qualification I tried with every fibre of my body to jump further than I did. I gave it absolutely everything and all I was able to muster was 7.93m. That was a big worry for me, because I wasn't sure if I was going to be able to jump any further the following day. The European Championships were meant to be relatively easy for me, but deep down I was concerned.

When I spoke to the media afterwards, I pointed out that I'd qualified for a European Championship final and made a joke out of it, saying I was just rusty and I'd be fine the next day. But I was worried. Andrew and I talked about whether I'd almost taken the competition for granted, and maybe not got excited enough about the prospect of winning there.

Throughout that qualification, I felt absolutely nothing, just completely numb. Understandably, I'd been stressed out with my ear problems, and again I couldn't hear properly, which was really bugging me. I was walking around with headphones on the whole time, because having the closed audio helped the pain and distracted me from the annoyance of not being able to hear.

The trouble was, feeling no emotion about the event meant that I had no adrenaline. I rarely need to rev myself up, but my head was simply not in the right place. So Andrew and I sat up late, in a Starbucks in Amsterdam airport, and had a long conversation. We decided that, on this occasion, what I needed to do was change my approach and work myself up as best I could, to create an emotional investment that normally happened without trying. We started talking about the event in a way that would amp me up a little more, emphasising what an honour it was to have won the championships I have, but also what a privilege it was even to be at a European Championships, an opportunity not to be taken for granted. And then we did exactly the same before the final the next day.

Something else that really helped was interacting with the other athletes competing at the championships. When I was a youngster going to majors, I would look at some of the big names and be totally in awe of them. I'd see them around the hotel or warm-up, and look up to them. And now I had athletes asking me to take photographs with them. It was so bizarre to me that I was now considered a big name in my sport, even by my peers. When I was doing drills in the warm-up, one athlete and his coach politely stopped me and asked for some photos. Perhaps in the past I might have found that a distraction. But it actually helped get me amped up.

I started feeling and moving a bit better too. And when the final got underway, I knew I was in there fighting. I opened up with 8.12m, which took a bit of pressure off. But then Michel Tornéus of Sweden, an old friend on the circuit, jumped 8.21m and the pressure was right back on. I then had two fouls, followed by an 8.13m, and my title seemed to be slipping away. We were now in the fifth round, and I had that conversation with my body again, asking it for one more effort, just one good effort. 'Please let's do this together, work with me on this one, and then we can rest.'

I wasn't feeling great, my ear wasn't good, but I begged my body for that jump. Somehow it worked. A leap of 8.25m meant I had defended the European title I'd won in Zurich in 2014. It wasn't great, but sometimes good is good enough, especially when it means you continue an amazing winning streak in your last major competition before the Olympic Games.

CHAPTER 29

Bronze in Rio

From the outside, it probably looked as if I was back on track for the Olympics. After all, I'd just won another major title. However, I was more pessimistic. While I had shown yet again that I could conjure up enough intensity and sheer bloody-mindedness to come through even when I wasn't in great shape, I knew that in Rio that wouldn't be enough.

There were just four weeks remaining before the Olympic final and I desperately needed to regain my mojo. So the week after the Europeans, I flew to Malaga, hired a car and drove to a low-key competition in Andújar. It wasn't a big event, but I love these small meets – there might not be huge crowds but the people who do turn up really get behind you, and there is an overwhelming feeling that they are there because they thoroughly know, and love, athletics.

The track itself was lovely and the conditions were perfect. And although the competition wasn't that stiff – I won by around 45cm – I left with a real sense of disappointment, because I felt it was a day to jump really far but could only manage 8.15m. I guess I should have thought of it as another half-decent competition before the Olympics. But it definitely wasn't how things had been before the World Championships in Beijing the previous year, when I was absolutely flying. I was scratching around, trying to find the confidence to make me believe I could retain my Olympic title.

If there was anyone who could help me locate it, it was my coach Dan Pfaff. So I flew back to Arizona for the final camp before Rio. I actually arrived three days later than planned because I'd managed to lose my passport, which was less than ideal. When I finally got there, I spent a couple of days recovering from the flight before heading to the track, where I immediately felt that I was training really well. I jumped, did sprints in spikes, and felt really fast again. I started to think that perhaps it was all coming back to life.

That optimism lasted a few days, then on the Thursday morning – 15 days before I was due to compete in qualifying in Rio – I woke up and couldn't bloody walk again. I'd felt the smallest, tiniest of sensations in my knee when running the day before, but nothing that might indicate an injury. I'd run two reps at high speed after that, and felt nothing. But then I'd woken up with a pain high up in my groin, which came completely out of the blue.

I iced it for a few days, and thought perhaps it was just my body reacting to some fairly intensive training. Maybe if I took it easy for a few days, I'd be able to do a light session on Monday.

But it wasn't getting any better, so I went to see Dan who was also baffled by it. 'Look,' he said, 'it's the Olympics – what are you going to do? You either choose not to jump and you pull out now, or you go and jump.'

It's a real test in holding your nerve in the run-up to an Olympic Games; you are on the edge of breaking, both mentally and physically. You want to train hard, but anything you do at this stage is almost completely pointless; so you rest, train lightly, and try not to go insane. Obviously, I agreed with Dan. What else was I going to do – pull out? Any injury or problem, no matter what it is, just has to be dealt with this close to the Games. Being the genius he is, Dan figured out treatment and then a training plan to strike the complex balance between rest and activity, to keep me distracted and happy.

So after three days of good rehab, I was then able, every third day, to do a little jumping. Dan was determined to get me jumping as much as possible, to keep that ticking over while at the same time not placing too much impact on the body.

I wasn't in ideal shape, though. I jumped three more times before we left for Rio, and each time I could hardly walk again the next day. I also found I was having to hold a very specific posture in order to offload the pain when I jumped – I had to suck in my abs or tighten them as much as I possibly could and tilt my hip forward. It's all well and good holding that position off a short training run, but as soon as you put maximum speed in, it becomes very difficult indeed. The fundamental issue lay in the fact that I was now jumping in a different position from the one in which I'd jumped and won every major in my career, but I had no choice.

Obviously, I wasn't exactly spreading this news around. The guys down at the track who saw me all the time must have realised something was up, but I tried to play it down. I was still able to lift weights, which was good, but I couldn't do what I needed to do: sprint. However, not defending my Olympic title, especially at my age, was never an option. I knew I was injured, but it wasn't severe enough to keep me away from Rio. I would have had to have been on crutches to stop me from going.

Before flying to Brazil, I – along with most athletes and national anti-doping agencies – was stunned when the International Olympic Committee decided not to ban the entire Russian team from Rio 2016. I couldn't believe it. The IOC had missed the perfect opportunity to make a statement about cheats following a completely damning report by the Canadian law professor Richard McLaren, which had revealed widespread state-sponsored doping in Russia, involving the government, security services and sporting federations. Really, what more did the IOC want?

At least athletics had taken a stand, though, banning the track and field team. I was really proud of my sport at that moment. But after hearing IOC president Thomas Bach unconvincingly try to explain away the decision to let most Russians compete in other Olympic sports, I felt compelled to say something – so I made my feelings clear to the *Guardian*, calling the IOC's decision 'spineless'.

As I also told the paper, I was a little surprised and saddened that there weren't more athletes prepared to speak out about the IOC's decision, especially those with a powerful voice in Olympic sport. Part of me had been tempted to join them in keeping quiet for once, and to focus on my own performance in Rio, but I felt too passionate to stay mute on the sidelines. What I didn't mention at the time was that McLaren's report had given me another reason to pause before saying something, because he had revealed that the Russians had found a way of breaking into the tamper-proof urine samples. If that was true, should I shut up in case a sample of mine was mysteriously tampered with? Was I making enemies I did not want to make? This may sound crazy, and perhaps a little paranoid, but you just never know.

I was also fascinated to learn that in some way, an interview I had given to the journalist Martha Kelner in 2013 played a small part in revealing the Russian doping regime. In it, I discussed my concerns about the suitability of Moscow as a location for the World Championships, considering the country's reputation for doping, and apparently, as a result of this article, Martha was contacted by a whistleblower, which triggered the process of blowing the lid off the whole thing.

One point that's important to make is that while I don't think doping is as widespread as it often seems, I am sure that Russia are not the only culprits. However, their federation is the first for whom we've been presented with compelling evidence of an institutionalised approach to cheating. Hopefully we'll see more investigations into other federations in the future.

Soon, though, it was time to go to Rio and focus on

defending my title. I didn't train for the first few days there, as it seemed like a good opportunity to let the injury recover. I arrived on 6 August, and didn't see Dan until three days later. He met me down at one of the tracks, and we decided that evening we would do a few accelerations and easy pop-ups without landing.

I ran through and, although I felt a bit of soreness, it was nothing major – it was the best it had been since before I'd pulled it. I felt really heartened by this. The mind is such a powerful weapon, as I knew, so I told myself it was fine because I'd been through this before. Ahead of London in 2012, I'd had the hamstring issue. In Beijing 2015, I'd woken up feeling really ill. I'd had appendicitis and the ear problem and won the Europeans the previous month. Almost always I'd managed to bounce back. And I was telling myself this would be the same – I'd bounce back, I'd go out, and I'd succeed.

So we went into qualification. Before I had got injured, I'd mentally rehearsed what I would do next a thousand times: I was going to go out in qualification and jump 8.40m and really scare everyone. Then I was going to go into the final and break the national record.

That, clearly, is not how it worked out. When you have an injury, big or small, you end up doing things differently, whether you like it or not. Your body instinctively tries to guard against the pain – or doing further damage. So I had to change the way I ran down the runway and also the positions and cues I was hitting. In practice, my two jumps were absolutely miles over the board. Normally, I'm slightly out with the first one, then I adjust, and the second one is smack on. Then I know I'll jump well in the competition. This all went rather differently.

When the competition arrived, I still couldn't get it together and I ended up fouling my first two jumps. That left me with one solitary jump to qualify for the Olympic final. Strangely, I didn't feel too much pressure, although I'm sure my family were having kittens. I jumped 7.90m, which wasn't great, but enough to put me in the final – phew.

I wanted to brush it off, and say I'd be fine tomorrow. But those three jumps I'd taken – even if only one counted – weren't ideal. Dan had been keen for me to get through with the minimum effort possible and he was really pissed off. I don't think I'd ever seen him get properly annoyed with me before, but he was now. I remember he said something like, 'Well, you've now given the Americans the biggest mental boost that you could ever give them by making yourself look like a second-rate jumper.' I knew he had a point but I told him, 'Don't worry, honestly it will be fine. I know where to run from now – tomorrow I'll get it right.'

On the plus side, I didn't hurt after taking the three jumps. I was actually getting quite excited because, now that my body wasn't in pain, I felt I'd probably have the freedom to go out there and do something the next day.

Obviously, given my history, I shouldn't have counted my chickens. Lo and behold, I woke up the following day and could feel the injury again. It was stiff and a bit sore, but nothing too horrendous. The whole day, I went through my routine – talking to Dan, talking to Andrew, talking to Susie, who was back home with Milo because of my concerns about the Zika virus. Each time I told them: 'It doesn't hurt, I'll be fine.' And I guess it was partly true, but only partly.

Going into the warm-up, I initially felt really good. The pain was easily manageable as I went for a jog. Then my physio Andy treated me and I started to notice that it was getting slightly more painful. I did some of my drills and, as I went through one of them, all of a sudden pain came rushing back into my groin. I was on the side, and I saw Jeff Henderson and his coach about four metres away from me, standing there. Many of my other rivals were close by too.

If you had looked at me in that precise moment, you would have seen a big smile and then an incredibly arrogant expression on my face – because I know how mentally weak some of my competitors are, and how to shake them. But if you could have seen what was going on inside my head you'd have found the complete opposite. It was taking everything in my power not to limp because the pain I had high up in my groin was crushing me. I was desperate not to show any weakness outwardly.

So I went to see Andy and we stuck a ton more tape on the problem area, at every conceivable angle, to try to mitigate the pain. I was more tape than man at that point. Generally, it works as a kind of distraction, pulling the fascia in different directions and forcing the brain to not focus so much on the pain, but it didn't really work on this occasion. My warm-up was completely compromised. Again, you wouldn't have known this from the outside, as on the surface I was putting on my best game face. You'd probably have thought I was a certainty to be Olympic champion again.

Even Dan and Andy thought I looked good. But I'm adept at hiding the fact that I'm in pain. And what could I say to Dan? We were warming up in an Olympic final. I didn't want to pile on any more stress because he was already having to deal with so much out there. He'd travelled to Rio even though his doctors had said he shouldn't. And Fabrice Lapierre, my training partner at Altis who was also coached by Dan, had exited the competition in the qualification. So I guess I saw myself as Dan's hope for a good Olympics.

On the way out to the final, I said to myself, 'It's going to take an absolute miracle for me to stand any chance of winning a medal tonight, let alone retain my title.' I was still smiling, chirpy, chatting to people. I was showing nothing of the emotions that were going on inside. But the inner conversations I was having were worrying. I'd double-dosed on paracetamol, been massaged as much as I could, had tape everywhere – and nothing was working.

Out in the stadium, the adrenaline finally kicked in. I'd told myself going out there that if I got a decent one in the first round, there was a small chance I could pressurise the field, and get rid of a couple of the major guys. So I went down, and jumped 8.18m. I was hugely relieved to get a decent mark out in the first round. Despite the level of pain I was feeling in my groin, I actually managed to jump a hell of a lot better than I had done the day before.

I saw, straight away, in my competitors' faces, this look yet again of, 'Oh, for crying out loud, he's back.' It's an exasperated expression some of them have when I'm jumping well. It seemed to have got to the stage where, if I was able to exert pressure on my rivals by jumping well, some struggled to find the mental reserves to beat me. Normally, when I'm fit, I can maintain that, and then push it on to another level. But I wasn't fit, however it might have looked from the outside.

In round two, I jumped 8.11m – no improvement. Meanwhile, the gold was changing hands all the time. In the third round, I jumped 8.22m to retake the lead, only for the American Jarrion Lawson to immediately go three centimetres further. For the neutral, it must have been a thrilling competition.

In round four, I dug deep and produced what I thought was an improvement – only to be given a red flag. I wish I had contested it more, but the official seemed convinced it was a foul so I let it go. After the competition was over, they ended up reinstating it and giving me 8.26m, which would have put me second, two centimetres behind the South African Luvo Manyonga.

As it was, I was slipping down the field. And after the fifth round, I was out of the medals in fourth place. It was time for that conversation again. I lay there on my towel, begging my legs to give me something. 'Just give me a big one – one to win – then we'll stop for the year,' I promised. 'I'll give you the whole of the year off. I will stop putting you through all this anguish and pain, I promise.'

I'd really started losing the ability to run by this point. I just couldn't generate the normal amount of power on the runway. Instead, I was taking big, long, looping strides, which aren't great for jumping. I'm not a light, floating kind of jumper; I rely a lot on my speed and power, so when they're missing, it poses me some serious problems.

Meanwhile, just as on that fateful Saturday in 2012, I watched Mo retain his 10,000m title. I was trying to summon some of that energy myself. I had a picture of Milo with me, which I carried everywhere. I slid the photo up the leg of my shorts, so that it was resting on my quads. Yes, I jumped with that picture of my son in there.

It was just a little reminder. When the going gets tough, sometimes you need to tell yourself again why you are doing it. I needed something to go right, if only to justify the amount of time I'd spent away from my wonderful little boy. And that did help. As I stood on the runway for that final jump, I touched my leg – the photo – one last time. And then I summoned every last bit of energy I had left, and jumped.

It was better, but not enough. That leap of 8.29m put me back in the medal positions – just not the colour I wanted. It was fantastic, but also gutting. I simply didn't have it in my body to jump a centimetre further.

Meanwhile, an odd ending to the competition was unfolding in front of me. Lawson put in a huge jump, but was stunned when it was only counted as 7.78m because his hand had dropped back into the sand. That meant my bronze medal was confirmed. Or was it? I found myself in the weird position of being draped in the Union Jack with loads of people cheering me – there were a lot of Brits in the crowd – while Lawson's coach was going absolutely crazy and demanding the jump be looked at again.

So I now couldn't celebrate, because who wants to be the guy who trots around the stadium thinking he has a bronze medal, only to be knocked down to fourth? Instead, I stood there, talking to Dan. It was such a strange feeling; having to restrain my emotions even for that short period of time was really difficult.

Finally, they upheld the original distance. And then, funnily enough, just after that the official came up to me and said, 'Oh, just to let you know, we've reinstated your jump from round four.' Part of me was slightly confused. Then I began to wonder whether, had they given me that jump at the time, everything might have turned out differently. Because it would have been further than Henderson, and Lawson too at that point. So I would have gone into rounds five and six in a medal position again, putting pressure back on my rivals. It's a lot easier to catch a bigger jump when you know you've guaranteed yourself a podium spot.

By the time I got to the BBC interview, I had started to cry. I just felt this awful, sinking, overwhelming sensation that I'd given up everything in order to retain my title, and I had failed. For the first time in years, giving it everything hadn't been enough. It was really difficult for me to take.

Then obviously I was thinking about people at home, friends and family. I just about managed to compose myself when the BBC's Phil Jones asked me on camera, 'So the emotions are running high. What are you thinking about – your family? Is that what's going through your head?' It was exactly what he needed to say in order to set me off again and I couldn't stop the tears.

I felt as if I'd let everybody down. Because, as an athlete, you are very selfish by default. You know it, so you try to make up for it in other ways. But I'd devoted myself, to the exclusion of almost everything, to achieving my goal of retaining my Olympic title and all I could do was go home with a bronze medal. I was deeply, deeply upset about it. And pretty grumpy too. It's almost impossible to put into words how much I'd wanted to win. And how much I'd felt I needed to, to justify everything I'd sacrificed. As I've said before, the goalposts always move in sport. No matter what you've accomplished before, there is a tendency to value yourself only on your most recent competition.

There were, however, little things that slowly lifted my spirits . . . For example, looking at the faces of some other athletes who I know would give anything to win an Olympic bronze – what did I have to complain about? Also, the number of people telling me what a great performance I'd put in. And the former head of UK Athletics, Charles van Commenee, told me bluntly not to be an idiot, that I nearly didn't get a medal at all – saved by Jarrion Lawson's hand touching the sand – so I should shut up and be happy. Typical, direct, Charles!

But you can only judge yourself by the standards you set for yourself. Sure, I'd come third, but that's not what I wanted. Ultimately, in track and field, we are defined by how we do in the Olympics. Generally, the public doesn't know or care about the other events that take place, so what we do at the Games can make or break you. Your career, how people perceive you, everything else. As soon as you fail to win, and you don't get the result you wanted, you realise that your value in the eyes of the wider world is diminished, and it takes some swallowing of your pride to adjust to that.

I know, logically, that very few long jumpers have ever

medalled in two Olympics. But, equally, I believe that if I hadn't been hurt, I could have won. My winning distance from the World Championships the previous year would have delivered me gold in Rio. But no successful sportsperson is in sport because they're logical. If I had been logical, I would never have even attempted to be an Olympic athlete. The odds are stacked dramatically against you, and you train and work off dreams and aspirations, not evidence.

Even now, a few months on, that bronze medal is still really difficult for me to get my head around. My body let me down at the most crucial time, and at a moment I can never get back. Whatever my previous record, this missed opportunity truly hurts me. My head tells me to be proud, to be realistic and measured, but my heart knows otherwise. I guess I'll have to accept, begrudgingly, it was the one that got away.

FINAL THOUGHTS

Despite the lingering pain of that night in Rio, I know I can look back at my career with pride. Eight major championship medals – including golds at the Olympics, World Championships, European Championships and Commonwealth Games – is a decent enough return, even if some people still persist in calling me a fluke. If that's the case, then I am the luckiest and most consistent fluke alive.

I believe I can add to that medal tally, but at the same time I accept I haven't got that much time left as an elite long jumper. In November 2016 I will turn 30, and, although entirely possible, it's probably unrealistic to assume that I will be among the favourites for gold at the Tokyo Olympics, when I will be pushing 34. As things stand, my plan is to carry on for a couple more years, which will take in the 2017 World Championships in London, where I'll aim to retain my world title in that fabulous Olympic Stadium, and the Commonwealth Games on the Gold Coast in Australia in the spring of 2018, where I plan to hang up my spikes. That date is not set in stone: as with everything, it depends on injury, form, and – most of all – my family.

Whatever I do when I finally call it a day, I am never going to be satisfied with resting on my past achievements. There's so much out there in the wider world that fascinates and engages me, and I want to be part of it. I want to do something interesting, something great. I also want to be a role model for my son – and any future siblings he might have. I'm not someone who will put on five stone in retirement and lose my drive, as seems to happen all too often with ex-sports stars.

I still love the notion of changing sports: the idea of being great at a completely different discipline is hugely appealing to me. Whether I could really become good enough in something like bob skeleton to have a realistic crack at the 2022 Winter Olympics is a bit debatable, though. It would be a tall ask.

I have also loved being on TV and working in the media. Appearing on *Strictly Come Dancing* in the autumn of 2016 has been particularly enjoyable and I hope it's shown a different side of my personality. That said, I found it a steep learning curve! On our first group training day, I had a complete meltdown because I was struggling while everyone else seemed to be picking things up instantly. I ended up going to another room to cool off – until my dance partner Natalie Lowe found me and hauled me back to the class.

I knew I had to find a way to make up for my innate lack of dancing ability, so Natalie and I started to put in ten-hour training days to try to get up to speed. People expect that because I am an Olympic athlete I should grasp things fairly quickly, but the long jump is about repeating the same things over and over while dancing requires using completely different muscles and learning to use your body in a very different way. No wonder I sometimes felt like I had two left feet.

Yet, despite all those occasions when I found myself lying on the floor, feeling physically and mentally shattered and with my head exploding with too much information, it was all worthwhile for the incredible buzz I felt when Natalie and I had our first dance on TV – and the crowd's reaction at the end. The judges were kind too – giving us the top score on the night. I knew they wouldn't always be that generous, but at that moment I didn't care: I had danced in front of millions of people and hadn't disgraced myself. My teenage self, break-dancing badly at Rollers in Milton Keynes, would have been shocked, to put it mildly.

I'd like, too, to do more to stand up for athletes' rights across the globe. One of athletics' greatest strengths is its purity: anyone can run, jump or throw something. Yet the sport is slowly dying for many reasons: because of suspicions about who may or may not be doping, because most athletes struggle to make any sort of living for themselves at all, because of corruption among agents and meeting organisers, and because too many administrators are hugely out of touch with ordinary athletes and fans. When former senior members of the IAAF, the sport's governing body, are banned for life for accepting bribes to cover up doping, you can't blame the casual viewer for turning away in disgust.

One illustration of this sticks in my mind. When I was having the long pit built in my back garden in 2015, the builders who put it in were chatting to my dad. 'What drugs does Greg take?' they asked him. Obviously, my dad said, 'Nothing!' – but they just didn't believe him. They thought it was a simple matter of fact that I must be taking drugs, because everyone does, right? If you succeed in sport, you must be cheating. Fundamentally, track and field – in fact, all sports – must do more to prove to people that they can trust what they are seeing. It is a serious problem if, when audiences witness an amazing performance, the first question they ask themselves is, 'Was that real?'

Of course the issues facing track and field are wider than just doping. We are being destroyed from the inside by the very people who run the sport. Athletes know it, but may not quite have realised to what extent, and certainly many are often worried that if they speak out, if they complain or point out inefficiencies, they'll lose their funding or their sponsors. I've just never in my life been one to wind my neck in and go with the status quo, to a fault many times I am sure, but I'd love to be involved in setting up a formalised athletes' union whose remit would be to do everything possible to give all athletes a voice: to ensure that we're all treated with more consideration by the sport's organisers and sponsors. Finding new ways of taking athletics to the people is essential too, as is ensuring more athletes can make a viable living.

The way Olympic sport's revenues are distributed is truly unacceptable. As an example, for every televised major championship, the organising body is taking extremely large sums of broadcast revenue. In the IOC's case, the Olympics generate something in the region of $4 billion, yet absolutely none of this goes to the athletes. We are asked to compete entirely for free, which we are perhaps foolishly happy to do. In the USA leagues of the NFL and NBA, as a comparison, the unions managed to negotiate that 50 per cent of the league's broadcast revenue has to filter down to player salaries. Imagine if 50 per cent of the Olympic broadcast revenue were distributed equally to all competing Olympic athletes, across all sports. That sort of money could completely change so many athletes' lives, especially those from Third World countries. The irony is, without the athletes the organising bodies would have no product to sell at all. It's just plain wrong.

If there were no money being made, then there'd be no problem. But the reality is, somewhere, someone is getting unfathomably wealthy off the exploits of underpaid athletes. It is only right that a share of the sport's revenue should provide for those who work so hard, sometimes in the face of extreme adversity and poverty, just to provide a good show on the track.

I say this as one of the lucky ones. I have been paid outrageous sums of money to turn up and do the long jump, but that wasn't always the case, and it's important that I don't forget this fact just because I'm OK now. In my opinion, too many successful athletes forget the struggle.

Time is of the essence. The sport is in such decline that, if the issues plaguing it aren't addressed, God knows what it will be like in 20 years' time – if it's around at all.

Yet for all the fun I've had on *Strictly*, and my ambitions to cultivate a career outside sport, I am still very much an athlete for the foreseeable future. I do, however, realise, more than ever before, that something else in long jump motivates me now just as much as winning gold medals. That motivation is catching a massive, career-defining jump.

In long jump circles, a distance of 28 feet – 8.53m – has

semi-mythical status and I certainly think I'm capable of that – and beyond. I have the runway speed, after all (if I could sustain my 50m speed over the full 100m I would be running in the 9.8s – good enough to trouble most of the top sprinters), and if I can remain injury-free I believe it is not impossible for me to jump into the 8.60s. And while I don't believe in fairytales, if I could win gold at London 2017 with a big personal best, I would retire on the spot. What else would I have to prove – or chase?

For now, though, I am like a restless surfer who spends their every moment in the sea hunting for the perfect wave. I know that jump is out there lurking, waiting for me to nail it. And when it comes, I'll be ready. Ready to defy people's expectations, ready – as far as humanly possible – to defy gravity.

ACKNOWLEDGEMENTS

I have so many people who I wish to thank, and I apologise to anyone I may have missed off.

Firstly, thank you to my family – my father Andrew, my mum Tracy, brother Robert and sister Natalie, for providing me with all my sporting opportunities and for their unwavering, incredible support, in the face of many challenges.

Susie and Milo, you two are my world; thank you for everything and I'm sorry for the special moments I have missed while away training or competing.

Thanks to my best friend, team-mate, fellow coffee enthusiast and now manager Andrew Steele, who opened my eyes to the world and has kept me focused over the years.

Huge thanks must go to my coach, Dan Pfaff, for transforming my performance and outlook on both my sport and life. Without Dan, there is no doubt I would not have enjoyed the success I have been lucky enough to achieve.

Thank you to Gerry and Andy, for working your magic and keeping my body in one piece.

Thanks to Sean Ingle and Andrew Steele for pulling this book together in record time. Also thanks to my publishing team at Simon & Schuster for helping bring my story to life.

Finally, thanks to my dogs, Murphy, Dexter and Gus for being the most loyal training partners.

Greg Rutherford

Sean Ingle would like to thank: Kate Carter for all her help and patience – not many wives would tolerate the first couple days of a family holiday turning into a mammoth writing session, let alone spending hours (and hours) going through the first draft. My kids Lily and Rosalie, for being lovely. The *Guardian*'s head of sport Ian Prior, for giving me the time to help Greg with this book. And Paula and Ian from www.transcriptions.co.uk for turning around hours of conversations so quickly and accurately.